RELIGION
IN THE MAKING OF
WESTERN MAN

Edited with an Introduction by

Frank J. Coppa

Published by the

St. John's University Press

Copyright 1974© St. John's University, New York

Library of Congress Catalog Card Number BR115.C5C63 74-2431
SBN 0-87075-072-0

To Our Colleagues,

Walter L. Willigan
Arpad F. Kovacs
Borisz de Balla

for many years of distinguished and loyal
service to St. John's University, New York.

CONTENTS

INTRODUCTION

Today, more than ever, historians are prone to stress the impact of scientific and technical innovations in the shaping of modern man. Science and technology have achieved a remarkable sophistication and have enabled man to pierce the darkness of outer space and substantially modify the environment of our own planet. Since their findings have contributed to many of the miracles of the twentieth century world, and have created the conditions which permit our urban, consumer oriented culture to survive, there are those who would attribute to them not only the reshaping but the actual making of modern man. Unquestionably science and technology have played an important role in the transformation of the occidental mind and mode of life; they do not provide a complete or adequate explanation for the evolution of western civilization.

Religion, defined in the broadest sense as the relationship between man and the superhuman power he believes he is dependent upon, has played a crucial role in the genesis and growth of civilization in the West. Admitting that at the beginning of human history there is a great darkness, ethnologists, archaeologists, and anthropologists have found no trace of men who were without some religion. "Religion is as necessary to reason as reason to religion," wrote President Washington, "The one cannot exist without the other. A reasoning being would lose his reason, in attempting to account for the great phenomena of nature had he not a supreme being to refer to . . . ."

Although the supernatural transcends experience and cannot be examined by the tools of the physical sciences, its impact can be historically ascertained. Such an analysis reveals that man's search for truth, tranquility, as well as life after death have all been influenced by his religious impulse. This shaped his outlook and concept of reality while motivating many of his activities from the study of the stars to the development of drama. According to Max Weber, the outstanding German sociologist and student of the modern state, economic and social factors almost always interact with religious ones to render all three interdependent. Even in our increasingly secular society, where many religious beliefs have been eroded and practices abandoned, the Bible remains at the center of the English language and a dominant factor in its literary development. Scripture is in fact the common and unavoidable inheritance of believers, agnostics and atheists.

It is frequently forgotten that the values of the West, which made possible the scientific revolution and industrial transformation of the world, are based upon the moral and ethical principles of the Judeo-Christian tradition. Alfred North Whitehead, the outstanding philosopher of modern science, never tired of emphasizing the important medieval Christian contribution to the development of the scientific approach. Without its imput, without its essentially rational and Aristotlean outlook, he asserted, there might not have been a scientific revolution in the seventeenth and eighteenth centuries. Since this was a prelude to the technological innovations of the nineteenth and twentieth centuries, the medieval Christian world helped to usher in the modern, industrial one. In numerous other ways religion is at the root of present day practices and events.

Most of the religions of the ancient orient, while extremely influential in the societies of their day, did not always exert a moral influence upon the course of history. In Israel, however, the need for a redeemer and the search for the lasting Kingdom of God created religious tensions transmitted to Christianity and Islam and profoundly affected the course of western history.

The ten essays which follow reveal that the western mind has been influenced by religion from the dawn of civilization to the conflicts of the Reformation and the Wars of Religion. Commencing with the extinct religions of the ancient near east, particularly those of Babylonia and Egypt, this volume will then turn to the extinct religions of Europe, notable those of Greece and Rome, before concentrating on the religions of biblical revelation and their impact upon modern man.

While examining the impact of Judaism and Islam, this volume will concentrate upon the role of Christianity. This emphasis reflects not only the fact that Christianity has become a world religion transcending particular peoples and sects but also that it is the religion of a majority of Europeans and Americans and hence has played the most important role in their development.

Christianity in the West, during its early existence, served as a bridge between the classical world of Greece and Rome and our own. As it became clear that the old civilization was doomed, Christianity formed a fixed point about which a new civilization could eventually crystallize. Generalizing from this experience, Arnold J. Toynbee in his *Study of History* has observed that one of the important roles played by religion is to preserve the germ of life through the perilous period following the death of one civilization and the development of another. Nor was the preservation of the classical heritage the sole contribution of Christianity, for it contained within itself a crusading zeal which has contributed to the expansion of western civilization to almost every corner of the world. At the same time its rationalism and moral outlook contributed to the development of a philosophy which has directed political and social developments and influenced the economic evolution of the West.

Unfortunately this religious theme has not always been sufficiently stressed either in western civilization texts or supplementary readers. Many of the texts in this area are encyclopedic and cumbersome and their attempts to be scholarly and inclusive in one or even two volumes necessarily restricts their treatment of religious developments. The present collection of original essays, which examines the role of religion in ten crucial processes and periods, has been produced with the intention of filling this historiographical hiatus. Each of the essays is a work of synthesis rather than original research; together they clearly illustrate the importance of religion in the first millennia of western man's recorded history.

THE POLITICAL THEORY OF GOD:

Politics and Religion from the Roman Empire to the Reformation

Paul Lawrence Rose

Paul Lawrence Rose, *Docteur en Histoire*, Paris-Sorbonne, is Assistant Professor of History at New York University. He has recently completed a book entitled *Humanists and Mathematicians in Renaissance Italy* and is currently probing the notion of war and peace in early modern Europe.

Machiavelli, writing in 1513, was skeptical of religious explanations of politics. If one wished to explain the political successes of Pope Alexander VI, then one should seek political reasons such as the Borgia Pope's talent for raising money to hire mercenary armies. Religious explanations, such as God's will to exalt the papacy, may well operate, but as Machiavelli remarks ironically, such superior causes transcend human understanding. So far as man's reason is concerned, God and politics are quite separate one from another.

Yet if one is unable to understand how God influences politics, nevertheless one can discover by reason how man's concepts of God and religion affect politics. Man's view of God and religion is primarily a matter of personal faith. A man combines theological belief, spiritual experience and moral values to form his religion. But even such a personal view of God has immediate political and social repercussions. In the first instance a man's religious beliefs will affect his behaviour in society. Moreover, people holding similar beliefs form themselves into a church, or organized religion, which becomes an element in the political structure of the state. On a third level, the ruling class of the state may adopt a church as its state-religion. At this level certain social groups may subsequently adopt a religious heresy to express their dissent from the political-religious system of the ruling class. Churches, whether they intend it or not, cannot help but be political as well as religious organizations.

1

In this light it is evident that a number of apparently religious phenomena are in fact a mixture of political and religious factors. These phenomena include state-religion, church organization, heresy, wars of religion, and religious toleration and persecution. Together these concepts form what may be called the *political theory of God*, that is, a political theory tied up closely with religious arguments and institutions.

This essay will examine how a Christian political theory of God was established by the Roman emperors Constantine and Theodosius; how it was endangered in the middle ages by the claims of the papacy to control of the national churches; and how, after the failure of the papal threat, a new danger appeared with the success of Luther's heresy. With the Reformation, European religion and politics entered a crisis which lasted from 1517 to 1648 and beyond. This crisis, called the wars of religion, saw the surfacing of new views on the political status of religion and resulted ultimately in the abandoning of the political theory of God for a secularized politics. The crisis of the sixteenth century, in fact, marks the end of the middle ages and the birth of the modern world.

*   *   *

The pagan state-religion of the Roman empire had a dual purpose. In the first place it imposed some sort of unity on a multi-racial empire. As soon as a province was joined to the empire the province's gods were added to the pantheon of the Roman religion. This practice made it easier for any new province to conform to the state-religion. Secondly, religion was regarded as a means of inculcating social virtue. A man without *religiones*, (meaning technically a man without morality), was regarded as subversive of society. For these reasons intelligent Romans like Cicero privately viewed the collection of gods with disdain while publicly affirming their belief in those gods. As the emperor Valerian proclaimed, "those who do not profess the Roman religion nevertheless must not refuse to take part in Rome's religious rites". Roman religion, therefore, was political rather than spiritual.

One group which refused to add their god to the Roman pantheon was the Jews. Since the religious and national zeal of the Jews was well known to the Romans, no attempt was made to enforce their acceptance of Roman religion for fear of revolt. Difficulties arose, however, with the rise of an apparent offshoot of Judaism, namely Christianity. The Christians' repudiation of the Jewish authorities seemed to the Romans a form of social revolt. Moreover, whereas the Jewish religion had been restricted to the Jewish nation, Christianity asserted itself as a universal religion welcoming converts from all races, and sought to destroy the state-religion of Rome. Thus, the Christians soon found themselves denounced as both criminals and traitors.

Christianity spread as the Roman empire declined, and the two facts were thought to be connected. Thus, the great persecutions of the emperor Diocletian (284-305) were launched in an effort to restore the authority of the central government in the religious sphere and so halt the decline of the empire. Eventually, however, the power of Christianity was conceded when the emperor Constantine was converted (312). Constantine's conversion may well have been a matter of personal conscience, but the political benefit which resulted was considerable. Because of its social teachings — the belief in the equality of rich and poor before God, the free election of bishops by the whole congregation — the Christian religion appealed to the urban and agrarian poor. Certainly by the time of Constantine the Church had a vast membership composed mainly of the poorer classes, and as such was becoming a major threat to the old wealthy ruling classes of the empire. One effective way of dealing with this threat was to take over the leadership of the Church and to purge it of its inconvenient social teachings. The leading bishops of the Church agreed to the alliance since it acknowledged in a spectacular manner the truth of the Christian faith. Soon the old ideals of social equality and personal conscience were replaced by new principles of social hierarchy and of dutiful obedience to the state. Christ's precept "Render unto Caesar what is Caesar's", assumed a new significance after Constantine's conversion.

As well as turning a dangerous social force to his own advantage, Constantine's conversion brought new resources to the administration of the empire. The efficient diocesan administration which covered the empire was virtually annexed by the government to supplement its own weakened bureaucracy. Moreover, the internationalism of the Church, from being a rival to that of the empire, could not help but unify an empire which was beginning to disintegrate.

If the Christian system of state-religion were to last, two conditions were essential. First, the leaders of the Church had to be under the control of the state. Second, the Church itself had to remain one and indivisible; otherwise, it would foster disunity rather than unity. Thus, heresy was anathema not only theologically but also politically. These two conditions were to be enforced, first by the Roman emperors and then by the barbarian and national kings within their own states, until the Church was superseded as the main bond of society by more secular instruments in the seventeenth century.

Constantine set up the Christian system successfully and prepared the ground for Theodosius' formal adoption of Christianity as the sole state religion of Rome in 380 AD. Since Athanasius and Eusebius, the leaders of the Church, agreed politically with Constantine, there was no church-state problem. Athanasius in fact was a close friend of Constantine's and guided him spiritually, at one time rescuing the emperor from heretical Arian beliefs. Constantine was personally content to leave the *determination* of orthodoxy to the Church and the Church produced its definition of Christ-ian dogma in the Athanasian or Nicene Creed of 325 AD. The *enforcement*, however, of orthodoxy was very much the concern of Con-stantine and his imperial successors. Religious toleration was out of the question since a heresy might serve as a rallying point for the same discontented classes who had previously turned to Christianity. Moreover, in the wealthy African and Eastern provinces, which were the economic bases of the empire, the Arian, Donatist and Monophysite heresies were largely a mask for particularist movements aiming at secession from the empire. Thus, the extraordinary interest of Constantine and his successors in the profound abstractions of the Trinity controversy was motivated by the real fear of an esoteric theological dispute developing into a social upheaval. The abhorrence of heresy that started with Constantine was to prevent the success of any heresy during the next twelve hundred years.

Although the Western Roman empire fell apart in the fifth and sixth centuries, the Roman Christian state-religion was adopted by the barbarian kingdoms which succeeded the empire. This continuity was achieved by the series of extraordinary conversions of barbarians which took place from around 400-800 AD. The Lombard and Goth invaders of Italy, the Frankish invaders of Gaul and the Anglo-Saxon invaders of England all were converted *en masse* to Christianity. Many of these conversions were no doubt motivated by religious faith, but again, for Constantine as for the barbarian kings, the political advantages of adopting Christianity were quite striking. The conversion in 486 AD of Clovis, king of the Franks, is a case in point. Clovis inherited a kingdom consisting of a loose federation of tribal chieftains which lacked any real central authority. By 486 AD, however, Clovis had established by arms an effective central power, which he sought to both legitimize both politically and religiously. In the first place the Frankish king nominated himself Consul, so deriving his author-ity from the Roman emperors. Clovis then turned to Christianity to supply a divine sanction for his power. Constantine claimed to have been told "In this sign, thou shalt conquer"; the Frankish king in like manner asserted that his victory at the battle of Soissons was a sure sign that God wished him to be king. Having been converted, moreover, Clovis was able to call on the bishops of Gaul to help him set up some form of administration capable of holding his territories together. A final sealing together of Church and state was accomplished by Clovis' undertaking of wars against the Vis-igoths, whom he branded as both aliens and heretics. The general effect therefore of the conversion of Clovis was to civilise his barbarians, Christ-ianity led them out of tribalism into a more organised state.

For the six hundred years of the dark ages (450-1050) the officials of the Church served the temporal kings as civil servants. There was no conflict of church and state since the kings were the effective heads of their national churches and appointed the senior clergy. During this period the popes at Rome did not try to intervene in the domestic ecclesiastical politics of the national states and were content to leave matters in the hands of the kings. This acquiescence of the papacy ceased when Pope Gregory VII (1073-1085 AD) and his successors started to assert their rights to jurisdiction over all the national churches and over all clergy. The Christian clergy had always been caught between two loyalties. As royal servants and tenants of royal lands their loyalty was to the kings; as clergy, their loyalty was to God and his earthly vicar, the Pope. When the Papacy actively laid claim to the latter loyalty, the stage was set for the great disputes between the kings and the Popes which characterise the middle ages: the Investiture Contest, the Empire and Papacy struggle, Becket and Henry II.

As with the Trinity debates in the time of Constantine, it is important to understand what was at stake politically in the tedious and obscure squabbles between the kings and the Popes. To do this one must first recognize that the nature of the medieval state was feudal. In the feudal state all land-holders held their land (*fiefs*) directly or indirectly from the kings in return for a fee rendered in military service. The greater tenants (*barons*) had acquired, for the most part, extensive rights or liberties within their own fiefs by the eleventh century — for example, the right to dispense their own private justice. Such independent power was, however, at odds with the steady growth of the central royal power, especially after 1100. One aspect of this growth, taking again the example of justice, was the attempt to break down baronial liberties by extending the jurisdiction of royal judges into the fiefs. By 1500 the kings of England and France had advanced the central power so much that their governments had become transformed from feudal into so called new monarchies.

To kings bent on achieving a new monarchy it was necessary to have control over all citizens, not just over the barons. The claims of the Popes to the allegiance of clergy were intolerable to medieval monarchy, and it was for this reason that the medieval disputes were pursued bitterly. The Investiture Contest was a dispute over whether the king or the Pope (or their representatives) should invest the new bishop at his consecration with the insignia of episcopal office. At stake were the wider issues of whether the bishop derived his office from the crown or the Papacy, and whether, as a consequence, the bishop owed his loyalty to the king or the Pope. At stake also was the crucial question of who held the right to appoint bishops, for it was the appointer of bishops who effectively controlled the national church. Henry II of England's appointment of Thomas Becket as archbishop of Canterbury, for example, had been part of a general effort to reduce all his subjects, lay and clerical, to obedience to the crown. The judicial innovations of Henry had weakened baronial power, but the existence of clerical courts and appeals to Rome took the clergy outside his jurisdiction. It was in order to cut off the outside loyalties of the clergy that Henry nominated his old friend Becket as archbishop. The appointment, however, backfired for Becket became a strong defender of clerical rights.

In general, however, the medieval kings were successful in keeping control of their national churches and in excluding papal jurisdictions from their kingdoms. By passing anti-papal laws such as the Statute of Provisors, and by fomenting anti-clericalism England and France had succeeded by 1500 in rescuing the old Roman Christian state-religion from the dangers to which it had been subjected by the internationalist claims of the medieval Papacy. The pretensions of the Papacy, as one medieval author had written, had occasioned a perilous rift in Christianity, but by 1500 the medieval church-state problem had more or less been solved. A new crisis, however, involving the old danger of heresy, was about to erupt.

Heresy had been denounced by both kings and Popes throughout the middle ages. Both sides had recognized that here was a weapon too dangerous to be used freely, for it could be seized upon by the discontented groups of medieval society. Wycliffe's heresy in England at the end of the fourteenth century, for instance, had been sponsored for a while as part of an anti-papal campaign by John of Gaunt. When Wycliffe began to attract a large following, however, John quickly dropped his former protegé and suppressed the heresy in 1382. Some years later, in 1455, a Bohemian counterpart, John Hus, was burnt for a similar heresy. Two centuries previously in 1229, the heretical French city of Albi and its lord the Count of Toulouse had found itself the victim of a crusade and massacre. In medieval Europe, therefore, heresy was viewed as a social revolt against a Church identified with the ruling classes. In 1517, however, Martin Luther gave the German princes the opportunity of converting heresy from a revolutionary doctrine to a conservative one capable of asserting their absolute power.

The German princes had encountered more obstacles in their pursuit of absolute sovereignty than did the national monarchs. The interventions of the Papacy had frustrated both kings' and princes' efforts to control all of their citizens. In addition, German rulers were subjected to the claims of another internationalist power, namely, the Holy Roman Empire, whose Habsburg emperors sought to reduce the independence of their princely vassals. Within their own domains too the princes were experiencing threats to their absolute powers from the estates or representative assemblies of the town classes.

Luther's heresy turned out to be the vehicle that the princes needed. Starting as an anti-papal outburst the heresy was soon transformed into a political protest. In his *Address to the Christian Nobility of the German Nation* in 1520, Luther accused both the emperor Charles V and the Pope of disrupting the unity of the German nation. Whereas in the middle ages the empire had opposed the Papacy, now Charles V was allying with Rome to suppress the liberties of the German princes, in particular the liberty of the prince to control his own state church.

Although Luther defended the right of his princely supporters to hold heretical beliefs, he naturally denied this right to the princes' subjects. This was because any general right of citizens to their own religion would lead to the break up of the state-church and so weaken the power of the prince. At first Luther had failed to realize the dangers of this situation and had enunciated the "priesthood of all believers" as a principle which applied to all, no matter what class. According to this principle every Christian believer could read Scripture and decide for himself how he should individually interpret it. It soon became evident, however, that sects like the anabaptists which were hostile to the princes were using Luther's notion of the "priesthood" to justify their own revolutionary heresies. In order to rescue heresy from the revolutionaries Luther had to redefine his notion of "believers", so that it applied only to the princes and their allies. He did this by insisting that there was only one true Christian religion to be discerned by reading Scripture. Luther claimed that he himself, the Elector of Saxony and the other Lutheran princes had arrived at the true Christian religion and had therefore become "believers". Anyone who came to a different view of Christianity was therefore not a "believer", and consequently did not have the right to interpret Scripture for himself, that is, did not share in the "priesthood". This revision of the "priesthood of all believers" meant that the right of heresy was restricted to the princes.

This transformation of Lutheran heresy from a revolutionary to a conservative creed is shown clearly by Luther's reaction to the Peasant's War of 1524-25. The peasants had appealed to the Bible for justification of their revolt and by doing so they had placed Luther in a difficult position. If he allowed them to invoke the "priesthood of all believers" in the cause of revolution, then Luther risked losing the support of his princely patrons. He was thus forced to narrow his definition of the "priesthood" and he ended up exhorting his patrons to "stab, kill and strangle the peasants" in order to preserve Lutheranism.

Luther succeeded therefore in replacing Catholicism with Lutheranism as the state-religion of many German principalities. Within these states the former Lutheran heresy became a new orthodoxy, just as tied to the government as had been the Catholic Church. In fact, the new religion was far more subservient to the state. Whereas the pope and Catholic clergy had had a theoretical right to censure the evil actions of a prince in the name of God, now the prince himself was theoretically the head of his church and no longer subject to the moral judgements of a pope whom he disowned. Consequently the prince was no longer responsible to any earthly man or body, whether it be the Pope or the prince's own subjects. The prince was responsible only to his own conscience and to God.

This doctrine amounted to a new variation of the political theory of God, or of the role of God and religion in political theory. The theory of Constantine and Theodosius, which had been adopted by the Middle Ages, held that a state-religion would strengthen the loyalties of a subject to the state. Luther's theory, on the other hand, used the ideas of God and religion to exalt the absolute power of the rulers. This was a much more sinister doctrine than the Catholic one since it removed all moral controls upon the conduct of governments. In the early seventeenth century it was formulated by James I of England as "the divine right of kings". It emerged again during the eighteenth century disguised as "enlightened despotism", though by that time the theological pretence had been abandoned in favour of an outright statement of absolute power on rationalistic grounds.

A hundred and thirty years of "wars of religion" followed Luther's revolt. The emperor and the Pope immediately allied to bring the Lutheran princes to heel, but found the task too difficult. In 1555 the independence of the princes was temporarily conceded by the Peace of Augsburg, which enunciated the principle, *Cujus regio, ejus religio*, meaning that the prince decided the religion of his own state. The peace was, however, no more than a truce for the Habsburg emperors soon began a counter-attack, known as the Counter-Reformation. This campaign, which the Habsburgs fought under the guise of a Catholic crusade (while really fighting for political hegemony), culminated in the greatest and last of the wars of religion, the Thirty Years War (1618-48). The Peace of Westphalia, signed in 1648, finally put an end to religious warfare in Germany and continental Europe.

The wars of religion, however, were not simply wars between the princes, emperor and Pope. Luther's revolt had been the signal for a general outbreak of heresy of a more revolutionary kind directed against the princes as well as against the Pope and emperor. The lower town classes had immediately revived the medieval tradition of using heresy as an expression of social protest. They had turned to such radical heresies as anabaptism and had justified them by Luther's doctrine of the "priesthood of all believers". These radical reformers, however, were usually attacked by the richer town classes as well as by the princes and nobility and in consequence anabaptism, though never completely extirpated, failed to establish itself politically.

A revolutionary heresy with a more secure power base was Calvinism. Calvin stressed the free city as the best environment for the Calvinist religion. This advocacy of municipal independence from Pope, emperor and prince, was attractive to the middle classes who would be the ruling group in these free cities. Moreover, Calvin's insistence on rule by the elders represented a curb on the political demands of the lower classes whom the burgesses feared so much. The typical Calvinist theocratic state was Geneva — municipal, middle-class and independent.

Calvinism represented a revolutionary heresey in the eyes of Catholic and Lutheran rulers alike. Although the princes had allied in the Middle Ages with the middle class parliaments and estates against the nobles, most sixteenth century monarchs had found it necessary to subdue the political claims of the now too-powerful middle classes. When these middle classes adopted Calvinism, therefore, a social dimension was added to the already politicised nature of the wars of religion.

A short account of the wars of religion in various European countries will show how the political and social conflicts interacted.

*   *   *

In Germany Calvinism was a thorn in the sides of both Catholic and Lutheran princes. Taking root in the free cities of the empire, the creed stiffened resistance to princely efforts to subdue the cities economically and politically (such an effort was made at the Diet of 1522). Within the principalities also Calvinism was often espoused by the estates as a protest against a Lutheran or Catholic prince.

It is true that two major princes did themselves become Calvinists, namely the Elector Palatine Frederick II in the 1560's, and John Sigismund of Brandenburg in 1613. These princes were, however, interested in pursuing a foreign policy connected with Calvinist states, and, more immediately, in secularizing further church property. The Peace of Augsburg had frozen the confiscation of church property at the 1552 level, but that settlement applied only to Lutherans, not to Calvinists.

The absolutist Catholics and Lutherans had, in fact, intentionally excluded the middle class Calvinists from Augsburg, and this policy was continued by the Formula of Concord of 1580, which temporarily reconciled the two Augsburg parties. Princely Calvinists too were ostracized. In 1620 when the Calvinist Elector Palatine was deposed from the Bohemian throne by the Catholic emperor Ferdinand II, the Evangelical Union of the Lutherans declined to come to the elector's aid. The Lutheran princes enjoyed the independence granted to them at Augsburg, and were anxious to maintain the favourable *status quo* which was being endangered after 1555 by the ambitions of Calvinist princes and towns alike as well as by the Catholic Habsburgs. It was only after the catastrophes of the Thirty Years War that all three German parties were brought together in the religious peace settlement at Westphalia in 1648.

One element in the Elector Palatine's activist foreign policy which had threatened to disrupt the *status quo* in Germany was his support of the revolt of the Dutch Calvinists against Philip II of Spain, a member of the Habsburg family. The Rhine valley was the route taken by the Spanish troops in transit from Italy to the Netherlands. Consequently, it was feared that Calvinist expansion along the valley would provoke Spanish intervention in Germany, possibly resulting in the extirpation of all Protestantism by the Habsburgs.

Philip II's intense Catholic faith has led to his depiction as the tool of the Papacy in putting down the Dutch revolt. In fact Philip's Dutch policy was politically directed at preserving Spanish government and state-religion in the Netherlands, just as in Spain his aim to keep royal control of the church led him to suppress certain papal bulls. The Dutch revolt was, however, much embittered by the rebels' open adoption of Calvinism as a nationalist and a revolutionary ideology. Calvinist preachers acted as commissars of a kind, organizing local resistance and revolutionary resources. Philip was thereby forced into treating the revolt as a war of religion, revolution and nationalism. French and English support for the rebels, arising out of fear of the Habsburgs, made the war even more intractable for Philip and provoked his catastrophic attempts to invade England and France.

The Tudor England against which Philip launched the Armada of 1588 is an excellent illustration of the political nature of religion in the early modern state. Like the French kings, the English monarchs had asserted their control of the national church throughout the Middle Ages. The Papacy acknowledged English independence when in 1521 pope Clement VII frightened by the German Lutherans, tried to enlist Henry VIII's support by acknowledging Henry as *Defensor Fidei* (defender of the faith). With this concession of royal control Henry, like the emperor Charles V, might have been expected to remain a Catholic. Instead Henry pushed on and tried to blackmail the Pope into granting him a divorce. When the Pope refused to give in, Henry immediately treated the matter as one involving the highest principle of state control of the church.

In repudiating the authority of the Pope Henry was far more careful than the German princes had been. Where the Lutherans had used such perilous justifications as the right to individual conscience (as in the doctrine of the "priesthood of all believers") the English king freely admitted that he was breaking with Rome by virtue of his absolute royal power. Henry was thus always able to affirm that he was no heretic but a Catholic king who was resisting the outrageous claims of the Papacy.

Henry's revision of English state-religion went very smoothly and during his lifetime there occurred only one major religious war in England, the Pilgrimage of Grace in 1536. Basically a regional Yorkshire revolt against the centralizing policies of Tudor government, the Pilgrimage took on a religious Catholic aspect. This was to be expected since perhaps the most blatant use of Tudor power was Henry's *fiat* that the state-religion be changed. Naturally, the revolt was put down without mercy. Henry was similarly merciless with Sir Thomas More's claims to be allowed to follow the dictates of personal conscience. More was advocating religious toleration, an idea that meant the end of all state-religion. This radical notion was to be experimented with in France only in the 1590's and as a desperate attempt to end forty years of religious warfare.

Two main factors enabled the Tudors to prevent a full-scale war of religion in England. In the first place England's island geography made difficult the kind of foreign interventions that bedevilled the Reformation on the continent. Secondly, the Tudors based their power largely upon alliance with a strong middle class which extended into the ranks of the nobility. To secure this alliance Henry ceded large amounts of confiscated church lands to the middle classes and so created a vested interest in the maintenance of the Reformation. These two factors in combination stimulated the fantastic growth of Elizabethan patriotism against such Catholic invaders as Philip II.

Some years after Henry's death his daughter Mary tried to overthrow the Henrician system by ordering a reversion to Catholicism as the state-religion. This policy was determined not by political motives, but simply by Mary's rather devout Catholic faith. Political reflection would, of course, have shown Mary that the Reformation was too well-anchored to be undone. The middle classes and their Parliamentary representatives upheld Henry's system, and by the end of her short reign, Mary's forced conversions and martyrdoms of Protestants had set up such political stress between crown and country that even her husband, Philip of Spain, was advising restraint.

The connections between Parliament, the middle classes, Protestant-ism and patriotism were recognised by Elizabeth I. Under Elizabeth the crown became closely involved with Parliament in the defence of a nationalist English form of Protestantism, and, as a result by 1603, when Elizabeth died, the absolute power of the monarchy had been somewhat modified by Parliament. Thus, under the Tudors England had been spared wars of religion on the continental scale. The new monarchy of the Tudors had ensured an easy transition from Catholicism to Anglican Protestantism. The Parliament and the middle classes were firmly on the side of royal Anglicanism and had been given sufficient political conces-sions to forestall a war of religion.

With the Stuart monarchs, however, the compromise between crown and Parliament broke down. James I and Charles I pursued an absolutist theory of the divine right of kings which would have been appropriate to the times of Henry VIII, but was at odds with the reduced royal power after Elizabeth. Parliament, for its part, turned more and more to Puritanism as a revolutionary heresy with which to curb the ambition of the crown. The result was the outbreak in 1642 of England's long delayed war of religion, the Civil War. The English Parliament had thus followed the German and French cities in adopting heresy as a means of political protest; in England as in the other two countries, this action sparked off wars of religion.

It was to the political and religious strife in France that the term "wars of religion" is usually applied. By the Reformation the power of the French

crown was absolute, and like most other absolutist states France demanded conformity to the state-religion. One French theorist of absolute
monarchy commented that "difference in religion and laws split a kingdom in two, and hence the old saying, *une foi, une loi, un roi*" (one faith,
one law, one king). Another writer remarked that "it is folly to hope for
peace, respite and amity between people who are of different religions".

In the 1550's the new monarchy of France ran into serious trouble
from both fractious nobility and ambitious *parlements*. Such a situation
was ripe for the outbreak of the religious strife, which, it will be evident,
denoted political crisis. The French wars followed a complicated course.
At one point a Catholic king would be suppressing Huguenot (Calvinist)
towns, while a little time later the king would be siding with the Huguenots
in order to crush the rebellious nobles of the Catholic house of Guise. Such
confusion could be solved only in political terms and there emerged the
party of the *politiques*, who tried to reduce the religious disputes to their
true political meaning.

Their preference for a political settlement, combined with their willingness to compromise, enabled *politiques* to abandon completely, for
the first time in European history, the Roman Christian concept of state-
religion. The Catholic kings of the Middle Ages had accepted the crucial
importance of religion in the maintenance of states, nor had they permitted
any religious disunity to spread lest it endanger the unity of the state. The
Lutherans and Calvinists, although they dissented from the Catholic state-
religion, firmly supported the concept of a unified state-religion within
their own states; they believed that within Lutheran states all should be
Lutheran, and that within Calvinist states all should be Calvinists. Henry IV
of France, however, threw away this rule of religious unity. In 1589, Henry,
a leading *politique*, renounced his Huguenot beliefs and became a
Catholic in order to ascend the throne and end the religious wars; Paris, as
he put it, was worth a mass. To reconcile the Huguenots to this apparent
Catholic victory, Henry then took the revolutionary step of proclaiming
religious toleration by the Edict of Nantes in 1598. This toleration of two
different religions within one kingdom (though in specified areas only)
meant the rejection of the traditional system of uniform state religion;
henceforth, it was hoped, a subject's loyalty to the state was not to be
judged in terms of religious conformity, but rather in terms of his political
obedience. This is, of course, the view of religion accepted in modern
liberal democracies, but in the sixteenth century the putting into practice of
such a view was astonishingly experimental.

Henry's policy of religious toleration paved the way for the central
concept of liberal democracy, namely the toleration of dissenting political
opinions. It was a departure from medieval and later theories of absolutism
to believe that any citizen could be permitted to hold dissenting views from
those of the ruling class. The absolutist systems of the Middle Ages and the

Reformation identified religion and politics and so treated religious dissent or heresy as political dissent. Both forms of dissent were therefore suppressed. Henry's policy, by allowing freedom of religious dissent, introduced into practice the principle of permitted dissent. Political dissent as such was not allowed of course, for Henry IV was not a liberal democrat but an absolute monarch in the traditions of the new monarchy. Nevertheless, the principle had been introduced.

In the unstable atmosphere of French politics, though, it was obvious that the coexistence of political absolutism with religious freedom could not last. Henry was assassinated and, with the peacemaker gone, the old tensions between crown, nobles and *parlements* reappeared. Eventually Richelieu, Mazarin and Louis XIV established royal power in a more absolute form than before, and, in furtherance of this policy, the independence of the Huguenot cities was destroyed and the Edict of Nantes revoked in 1685. At the same time the French Catholic Church was brought more firmly than ever under royal control. Thus ended an early attempt to separate religion from politics, and to thereby abandon the political theory of God.

*   *   *

The wars of religion were political and social conflicts between parties who adopted the banners of Luther, Calvin or the Catholic church. In these conflicts each of the three main parties was against the others. The Catholics and the Lutherans represented the absolute monarchies of the emperor and the princes respectively. At the same time the Habsburg emperor attacked the strongly independent Lutheran princes in the name of the Catholic church. Yet the Lutherans could not look for help to their fellow Protestants and victims of Habsburg Catholic ambition, the Calvinists of the Netherlands and Germany. To absolutist Catholics and Lutherans alike, the revolutionary aspects of Calvinism were abhorrent.

Although the Reformation and Counter-Reformation comprised important religious movements the purely religious currents of the Reformation and the Counter-Reformation were very much at the mercy of political factors. Luther succeeded because he received princely support for political reasons. Similarly, on the Catholic side the Jesuits were effective only when the political power of the Habsburgs or another Catholic ruler was covering them. As Machiavelli explained in political terms the successes of the religious institution of the Renaissance Papacy, so here the fortunes of the Counter-Reformation Papacy and its religious arms, the Jesuits and the Council of Trent, can be linked to politics.

The rigid divisions of political parties according to religion was, however, gradually weakening during the later sixteenth century, especially in France; the death blow to the system came in fact with the French intervention on the Protestant side in the Thirty Years War. The French were Catholics, but they intervened for the openly political reason of preventing an Austrian victory in Germany. Such a victory would lead to encirclement of France by the Habsburgs of Spain and the empire. This adoption of a purely political policy marked the final phase of the God-based political theory which had dominated European thought since the fall of Rome. Religious ideas thereafter were usually cut off from international politics as they were from natural science. Both separations of God, from politics and from science, typified the general secularization of thought which occurred in the Renaissance and which is customarily regarded as the origin of the modern consciousness. After 1648, therefore, there were no more wars of religion; the modern age of wars of nationalism and of ideology had begun.

BIBLIOGRAPHY

Baldwin, John W. *The Scholastic Culture of the Middle Ages 1000-1300*. Lexington, Mass.,1971.
Cohn, Norman. *The Pursuit of the Millennium*. New York,1970.
Courtenay, William J. *The Judeo-Christian Heritage*. New York,1970.
Dawson, Christopher. *The Making of Europe: An Introduction to the History of European Unity*. Cleveland and New York,1956.
Holborn, H.J. *A History of Modern Germany, I: The Reformation*. New York,1959.
Hunt, G.L. *Calvinism and the Political Order*. New York,1965.
Hyde, W.W. *Paganism and Christianity in the Roman Empire*. Philadelphia,1946.
Momigliano, A. (ed.). *The Conflict between Paganism and Christianity in the Fourth Century*. Oxford, 1963.
Rose, H.J. *Religion in Greece and Rome*. New York, 1959.
Russell, Jeffrey B. *Medieval Religious Dissent*. New York, 1971.
Southern, R.W. *Western Society and the Church in the Middle Ages*. Baltimore,1970.
Trevor-Roper, H.R. *Religion, the Reformation and Social Change*. New York,1967.
Ullman, Walter. *A History of Political Thought: The Middle Ages*. Baltimore, 1965.

RELIGION AND RITE
IN THE ANCIENT NEAR EAST

Theodore P. Kovaleff

Theodore P. Kovaleff, Assistant Professor of History at St. John's University, received his doctorate from New York University. He studied religion with the Niebuhrs and his articles have appeared in a number of journals including the *Journal of Church and State*.

Egypt is a land of contrasts; lush, verdant and bountiful in one spot; dry, brown and infertile scarcely a yard away. The topographical condition and the location of Egypt, even today, affect every phase of the life of its inhabitants. Were it not for an exotic stream, Egypt would be a total desert, incapable of supporting even a small portion of her teeming population. Luckily, however, the Nile, which rises in the tropical mountains far to the south, flows from its source to the Mediterranean Sea. The flood stage of the river comes gradually and, extremely important, at a beneficial time of the year, after the first harvest and before the sowing of the second. The river gently overflows its banks and covers the dried soil and, besides soaking it with life-giving water, revitalizes the soil with a new layer of fertile silt brought from further upstream. As soon as the river retreats, the farmer is ready to sow the next crop.

Before the completion of the Aswan Dam, only about 4% of the total land area of Egypt was arable and there almost all the population lived and worked. While no figures are available for ancient Egypt, and while her population could not have been as great, the main feature was undoubtedly the same: a river flowing between fertile and densely populated shores in an otherwise almost uninhabited desert.

The geographical picture cannot be over emphasized. While constricting, the desert also provided the Egyptian with a defense perimeter that protected him from almost all invaders. Also, the concentration of life along the Nile led to a quasi-urban civilization. Very likely on account of the high population density, Egypt developed a type of sophistication that manifested itself most obviously in a tendency to synthesize different modes of thought. What results, therefore, especially in religion, is a group of divergent concepts woven into an apparent patchwork of old and new religion.

The religious concepts of about 3000 B.C., or before the unification of Upper and Lower Egypt, were diverse and primitive. Each independent area had its own gods, often depicted as animals, or as having animal-like characteristics, for instance the head of a beast. Not only did the early Egyptians worship the more usual animals such as bulls, rams and lions, but they also idolized such unexpected animals as wart hogs, jackals, frogs, mice and cats. There appear to have been 42 different city states prior to unification and each had its special god. As time passed, and as the city states were conquered the various gods were often amalgamated resulting in "hyphenated gods" such as Osiris-Apis. While these gods were regarded as guardians of an area, they were viewed as neither omnipotent nor even possessing hegemonic leadership. There were also many gods and spirits for objects such as trees and mountains, and for concepts such as truth and beauty.

After the unification of Upper and Lower Egypt, the religious mixture of the area became less diverse. Several of the gods were especially prominent and are worthy of note. The personification of the atmosphere, Set, was pictured as a human with the head of a composite animal. Re (or Ra) was the means by which the sun was worshipped; he, too, is depicted as having a human body, but with the head of a falcon. Osiris was, among other titles, the god of the dead and the ruler of the dead; hence he was often pictured as a mummy. There were also female goddesses. Isis, for example, who was both the wife and sister of Osiris, was goddess of motherhood and was the exemplary faithful wife.

As an outgrowth of a myth that described the first rulers of Egypt as gods, the pharoahs, as their descendants, were also considered divine. There is little evidence, however, that any of them were worshipped until after their death.

The relationships of the gods is of interest in trying to understand the civilization of the early Egyptians. While her thinkers never produced any all-encompassing system of philosophy, theological speculation did exist. Osiris was originally a warrior god, but in one of his conflicts he had been slain by Set. It was at this point that he acquired his greatest drawing power, because he had subsequently risen from the dead. After this, he had become also pictured as a god of the Nile (which every year rises from the dead as it rises to flood stage) and of nature (which also rises from the dead each year). As such, Osiris dominated the various popular cult religions. Not only the masses, but many monarchs appear to have believed in Osiris. As a god associated with death, a universal experience, and the life after death, an almost universal aspiration, he appears to have had a large following. There are remains of elaborate tombs and shrines which must have been built by the wealthy. Similarly, archeologists have found traces of small, rude shrines that must have been constructed by the poor.

Whereas Osiris was basically of the underworld, Re was celestial. There are stories of his creation of the world and of his giving of a government to the Egyptians. It was the cult of Re that was the "official" religion of Egypt. Not only was the pharoah related to Re, only he could deal with the god. While a priestly caste would evolve, it would only act for the pharoah. All sacrifices and offerings were made in the name of the pharoah. Naturally, as time passed, and as Egypt grew more wealthy, the worship grew more complicated and different orders of priests divided the duties.

The Egyptian temples were all similar. On the outside walls were pictures of scenes which likely had religious overtones. One could enter the building in only one place — through a small entry leading to an open courtyard. Beyond was a covered area in which services were conducted. Further on, was the most important area of the temple, the dwelling place of the god. Naturally, only the priests were admitted to this holiest part of the temple. Inside was an image of the god before which incense was burned and the offerings of food were placed. Daily the priests performed an elaborate ritual cleansing. Elsewhere in the temple were other shrines, storehouses with large supplies of grain for both deity and the priests. To support this vast operation, revenues from land ownership, endowments, and offerings were collected, but they do not appear to have been adequate, for there are records of substantial contributions from the state.

Magic played an important role in both popular and official Egyptian religion. The gods allegedly had various magical powers which could be set in motion by the utterance of various words, sounds, or texts, or the performance of specific acts. If man could learn them, he could gain control of the magic, and hence control the gods. *The Book of the Dead*, a collection of many such procedures, is the best record extant. There appear to have been many different versions and editions of the text, some even dating back to the days before Unification. They all contain the proper ritual for funerals, for the book was a handbook for the dead soul as it made its journey through the underworld towards a hoped-for Osirian resurrection.

There was even a short-lived experiment with monotheistic theology. Because of the tendency of historians to seek the earliest manifestations of an idea, the monotheistic reforms of Ikhnaton (Amenhotep) have been given far more attention than they deserve. Aton, a type of sun god, was pictured as creator.

Thou dawnest beautifully in the horizon of the sky

O living Aton who was the Beginning of Life . . .
. . . Beside whom there is no other.
Thou didst create the earth according to
                                        thy heart.

All traces of the old religion were to be expunged, but Ikhnaton did not live long enough to achieve this necessary change even in his own family, for he would be succeeded by his son-in-law who was receptive to the wishes of the displaced priestly class. They would restore the old religion. Once again it would be a strong force in Egyptian civilization and would remain so until the advent of Christianity.

In many ways, the environment of the Fertile Crescent is similar to that of Egypt. Instead of the Nile, there are two rivers, the Tigris and the Euphrates, and each overflows its banks and leaves behind rich alluvial soil, almost inviting cultivation. The two climates are roughly similar, and thus the agricultural produce was also alike.

Upon deeper investigation, however, the comparisons, while valid, only serve to make the contrasts more marked. Although Egypt had been protected by its geographic position surrounded by deserts and water, and hence had been able to develop without having been conquered, Babylonia had had to protect herself against attacks by the desert peoples to the south and southwest. The mountain country to the northeast also held dangers for the Babylonians; and, to the northwest, the valley between the two rivers offered no impediments to invading armies. Not only invasions, but also wars between the various city states were commonplace. The uncertainties inherent in such an environment could not but affect the beliefs of the peoples. Life was too hectic; it was not peaceful enough to think about the eternal.

In addition to man-made dangers there was the possibility of natural catastrophes. The Tigris and the Euphrates flow to the sea only half as fast as does the Nile. While the Nile, Tigris and Euphrates are all exotic streams, the Euphrates especially relies for its water on melting snow in the mountains to the northwest. The snow does not melt on the same day every year, and the miniscule slope of the river makes foretelling the advent of the flood nearly impossible. Not only is the flood stage irregular, but also it comes at an inopportune time. While in Egypt it comes *before* the planting, in Mesopotamia the Tigris and Euphrates rise in the north and flow southeast, bringing the melted snow later in the year. Therefore, the flood occurs *after* planting. In this context then it is easy to understand why the flood is viewed as not *good*, but instead as a destroyer that must be fought.

Although the Babylonians were not the first to settle in the Fertile Crescent, we shall deal with them. The Amorites, a group on the fringe of the area, appear to have first entered Babylon peacefully and then infiltrated all aspects of its life. Later, however, they came as invaders, or in such numbers that this time there was resistance on the part of the original inhabitants. Nevertheless, around 2060 B.C. they finally succeeded in placing one of their own on the throne of Babylonia. As time passed, the successors expanded their control of the area, and by the reign of Hammurabi (1958-1916 B.C.), they had conquered a large portion of the Fertile Crescent.

The gods and myths of the conquered people were usually amalgamated with those of the newcomers, and thus Marduk, the god of Babylon, was raised from obscurity to the position of one of the most important gods of Mesopotamia. Marduk would replace the other head gods, and the priesthood would build a theology around him.

While many describe the *Enuma Elish* as a creation story, in essence it is much more. Large segments of the story deal with the various battles and detailed preparations undertaken by the gods. Were the purpose of the poem simply to have been to explain the riddle of creation, much more emphasis would have been placed on that topic. The *Enuma Elish* must instead be viewed as a hymn in praise of Marduk, champion of the gods and creator of the heavens, earth and man. As Marduk, the god of Babylon, is pictured as having conquered all, the work must be regarded as a political writing as well as a religious tract.

The poem begins with a description of the state of the universe at the beginning — a watery chaos that consisted of sweet water, the sea and the mist. Many other gods are born of this situation. As time passes the gods multiply and they drive the waters to desperation with their revelry and clamor. In an effort to return to the good old days, they decide to destroy their offspring.

But while killing one's offspring may be easy to contemplate, it is not necessarily easy to accomplish. Marduk offers to help the young gods on condition that henceforth he be their undisputed leader. That being settled, he goes forth to meet the sea and split her open into two halves. One part became the sky, the other the earth.

After his great victory and the creation of the world, Marduk set about creating the heavens in order to establish the calendar. It is at this point that much of the creative activity is lost, for the clay tablets, on which the epic is recorded, have been damaged by the ravages of time. When the story is again decipherable, Marduk is in the process of deciding to create man. No description of the creation of man is supplied, for it was "not suited to human understanding."

The *Enuma Elish* is not the only document that the Babylonians have left us. The *Epic of Gilgamesh* is another which tells the story of a man's search for eternal life and his adventures along the way.

While the records are incomplete, one can piece together certain ideas and information about the practical relationship between man and the gods. Three hundred gods had been assigned by Marduk to live on this earth, hence divine power was expected to be visible on the earth either in animal or other form. For man, magic was a most potent means of communication with these entities. Charms depicting their forms were also often carried.

It was in the temple, however, that the Holy was expected to dwell. There were actually two different types of temples. Firstly there were those found in "natural habitats." Often located on mountain tops or near springs, the temple was built for its occupant to live like a king. Inside, in an area set apart especially for the god, was an image usually with a core of wood overlaid with elaborate decorations of gold, silver and precious stones, plus a garment of costly fabric. In the city, the temple was more ornate, yet no more accessible to the common man. On most days, the closest he could approach the sacred space of the god was to view the elaborate doors of the entrance way. Behind those doors, the priests were caring for the god. Following a most complex ritual, the god was awakened, then fed numerous hearty meals specially prepared in the temple's kitchen, and finally at night put to bed. Thus, the god was invested with human needs and qualities.

There were times, however, when it was possible for the ordinary man to confront the god. This was due to the extraordinary mobility of the image, which was moved from place to place by means of chariots, barges, or even human shoulders. In the observation of certain feasts, the image would be part of a long processional through the city, and short services would be conducted at various street corner shrines. The images were also taken to other shrines, usually in politically subservient areas.

Perhaps the most important festival was the one at New Year's. A special shrine was even built for the occasion, and then the image was transported to the edifice. The entire population would participate as spectators or minor aides in a celebration that included an enactment of the victory of Marduk over Tiamat. In this way all could be part of the new creation of the New Year. The importance of the people's participation in the annual rites of passage cannot be over-emphasized, for, besides helping them with a sense of identity, it aided the state by promoting unity.

The temple was the focus of activities other than worship. The religious institution was extremely rich and powerful, and thus it influenced many phases of life. It held large tracts of land which were utilized with the idea of profit foremost in mind. Clay tablets have been recovered from temples showing a clear-cut accounting system. Priests were involved in primitive medical activities, both preventive and curative. It can be assumed that their most effective medicine was the psychologically potent awe of the power of the gods. In addition, records reveal that the temple was involved with banking. It may even have played the role of a primitive Federal Reserve Bank by stabilizing the prevailing interest rate. Scientific measurement and inquiry were also centered in the temple. Besides setting the standards of measure, using the base six, they developed surveying, which was an obvious need after a flood which might well wash away many markers. Priests were astronomers, too, and kept the most complete and accurate records of the heavens which had been put in place by Marduk. Allied with astronomical study was their regularization of the calendar. The religious institution, therefore, permeated all facets of the life of a Babylonian.

In what today is called the Middle East, there were many religions, but perhaps one of the most widespread geographically was the worship of Mithra. Basically an old Indo-Euopean god, Mithra was taken even to India where he was known as Mitra. As soldier-god and the power of Light, he was an almost all-pervasive deity. Mithra was often associated with a stronger god, Ahura Mazda the Father of all, or Supreme Being. Nevertheless, the sun was believed to belong to Mithra, it was his means of transportation; even when the sun was down, however, Mithra was credited with being awake, he saw all with his thousand eyes and heard all with a like number of ears. As the sun was his, he was associated with light and what it could do, namely cause plants to grow. Hence, many times, Mithra was pictured as responsible for life. It is notable, however, that, despite his reputed powers, there was not even a tendency toward monotheism in the worship of Mithra until the coming of Zoroaster.

There is a rough consensus today that Zoroaster was born somewhere between the middle of the seventh century and the first half of the sixth century B.C. Legend tells that in his youth, Zoroaster went into a temple and denounced the worship of demons. As time passed, he grew in wisdom and then was "possessed by Ahura Mazda and was able to solve the problem of life." At that point he was ready to be a missionary. At first he was not overly successful, taking ten years to win his first convert, his cousin.

Flushed by this success, Zoroaster immediately decided to convert the local king. After waiting two years for an audience, he finally saw both the king and the queen who were impressed. Their response worried the priests of the establishment religion who succeeded in jailing the prophet. At that very moment the king's favorite horse fell dead. Zoroaster said that, if freed, he could heal the animal. He succeeded, and the king was converted. Thereupon the religion, Zoroastrianism, gained state backing and spread quickly. Until his murder at the age of seventy-seven by a priest of the displaced religion, Zoroaster spent his life as missionary and writer.

The teachings of Zoroaster are contained in the *Avesta*. Also included are various other types of literature: devotional, ritual and doctrinal. Here, for the first time, can we find a true ethical monotheism. Zoroaster taught that Ahura Mazda, Lord of light, was the God of the Moral Order who had called him to cleanse the religion of the other false gods (including Mithra). All other gods or divine spirits were amalgamated into the Primal Being, All

Father, Ahura Mazda, or they were demoted to the status of demons or aides of Angra Mainyu, the Evil Spirit, who was believed to have opposed Ahura Mazda from the beginning of time.

Ahura Mazda himself created the world and then created man with whom he consulted to determine how best to deal with Angra Mainyu. It was decided that man should be given the power to make the choice between good and evil. Therefore, within each man, the conflict between good and evil rages. That is life. The *Avesta* contains Zoroaster's principles to aid man: right speaking, right thinking, and right doing. Thus each person should be able to keep his mind pure and hold fast to that which is good. Not only must one abjure evil, one must fight the wicked with all one's strength; in this way one will imitate Ahura Mazda.

Classical Zoroastrianism left little room for ceremony. The old Aryan ritual to Mithra was suppressed in the amalgamation of Mithra into Ahura Mazda, and all magic and idolatry was purged from the religion. The only element that was saved was that of fire, which became a symbol of Ahura Mazda. Light in most any form was believed to be good and part of Ahura Mazda; darkness was believed to be bad and part of Angra Mainyu.

In this religion life was divided into two parts: the life before death when one performs the deeds that determine one's destiny in the second phase. While man is on earth, all thoughts, words and deeds are entered on a tally sheet in the Book of Life; strict accounting procedures are followed. After death, the soul leaves the body and journeys to the *Cinvato Pereta*, or Accountants Bridge. Beyond is Heaven, under the bridge the entry to Hell. At the entrance to the bridge, the account is added up. If the final tally shows credit, the soul goes to Paradise; if debit, it goes to the realm of Satan and the pains of Hell are his forever. If the score breaks even, the soul goes to an intermediate stage, where it remains until the ultimate destination is decided in the Final Judgment. At this point no one can change the tally except Ahura Mazda.

The final doctrine of Zoroastrianism is that Good, or Ahura Mazda, will emerge victorious in his struggle with the Evil Spirit. Then a general resurrection will take place; this will be the end of the world. All those persons alive at the time will be subject to an ordeal of fire and molten metal. For the bad, the ordeal will be impossible. For the good, the fire and metal will be as milk. This is the first instance of a doctrine of the last things, or eschatology in religion.

Zoroastrianism is perhaps the most important of the forgotten religions. Besides the first eschatology, its belief in an ethical monotheism must certainly be viewed as in the vanguard of religious progress. The Magi were probably of the Zoroastrian faith, and Cyrus the Great was a Zoroastrian. His successors, Darius and Xerxes, also were adherents, and had they defeated the Greeks at Salamis and Thermopylae, perhaps the religion would have spread further westward.

Of all the Ancient Religions, that of the Hebrews is the most relevant for man today. Throughout the Old Testament there is a dual theme that dominates and matures: Firstly, there is a god who is interested in a little band of people; that God becomes the god, not just of the Hebrews, but of everyone. Secondly, the god is ethical and righteous and influences the world. The Old Testament, it must be emphasized, is not a history book. Despite the fact that it contains much history, the thrust of the work is religious. What it tells, and how it was assembled, is most important for understanding its impact on Western civilization.

The Hebrews were originally a Semitic desert people probably from the northern part of Arabia. In common with other desert folk, they likely felt that stones were alive (dynamism), had spirits (animism), and that demons lived in many places. Lush green areas often were viewed as sacred, or at least verdant thanks to the power of a god or spirit. Hence, understanding their importance, and realizing that a power could take as well as give, rites aimed at thanking and propitiating gods were frequently performed.

By the time of Abraham, the conceptions of the gods had changed slightly; the element of choice had been added. This is not to say that the Hebrews were monotheist at this point: The Old Testament recounts the story of Abraham; nevertheless for many years it has been the vogue to dismiss the tale as an impossible legend. Now, however, archeological discoveries have placed his existence in a much different perspective. Today, few would deny the existence of an Abraham figure. It appears as if his migrations were also possible, for in the nineteenth century B.C., there was much ferment in his area. Abraham was likely to have been a leader of only one of many small migratory clans around Ur, and when he died, his place was taken by Isaac and then by his grandson Jacob. Approximately then, Indo-European invaders, the Hyksos, conquered Egypt and the tribe of Abraham probably followed and established themselves in the fertile Nile valley or Delta area. Success smiled upon the tribe until all of a sudden, the Egyptians arose and expelled the Hyksos (1580-1560 B.C.). Life remained unchanged for the Hebrews for over a century until a pharoah with a mental condition and a passion for public works saw that the Hebrews might be used for labor on his building projects.

In order to escape their situation the Hebrews needed a leader, and Moses fitted that description well; also necessary was some sort of diversion that would distract the Egyptians sufficiently to enable the Hebrews to flee. There is much tradition concerning Moses, and it is extremely difficult to extract the "historical" Moses. There is, however, no doubt that he, too, did exist. As for a diversion, there seems to have been the threat of, if not an actual, invasion from Libya. Escape thus was possible.

After a period in the wilderness, lasting according to legend for forty years, the Hebrews were ready and able to settle in Canaan. Scholars differ as to whether only exodus Hebrews entered the area at the time, or if others also joined with them. What really matters is that the Hebrews were able to settle where there was a well-developed urban-type culture.

While the Canaanites lived in cities, their religion was still primarily based on its agricultural precedents. They recognized and worshiped many *baals*, each of which held sway over a small section, and each was responsible for the fertility of the locality. Consequently, in this "agricultural" religion were many festivals associated with the passage of the seasons. It is not surprising that besides absorbing many of the Canaanites' more advanced ways, the Hebrews also adopted much of the local religion. It must be remembered that the Hebrews did not discard their god, Yahweh; they simply added the baals. It would take a long time for them to conceive of Yahweh as also the god of fertility. In addition, there was a danger in this attitude, for it would be easy for the Hebrews to begin to confuse Yahweh with more powerful baals. A group of people, known as prophets, would vehemently decry this tendency.

There was a long-standing tradition of men who spoke in tongues, acted frenetically and claimed to have communion with Yahweh. They have sometimes been called "inarticulate prophets". Later prophets, such as Nathan, had a much more composed deportment and spoke rationally and articulately to kings. Elijah was one of the first to take a strong stance against the increasing influence of the baals on the religion of Yahweh. For Elijah, the question was extremely simple: As the God's champion, he could only believe that Yahweh was the real power, the baal was not. Yet Elijah was not very successful. His successor, Elisha, is perhaps better known for encouraging King Jehu to destroy all vestiges of the baals. The bloodletting was severe, yet while the worship of the baals received a great setback, it was not eradicated, and would experience at least one more recrudescence.

The first of the reforming prophets, Amos, was born in a more desert-like region, away from the more fertile North. Coming from a more puritanical locale that had strayed little from the Yahwehistic tradition, Amos was horrified by the degeneracy of the religion and of morals in general.

Hosea, less interested in morality, was much more concerned about Israel's pursuit of foreign loves. Israel he described as a harlot who would be punished until she returned to the worship of Yahweh. In the first part of Isaiah we find an unhappiness with the undue emphasis on ritual in the temple. Describing the ritual as useless, he prophesied that destruction would result by the legions of Assyria, for Yahweh would use the other wicked states to achieve his own ends. For Isaiah, the future is not to be seen as doomed. Some will survive and, aided by Yahweh, they will rebuild; not only will they be able to rebuild Jerusalem, but also from them a prince of peace will arise.

Jeremiah lived and prophesied at an extremely crucial time for Judah. Egypt, Assyria and Babylonia at one time or another threatened his country. Almost always pro-Babylonian, Jeremiah not only decried the prevalent faithlessness and the worship of astral deities, but also he emphasized that the temple would not be a saving armament. God would work through the Babylonians. For this attitude Jeremiah would be arrested and would remain confined until the king of the Babylonians, Nebuchadnezzar, captured Jerusalem and subsequently freed him. The promise of a glorious restoration included in the book of Jeremiah is probably the work of another and later author. Only with such additions was it possible for the Hebrews to endure the exile in Babylonia.

In Babylonia, the Jewish religion was faced with a most difficult situation: Although the prophets understood that Yahweh was always with the Hebrews and He was all powerful, would the newly exiled people remember His power, or would they feel that He was weaker than the Babylonian gods? Even were they to remain unswerving in their faith, they believed that the temple at Jerusalem was the only place where sacrifices could be offered to Yahweh. It is in this context that "sabbath meetings" must be viewed. In what would later become a synagogue, the exiles would come together to pray, study their history, and discuss the sacred texts and their future.

The last of the major prophets, Ezekiel, wrote from 592 until 570 B.C. Therefore, his prophecies cover pre-Exile as well as the Babylonian captivity. His writings prior to the Exile are in the normal condemnatory vein of the prophets, and he, too, sees a foreign people, Babylon, as God's instrument in punishing His wayward people. Once in Babylon, however, there is an entirely different tone to his writings. There Ezekiel endeavors to comfort and instill hope. Hence, by Chapter 35, the exiles are promised a return to their own land. The last chapters are even more specific; a blueprint not only for the rebirth of the nation, but also for the rebuilding of the temple. Thus, the plans for a future theocracy were given to the people.

The prophets, in sum, contributed five ideas to the religion of Yahweh. Firstly, those at the bottom of the social ladder must be considered. Despite the fact that the nation was enjoying prosperity, this prosperity was not a reward, it was instead responsible for an erosion of values. Secondly, while Yahweh was the god of the Hebrews, He was also the god of everyone else, and He could just as easily work through another people. In fact, He could cause the defeat of the Hebrews without suffering any loss of His own prestige or power. This is a radical departure from the previous belief that the god of a defeated people had also been defeated. Thirdly, God is first pictured as a hegemonic leader, and then finally as *the* God, period. Fourthly, God is more than a jealous god, He is pictured as a moral god. Finally, man's relationship to the God changes. No longer does man try to bribe an anthropomorphic-type god with sacrifice of "sweet savor"; good conduct becomes the key.

Not only does the Old Testament contain prophecy, it also contains poetry, wisdom,literature and narrative. The Pentateuch, or first five books of the Old Testament, includes examples of the last three forms of literature. Except for the part of Deuteronomy dealing with the death of Moses written by Joshua, tradition ascribes the authorship of the Pentateuch to Moses. Today, however, scholars are convinced that many more than one author contributed to the composition of the Pentateuch.

The area inhabited by the Hebrews was the meeting ground for many civilizations. This is exemplified not only by the Jews' political fortunes, but also by their literature. The Pentateuch, written over a span of more than 450 years, gives evidence of many of their alien influences; in the first portion of Genesis alone, we can find all these characteristics. In the First Creation Story and in the *Enuma Elish*, in the beginning there was a watery chaos and the god or some of the gods were already extant. When God begins to create for the Hebrews or for the Babylonians, the order of creation is the same. It required seven tablets to write the *Enuma Elish* and God created the world in seven days.

It is notable, however, that there are also some striking dissimilarities. Firstly, the *Enuma Elish* contains a great deal more material before the creation story. Secondly, man's relationship to the deity is different: For the Babylonians, man is created to serve the gods. For the Hebrews, man, instead, is to have dominion over the plants and animals.

Since the priestly Code was written around 450 B.C., it is entirely possible that the religion of the Persians, Zoroastrianism, might have exerted an influence. While the order of Ahura Mazda's creation is slightly different — first he is recorded to have created sky, earth, heavens, plants, animals, man and then finally water, the concept of the god creating *out of nothing* could have been adopted by the Hebrews.

The story of the Garden of Eden and man's subsequent Fall reveal many old, if not alien, influences. First, there is a great confusion as to what kind of tree grew in Paradise. Was it the Tree of Life or the Tree of Knowledge of Good and Evil? What is the penalty for eating the fruit of the tree? Genesis 2:17 says "The day thou eatest thereof, thou shalt surely die: but if one ate of the Tree of Life, one would live forever (Genesis 3:22). Yet after eating, all that occurred was that Adam and Eve knew they were naked. It is very likely that in one of the early redactions the myth of the Tree of Life was added to the story of the Tree of Good and Evil.

There is a parallel account to the Tree of Life tale in the *Epic of Gilgamesh*. Gilgamesh, a youthful ruler of the legendary kingdom of Uruk, experiences many adventures in his seach for the tree of life, or at least an elixir to make him grow young again. After many exciting adventures, all graphically recounted in the *Epic of Gilgamesh*, he finds the tree, actually only the size of a small sapling, and then leaving it on the shore . . . "he went down into it (a pond) to bathe in the water and the serpent smelled the fragrance of the plant; it came from the water and carried off the plant." The idea of the serpent being bad or of evil is also evident in Persian mythology. Dahaka is one of the servants of Angra Mainyu, and he leads a whole family astray. In much the same way as darkness or its symbols is almost universally equated with bad, serpents are viewed as evil, or agents thereof.

The theme of brother rivalry, ending in killing, finds expression in many civilizations. While Cain's murder of Abel is exactly analogous to the Roman legend of Romulus and Remus, few links between the Romans and the Hebrews can be found. The idea, however, of Abel's blood crying from the ground shows evidence of the institution of the blood feud. The mark placed on the head of Cain to make sure he would not be murdered is reminiscent of a like mark placed on the foreheads of Hittite smiths. The necessity of the mark was based on the value and scarcity of such artisans. In Hittite law, the murderer of a man with a mark was given a much heavier punishment than that imposed upon the killer of an ordinary man.

While almost every civilization has a disaster story, and usually a flood story, it is not always possible to infer an exchange of information between the societies. Yet we have seen that there were Babylonian influences on the Hebrews. Another parallel between their legends is their Flood story accounts. In the *Epic of Gilgamesh*, not only is there a flood, but an ark is built and upon it is placed his family, relatives and animals. Noah did likewise.

Religion was an important and sometimes all-encompassing element of the earliest civilizations — those of Egypt, Babylonia, Persia and Israel — each of which influenced one another and all in turn influenced Western Civilization and Christianity.

BIBLIOGRAPHY

Albright, William. *From Stone Age to Christianity*. Garden City, N.Y.,1957.
Breasted, J.H. *The Dawn of Conscience*. New York, 1934.
Cumont, Franz. *The Mysteries of Mithra*. New York, 1956.
Dhalla, M.N. *History of Zoroastrianism*. New York, 1938.
Eliade, Mircea. *Patterns in Comparative Religion*. New York,1958.
Heidel, Alexander. *Babylonia Genesis*. Chicago,1942.
Horne, Charles H. *Sacred Books and Early Literature of the East*. New York,1917.
Kramer, Samuel Noah. *From the Tablets of Sumer*. Indian Hills, Colorado, 1956.
Masani, R.F. *The Religion of the Good Life*. London,1938.
Mendelsohn, Isaac (ed.). *Religions of the Ancient Near East*. New York,1955.
Moore, George Foote. *History of Religions*. New York, 1931.
Noss, James. *Man's Religions*. New York, 1949.
Petrie, Flinders W. *Religious Life in Ancient Egypt*. London,1924.
Rogers, R.W. *The Religion of Babylonia and Assyria*. New York, 1908.

ISRAEL
ON THE EVE OF
CHRISTIANITY

Ronald S. Cunsolo

Ronald S. Cunsolo, Professor of History at Nassau Community College and Chairman of the Columbia University Seminar on Modern Italy, received his doctorate from New York University. Although primarily interested in modern European history, he has maintained a keen interest in biblical studies. He has presented papers at state and national conventions of the historical profession.

The Israelites, Hebrews, or later day Jews, have been singled out as the classic example of a people who have enjoyed a high degree of self-consciousness, based on a common culture and similarity of religious feeling, even though they have been denied throughout most of their history the normative sanctions of nationalism — territorial propinquity and political independence. Not even purity of race can be claimed for the Jews, much less a uniform language. Over the centuries spanning their existence and travels, the Jews have borrowed spiritually and intellectually from their wider contacts and broader surroundings, and have adapted these to the enrichment of their original ways and unique set of beliefs.

Devotees of the Jewish and Christian Faiths have accorded the Jews an indispensable role in the unfolding drama of God's search for Man and Man's inquiry after God and things eternal. Jewish history, therefore, is not just the account of a people fulfilling its own destiny. It provides those moral exertions and spiritual yearnings which are the foundation stones of our Judaic-Christian heritage — the quest for permanence, communion with the forces beyond, respect for life, social justice, the components of a well-ordered state, in sum, the realization of God's Will and the furtherance of His Kingdom here on earth. This is what gives the Jewish experience its inner vitality and far-reaching thrust.

This traditional view of the Jews as essentially a messianic people is now being rigorously challenged. Revision reflects perhaps the establishment of the state of Israel, the protracted Arab-Israeli dispute, the availability of newer documentary sources, and the extent and level of acculteration of Jewish minorities in other countries. Whatever the causes, a noticeable secularization, so to speak, of Jewish history has been initiated. The thesis advanced is that the positions taken in critical situations were motivated by class interests and material concerns as well as religious exigencies.

Jews trace their lineage to Shem, first son of Noah, from whom sprang twenty-six branches or offshoots of the Semitic race of people. They surface onto the pages of recorded time through the great patriarch, Abram (renamed Abraham) who, promised divine favor, abandoned in the eighteenth century before Christ his ancestral home in Haran in northwestern Mesopotamia and journeyed south into the area which was to be called Palestine. There a number of ancient peoples, mostly Semitic in origin, and given the general designation, Canaanites, were locked in a struggle for supremacy. Isaac, from Abraham, and Jacob, called Israel, of Isaac completed the patriarchal trinity. Israel fathered twelve sons, from whom the twelve tribes of the nation of Israel were immediately derived. After a sojourn of 430 years in Egypt, the Israelites in the thirteenth century before Christ were liberated through Moses. Eventually, under Joshua's leadership they subdued and settled in major sections of Palestine, the Promised Land, "the land flowing with milk and honey," as it was depicted by the Jews.

The initial communion struck by Yahweh (Jehovah, God) with Abraham evolved into an intricate religious system between God and Abraham's descendants. As a developmental relationship it was given the status of a high level contractural agreement, understood by the term, Covenant. Joint privileges and mutual responsibilities were stipulated and elaborated in a functional manner in the Torah (Law), which assumed written form as the first five books of the Old Testament (Pentateuch), codified and compiled between 950 and 550 B.C. Religious prescriptions and ceremonial rites were suitable to the frontier conditions and seminomadic character of life in the area, where the worship of the one true God had to contend for ascendancy against the many local deities.

Political consolidation, state building, and religious centralization actually began with Saul, the first king of united Israel. They were brought to their culmination under David and the earlier Solomon. David's forty-year reign was exceptionally productive as hostile peoples were driven back, and Jerusalem captured and designated the capital. Preparations were introduced for the construction of the temple, the installation of a purified, supervised and expanded sacramental order, with a division of labor to be instituted among the three levels of priests, the Zadokites,

Aaronides, and Levites. The first years of his reign increased the prestige of the Kingdom of Israel. The south (Negeb) was made secure; iron deposits and copper mines were tapped. A fleet was built and a naval base constructed at Elath, off the Gulf of Aqaba.

All too soon divisions appeared, primarily as a result of the misrule of the later Solomon and the defiant attitude of his son, Rehoboam. Many were thrown into despair by the confiscatory taxes, forced labor, foreign marriages, court extravaganzas, and the encouragement which Solomon and Rehoboam offered to the veneration of alien gods. As a consequence, the ten northern tribes or provinces revolted in 933 B.C. and combined to compose the Kingdom of Israel under Jeroboam; Judah and the adjacent tribe of Benjamin remained with the house of David as the Kingdom of Judah. This trend toward disintegration could not be reversed in spite of attempts at religious reform and political renewal under Jehu (c.843-816) and Jeroboam II (786-746 B.C.) of Israel and Hezekiah (715-687) and Josiah (640-609 B.C.) of Judah. Divided and weakened, Israel suffered rank humiliation when in 721 B.C. the northern kingdom was conquered by Sargon II of the Assyrian Empire, and in 586 B.C. Nebuchadrezzar of Babylon destroyed Jerusalem. Having captured Babylon in 539 B.C., Cyrus II, founder of the Persian empire, became the heir of the Babylonian possessions in Palestine. Following each takeover, tens of thousands of the Israelites were deported. Regardless of the political split which had occurred and the ensuing captivity, the Jews still conceived themselves as comprising spiritually and culturally one people as symbolized by the comprehensive term "Israel."

The Persian occupation was of immense significance because it inserted Palestine into the wider world. Palestine was a conduit from Mesopotamia to the lower Eastern Mediterranean and to Egypt. It was also the gateway to the Middle East. Convinced of the dependability of the Jews and of their appreciation for the semi-autonomous status accorded their territory, the Persian government not only recruited soldiers from the region but lifted some 2000 Jewish families at one time and transplanted them into key cities in Asia Minor which had been recently won from the Greeks. Seizure of the cities and the unrelenting imperialistic ambitions of the Persians ultimately threatened the city-states of Greece proper. This provoked a clash with Alexander III the Great of Macedonia who in 333 B.C. at the battle of Issus inflicted a disastrous defeat on Darius and the Persians bringing their dreams of world conquest to an end.

The exploits of Alexander the Great including his occupation of Palestine in 332, brought about noteworthy changes. Alexander was head of a vast dominion which stretched from the Greek mainland to the frontier of India. Composed of many different peoples and cultures, Alexander concluded that the only way to hold the centrifugal forces in check was by deliberately fostering a broad tolerance, a blending of Greek and Oriental customs and ideas, a phenomenon we recognize by the word, Hellenism. Hand in hand with Alexander's armies went the exportation of the language and culture. Cities were established throughout the far-flung empire on the Greek design, with their high degree of self-rule, complete with typical Greek civic institutions and governmental-administrative structures. A minimum of thirteen were called Alexandria in honor of Alexander, of which Alexandria in Egypt became the most famous. Alexander personally encouraged the marriage of his top officials to Persian women. Eighty of his generals were joined to local princesses and as many as 10,000 of his soldiers selected brides from among the women of the conquered population. Alexander himself took as his wife the Persian Roxana, daughter of Oxyartes, ruler of Bactria.

One should guard against any exaggerated notion of the influence Greek philosophy and manners had among the Jews. Although current excavation projects in Palestine indicate that the Greek presence was more extensive than many students had conceded, it is too risky to ascribe to it direct and widespread influence. The intellectual and commercial classes were apparently touched. The countryside where the overwhelming majority of the people lived, remained a stronghold of orthodoxy and exclusiveness. The gulf which separated the sober, devout, and extremely nationalistic Jew from the speculative, sports loving, and idolatrous Greek was impossible to bridge.

With Alexander's untimely death in 323 B.C., a struggle broke out among his top generals, the Diadochi, over control of the empire. Palestine, as part of what was known as Coele-Syria, later just Syria, became a major theater of action between the two main claimants, the Ptolemaics based in Egypt and the Seleucids who ruled over most of the Middle East. The Ptolemaics were the first to enjoy the upper hand. Their period of domination ceased in 198 B.C. when the Seleucid leader, Antiochus the Great, crushed the Ptolemaic-Egyptian forces at Panias.

Proud and arrogant, the Seleucids esteemed themselves the sole custodians of Alexander's imperial idea. In contrast to the decentralized type of rule initiated by Alexander and the congenial cosmopolitanism advocated by him and adhered to by the Ptolemaics, the Seleucids sought political and cultural uniformity through their own vigorous efforts. The attempt to force the issue of philhellenism in Jewish territories was bound to cause trouble since the bulk of the Jews were not about to sit by and allow a disruption in their pattern of religious devotion. Matters came to a head during the reign of Antiochus IV Epiphanes (175-163 B.C.). In 168 Antiochus promulgated several sweeping decrees which to all intents and purposes declared Judaism illegal. The rite of circumcision was ordered terminated, Sabbath and holy day observances cancelled, compliance with dietary laws prohibited, the temple commanded to be rededicated to the Greek god, Zeus Olympus, scrolls of the Torah publicly burned.

Finally, to provide a refuge for pro-Seleucid elements, Antiochus had a city-citadel built in the heart of Jerusalem, known as Antioch-in-Jerusalem.

Desecration and flouting of Jewish religious and patriotic sensibilities provoked a revolt among the Jews in Judea, the rebellion led by Mattathias from the Hasmonean priestly family. Mattathias had five sons, three of whom, Judas Maccabee (the Hammer), Jonathan, and Simon succeeded in turn to the leadership. The battle was enjoined against the foreign Seleucids and their Jewish supporters. Unable to engage the Seleucids in open encounters, those who rallied to the defense of the Covenant took to the hills where they set up bases of operation from which to harass the enemy. When the embroynic Hasidim sect came forward under Judas Maccabee and Jonathan and made of the revolt a religious-political crusade of the highest magnitude, the drive for self-assertion and national vindication acquired the volunteers, the zeal, and tactics required for victory. By 164 B.C. the temple had been purified and the former sacramental customs restored. Jews throughout the world commemorate the event with Hanukkah, the Feast of Dedication or Festival of Lights, celebrated for eight days, from the 25th of Kislev (third month) into Tibet (fourth month). Antioch-in-Jerusalem was razed in 160. Its dismantling convinced the Seleucids to grant Judah its autonomy.

In 141 B.C. Simon was chosen and acclaimed in solemn assembly ruler, military commander, and high priest. With political and spiritual power centered in one individual, the arrangement tended to make the state a theocracy. Since Simon was the last surviving son of Mattathias, and the offices he held declared hereditary in his immediate family, Simon's son, John Hyrcanus, succeeded him upon his death in 135 B.C. By 130 B.C. full independence had been attained. During the reign of John Hyrcanus (135-04) and that of his successor, Alexander Janneaus (104-76), the first to have assumed the title of king, the waves of jubilation set off by victory carried over beyond Judea into adjacent lands. In retaliation for the aid given the Seleucids during the war of liberation, the belief that all Palestine belonged by right to the Jews, the need for protection on Judea's flanks, and due to sheer expansionist fever, military campaigns were conducted towards the south (Idumea), the east (Transjordan), and north (Samaria, Galilee). Areas which had once formed part of the united Kingdon of Israel and had been detached and peopled by strangers were reclaimed. Circumcision became the test of repentance and adoption of the religion of the Jews. By 90 B.C. the area comprising the Hasmonean state compared favorably in extent with the Israeli state of David and Solomon.

It is doubtful that the Hasmoneans would have prevailed without the friendly disposition of the Romans. Aware of the crucial nature of Rome's attitude, Judas, Jonathan, and Simon, backed by the express wishes of the Jewish Senate, curried the good will of the Romans, entering into alliances with them. Agreements were sealed and periodically renewed by the monetary gifts Jews forwarded to Rome as tokens of the esteem in which the Romans were held. Rome reciprocated, accepting the gestures of best wishes conveyed by the gifts. In the Treaty of 142 B.C. with Judea, Rome recognized the independence of Judea from the Seleucids.

Rome's behavior may have been an indication of the influence of the Jewish communities in Italy and antedating Roman rule in the Middle East. Of more telling importance is that Rome's designs overseas and her plans for stability in the Mediterranean and the Aegean had been thwarted over the years by the aggressive Seleucids who insisted on seeing themselves as the only legitimate executors of Alexander's legacy. Rome had covetous eyes of her own cast towards Egypt, Greece, and perhaps Asia Minor, and Palestine. From the second century B.C. on, Rome felt obliged to engage the Seleucids in a number of wars, having as their objective their removal from Greece and Asia Minor. Final resolution, however, had to await the settling of other accounts. One of the results of the Second Punic Wars (218-202 B.C.) between Rome and Carthage was the registration of a Roman protectorate over Egypt. By the Third Punic War (149-146 B.C.), Carthage was permanently eliminated. Macedonia became a province of the empire and Greece a protectorate, thanks to the Fourth Macedonian War (149-148 B.C.). In the meantime Rome had fought a series of wars against the Mithridates, rulers of Pontus in Asia Minor, who were bent on hastening and exploiting the total disintegration of the Seleucid kingdom. In 74 B.C. they annexed Syria. Having cleared the entire Mediterranean of pirates between 68-67 B.C., Gnaeus Pompey was then able to concentrate his attention on the Mithridates threat. Within two years Mithridates Eupator VI was in flight across the Crimea. By 63 B.C. the provinces of Asia (Asia Minor) and Syria were Rome's. Seleucid power never recovered from the blows inflicted by Pontus and Rome.

Having begun to intervene in the Middle East, the Romans found it necessary to extend their concern into Palestine to a degree to which they had not anticipated. There the internal situation was rapidly deteriorating because of the inability of the Hasmonean house to retain the loyalty of its subjects and to exercise control over the entire kingdom. Divisions arose over the nature of the state and society, the intrusion of the government in religious affairs, the widening gap between rich and poor, and the increasing adoptions of foreign fashions. The emergent Pharisee sect became especially embittered over the centering of all religious authority, as well as the political, in the hands of one ruler and his family. Once hailed as liberators, the Hasmoneans were now being assailed as usurpers and corruptors. With the erosion of support a number of individuals appeared as champions of the downtrodden. Together with their followers they repaired to the countryside and set up headquarters for their attacks against the state. The incursions of the Seleucids striving to recapture territory they had lost added to the woes of the government. For many individuals the political and social upheavals led them to seek solace in the coming of the awaited Messiah.

As Roman Commander in Asia Minor and the Middle East, Pompey mediated between the Hasmonean brothers, Hyranus II and Aristobulus II, who sought the throne. Furious over the dilatory tactics and alleged duplicity of Aristobulus, Pompey joined with Hyrcanus in military action against Aristobulus. Once the conflict began, it was not to end until Jerusalem had been captured (63 B.C.), the Hasmonean monarchy abolished, one Hasmonean prince, Aristobulus, killed, and the other, Hyrcanus, appointed high priest and placed in the position of civilian ruler under the authority of the Roman governor of Syria. Having cautiously entered the sacred precincts of the temple, Pompey ordered the temple to be ceremoniously cleansed and daily sacrifices to resume. The toll in human lives in the battle for Jerusalem was high. A fine of 10,000 talers ($100,000,000) was levied upon the Jews. Many were taken as slaves and considerable quantities of gold and silver were shipped to Rome.

Nothing demonstrates more poignantly the steady decline in the fortunes of the Jewish state than the fact the Hyrcanus II was to be dominated by an ambitious and ruthless Idumean, Antipater by name, who maneuvered to secure for his son, Herod, the future Herod the Great, and for Herod's brother, Phasel, the territorial governorships of Judea (which included Samaria) and Galilee, respectively. Antipater and Phasael soon passed from the scene. By stealth, and astute devices, Herod managed to ingratiate himself with the Romans who believed he could be trusted to keep the peace. Granted Roman citizenship in 47 B.C. by Julius Caesar as a reward for the military assistance Herod had extended Caesar's forces in Egypt in his duel with Pompey, Herod in 40 B.C. induced the Second Triumvirate (Augustus Caesar, Mark Antony, Marcus Lepidus) to recommend to the Roman Senate his nomination to the kingship of Judea. Having taken Antony's side in the civil war with Augustus, Herod, after the Battle of Actium (September 2, 31 B.C.) won by Augustus, was summoned to Rome where, ever ingenious, he was not only able to placate the indignant Caesar but also gained from him the enlargement of his kingdom.

In the political arrangements Rome instituted within her empire we see in operation the practical outlook and pragmatic approach of the Romans. They refused to rule every area directly. Such a task would have been a monumental one, given the wide disparity in experience, customs, and temperament. Instead, they devised types of control geared to the locale and suited to the occasion, designed to insure the free flow of goods and services upon which Rome and the empire depended. Certain regions were annexed outright and governed immediately from Rome. Elsewhere, client states or satellite kingdoms were organized, as in Palestine. A measure of home rule in internal matters not only facilitated the job of governing but was also pacified nativist elements. Legates selected by the emperor and stationed in strategic cities were sufficient to remind the people of the Roman presence in the area as did the centurions and the small but efficient constabulary contingents they had at their disposal.

The Palestine under Herod's jurisdiction was bounded by the province of Syria on the north, the Nabataean kingdom on the south, the Mediterranean Sea on the west, and Decapolis, a league of ten self-governing cities dating back to Alexander, on the east, situated between the Jordan River and the Arabian Desert. Herod's kingdom comprised Judea and Samaria in the center, Galilee on the north, Idumea on the south, and Perea, modern day Transjordan. Bordering on Syria, Decapolis, and the Arabian Desert were the districts of Gaulanitis, Batanaea, Auranitis, and Trachonitis, all of which were ruled by Herod.

Although the ethnic stock of Herod's Kingdom was predominantly Jewish, there were pockets as in Samaria and Galilee where non-Jewish and non-Semitic elements were quite possibly in the majority. The term "Galilee" means, in the Greek, "district" or "circle of the foreigners." Greek influence in Galilee, Perea, and Decapolis was more pronounced than elsewhere in Palestine, with the Greek language enjoying in those areas equal popularity with Hebrew and Aramaic.

Economic pursuits were dictated by natural resources and geographic factors. The broad expanses on the south (Negeb) were barren. The thin soil, hard, stony ground, hilly conditions and dry climate characteristic of most of Judea and Samaria lent themselves to sheep grazing and goat tending. With its richer soil and more sufficient rainfall, Galilee found grain more profitable. Fishing particularly in the Sea of Galilee and on the Mediterranean coast, was the major industry. Most of the disciples of Christ earned their living by fishing in the Sea of Galilee. Cheese, wine, olive oil and fruits were also produced in Judea, Samaria, Galilee, and Perea. Weaving, pottery making, tanning, smelting, and general construction employed their share of workers. Neither should the army, the police, nor civil service personnel be omitted. The daily operations of the temples and shrines required various occupations to maintain them, from priests to money-changers. Commerce also provided jobs. A fine network of roads, with main spurs from Damascus to Egypt and trunk lines to the Jordan and the Mediterranean, served as a means of transportation for internal trade and the import-export market. Christ's parable on the rich man and the poor, his reference to the widow's mite, and to the grasping antics of merchants and landed gentry offer evidence of the wide disproportion which existed in possessions and opportunities between the fortunate few and the many who were deprived.

Herod was a man of intrigue and brutality in an age which invited conspiracy and cruelty but this does not satisfactorily explain his longevity as king (40-4 B.C.). A thoroughly detestable fellow, who at no time in his long reign ever gained the affection of his people, he succeeded in alienating so many groups and associations that his survival capacity becomes all the more remarkable. Undoubtedly, he enjoyed the abiding confidence of Rome, no mean asset to any puppet of Rome. Like his father, Antipater, he was clever, and an adroit manipulator. Apparently, deception and the urge to outsmart potential opponents was a family trait since Christ saw fit to speak of Antipas, Herod's son, as "that fox" (Luke 13:32). One detects also an inference of inferiority in the judgment of Christ since the Jews considered the fox to be a sly creature and one lacking dignity. As a half Jew from Idumea many of Herod's subjects could never accept him. The king, as the prophets had foretold, had to be of full Jewish and Davidic descent. To add insult to injury although partly Jewish in nationality he was not Jewish in religion, customs, and attitude.

An individual who engendered suspicions from the start, Herod experienced an unforgettable humiliation when at the moment of his ascension to the throne Jewish groups had attempted to thwart his expectations, petitioning Rome that the masses of the Jews preferred to have the realm joined with Syria and governed directly by Rome than to have a semi-autonomous state under an upstart and foreigner. In an effort to calm Jewish feelings and to disarm his enemies, Herod vetoed the festivities which had been planned for his coronation. Herod had to be wary of the several factions in Jewish society and the fanaticism which occasionally marked religious life. He had reason to fear the messianic impulse of his people which periodically surfaced and if unchecked, could easily provoke clashes and summon Roman retaliation. When the Wise Men having found the Christ-child went their way without notifying Herod of their success, Herod, we are told by Matthew, became "exceeding wroth, and sent forth, and slew all the children that were in Bethlehem, and in all the coasts thereof, from two years old and under, according to the time which he had diligently inquired of the wise men" (2:16).

Harassed by a number of foes and fears, Herod concluded that he had no choice but to retain the favoritism of Rome. When deemed advisable, Herod journeyed to Rome to maintain his private contacts with the Caesars and the Senate, and to defend his stewardship against the complaints lodged by Palestinian Jews. On the morrow of his coming to power, Herod required of the citizenry an oath of allegiance to himself. He then exempted many of the Pharisees and the Essenes who could not subscribe to such a pledge because of religious scruple. To conciliate the Pharisees, Herod acceded to their wishes by separating the religious sphere from the political. If he selected Hananel to head the priesthood, and not one from their own order, he at least had not offended them by offering the post to a candidate from the Sadducees, their arch rivals.

Between Herod and the Sadducees an implacable hatred existed. Since the Sadducees had been a main pillar of support for the Hasmonean state, and regarded Herod as a halfbreed and stranger, Herod sensed that any attempt at a rapprochement would be futile. Hananel's departure from the high priesthood in favor of Aristobulus III was viewed by the Sadducees as a victory for them and proof of their strength. Unlike the Pharisees, the Sadducees thought it much more advantageous to have both the political and religious authority centered in the king as under the Hasmoneans. Since Aristobulus hailed from the Hasmonean house, the Sadducees may have stretched their luck, believing that Herod would be compelled by popular clamor to relinquish the crown to Aristobulus just as he had been forced to move Hananel from the post of the high priest and to bring Aristobulus in. They reckoned unwisely. The death of Aristobulus (35 B.C.) by drowning caught them by surprise. Having returned from Rome (30 B.C.), whence he had gone to explain to Augustus his backing of Antony, Herod had many of the Sadducees put to death, accusing them of having plotted with Aristobulus, Hyrcanus, and Mariamne the overthrow of his regime. If the Pharisees escaped persecution, they were soon to be estranged because Herod insisted in having bandit leaders and guerrilla chieftains done away with without trial and without involving the Jewish senate (sanhedrin) in the decision. By that time, however, Herod had secured for himself another major source of collaborators and adherents, the Herodians as they are referred to in the New Testament. They were an important group of officials, adminstrators, army personnel, royal guards, court personalities, reinforced by a corps of influential civilians, all of whom saw Herod as the only logical alternative to anarchy or outright subjugation to Rome.

To capture the imagination of his subjects Herod undertook an imposing array of building projects. With the reconstruction of the temple in Jerusalem, the conversion of the old Maccabean castle into a fortified residence for himself, the building of a second royal palace on the western hill, with three huge towers to defend it, and the erection of many public places (hippodrome, theaters, baths), Jerusalem was transformed from a teeming but unpretentious city to one of the most glittering metropolises of the Roman Empire. If not a practicing Jew, Herod, nevertheless, permitted full freedom of worship. Pilgrimages were encouraged to the Holy City to coincide with the more solemn days of the religious calendar — Rosh Hashanah (New Year's), Yom Kippur (Day of Atonement), Succoth (Feast of Tabernacles), Passover (Exodus from Egypt), and Shevoth)giving of the Law on Mount Sinai).

It is to be doubted that such contrivances on the part of Herod were convincing or that they gained for him many new friends. Herod's works were too much based on calculation and too little on sincerity. They could not atone for his reprehensible character and for his many scandalous misdeeds. Some might understand why Herod rebuilt Caesarea and dedicated it to Augustus on the occasion of the latter's fiftieth year (15 B.C.) and could also tolerate the fact that Herod had his children educated in Rome. They would not accept his pro-Hellenic sentiments. Pagan shrines, theaters, sports arenas, and the idolatry, frivolity and immorality they connoted, were an unspeakable abomination to the Jew. Citizens readily saw through the artifice behind Herod's marriage to Mariamne of the Hasmonean clan. Herod's many other marriages (at least nine), the secret investigations, false allegations, use of torture, and the violent deaths of members of his immediate family (Herod's sons, Alexander and Aristobulus, from Mariamne were executed in 7 B.C. on the standard indictment of conspiracy) could not win public confidence. Neither should one forget the heavy burden of taxation necessitated by the payment of the annual indemnity to Rome, the cost of Herod's construction program, the maintenance of state functions, and the squandering of funds due to personal excess. It has been estimated that the incidence of taxation took a minimum of 40% of the individual's income. Rumblings over the onerous exactions and the inequities of the tributary system were to grow and become a main factor in the Jewish revolt of 66-70 A.D. against Rome.

Turning our attention to schools of thought and affiliated groups, it is only recently that we have begun to appreciate the many facets of Judaism the schismatic tendencies it nurtured in its bosom, and the crosscurrents that agitated within its frame of reference.

A prominent association was that of the Pharisees. In Christian circles the Pharisees are rarely evaluated without drawing on the rebukes they provoked from Christ because of their doctrinaire attitude, air of religiosity and self-righteous spirit. Later generations of the Pharisees may have become pompous, rigid in their thinking, and complacent in their walk with God. Nevertheless the Pharisees were a stabilizing factor and did make a singular contribution to the Jewish state and the flowering of Jewish life and culture. The Apostle Paul surely did not feel he had anything over which he ought to have apologized when he described the pre-conversion Paul as "a Pharisee of the Pharisees."

It might very well be that the original nucleus of the movement was composed by the Hasidims, founded by the High Priest Simon the Just in the middle of the fourth century before Christ. The Hasidims, it will be recalled, was that mobilized and highly vocal religious-military-political elite which surged to the forefront of the Maccabean struggles against the Seleucids and the Hellenizing Jews. Because of the difficult task faced by the lower clergy in maintaining their livelihood and social standing, the nascent Pharisee sect drew many recruits from among them, especially when the Pharisees were becoming strongly identified with the synagogues and schools of learning. In the aftermath of victory over the Seleucids and the Hellenizing Jews, the Pharisees became a fixture in society, holding forth before the people and the state the holy calling and extraordinary position of the Jews. We can glean from the apocryphal book, Sirach, what virtues the Pharisees extolled. It was categorically stated that "there is no one superior to him who fears the Lord" (25:10). By contrast, "a merchant," it was submitted, "can hardly keep from wrongdoing" (26:7). Pharisees prized wisdom whose chief function was to detail and to clarify man's relationship with God. Wisdom was a quality which was available to all, rich and poor alike.

Since they emphasized the intellect, the Pharisees associated themselves closely with the Torah, both Written and Oral. To them it was a comprehensive code, which addressed itself to the entire range of man's existence public and private, the spiritual and the material. In the act of explaining the Torah and justifying its validity in everyday life, the Pharisees became the masters of exposition. This may have earned for them the reputation for being petty and pedantic. By the middle of the first century B.C., the Pharisees had become the authoritative interpreters of the Law and in undisputed control of the instruction carried on in the synagogues. The Pharisees also demonstrated their interest in education by sponsoring the establishment of academies where the pursuit of knowledge could be undertaken within a Jewish context. As their group matured, Pharisees adopted such concepts as the resurrection and final judgment as cardinal tenets of their faith: They took a less hostile and more positive attitude toward their Gentile neighbors. Those of non-Jewish stock in Samaria and Galilee who embraced Judaism did so primarily because of the fervent evangelistic efforts of the Pharisees in their midst.

After their alliance with the Hasmoneans, the Pharisees became disillusioned and broke with them. The worldliness of the princes, their insistence on arrogating for themselves both the kingship and the high priesthood, and their preference for the Sadducees antagonized them. Similarly, the Pharisees fraternized with Herod during the early years of his reign. They were soon given cause to change course as they saw his cynical behavior, and Hellenistic affinities. Strengthened by their wholehearted commitment to the Law, the Pharisees found it impossible to accept Christ as He did not conform, according to their rationale, to the Torah prescription concerning the Messiah and the signs announcing His arrival.

Challenging the Pharisees for religious leadership in Israel were the Sadducees. As the name indicates, the Sadducees were the latter Zadokites, the descendants of Zadok, the High Priest who officiated during David's reign. They formed the priestly aristocracy and wanted to perpetuate the *status quo*. Affluent and seemingly secure, the Sadducees were not looking nor awaiting for a messianic kingdom. In contrast to the Pharisees and other religious brotherhoods who were expecting both a messianic age and the day of resurrection, the Sadducees believed in neither. They had been content to respect the Hasmonean house as fully prophetic in nature and worthy of the total allegiance of all. Because Herod doubted their loyalty, he cut off the more outspoken of the Sadducees and subjected the remaining to police surveillance. Herod's circumventing of the Senate over the death sentence imposed on outlaws was partly motivated by the desire to get the Sadducees out of state affairs. He succeeded in intimidating them after the inital skirmishes of the opening years of his reign. The wealth and social conservatism of the Sadducees tended to make them unpopular among the people who, particularly in the towns and cities, gravitated towards the Pharisees. Many Biblical commentators indicate that the Sadducees formed the religious-social class Christ had in mind when he lashed out at those rich who trusted in their possessions, lacked faith in God, and showed no compassion for the poor.

The religious position of the Sadducees was based on the Jerusalem temple. As the temple provided for the worship of the one true God, it underlined the crucial role of the Sadducees as an upper ministerial caste. If the Pharisees elevated knowledge and urged submission to all of the precepts of the Law, the Sadducees clung tenaciously to longstanding ceremonial rites. Literalists, they tried to circumscribe the scope of the Law. They lifted from the Scriptural text the sacramental ordinances and elaborated them into a dogma all of its own. Sadducees opposed the spread of synagogues and learned institutes and the advance of the Pharaisaical and Rabbinical type of Judaism implied. No one was more aware than they that the temple, with its services and offerings, its historic buildings, the stirring memories it evoked, and the great names connected with it, represented not only the religious but also the emotional center of the nation. Any diminution in its appeal and authority stood to endanger the unity of the country and undermine their own personal position.

The Essenes were another variant of Judaism and flourished from about 100 B.C. to the Roman onslaught in 67 A.D. Adhering to a stern code, their tastes were plain and their life style uncomplicated. As a rule Essenes had a low opinion of man and his innate capabilities, contending that his character and fate were more predetermined and bound up to a greater degree with environmental factors than Jewish sectarian groups had been willing to admit. Forsaking the world and the desires of the flesh, the Essenes took up their abode in rural areas, organizing for themselves monastic and semimonastic communities. Avoiding the costly distractions of urban civilization, the Essenes preached and practiced holiness seeking through prayer and fasting individual salvation and national regeneration.

One Essene enterprise was established at Khirbet Qumran, five miles off the northwestern corner of the Dead Sea, where between 1947-1956 the library collection of the communicants was discovered. Popularly entitled the Dead Sea Scrolls, the manuscript materials included among its religious works the earliest copy yet known of the complete book of Isaiah. The scrolls were of leather parchments, several of which were wrapped in linen cloth and placed in large jars, deposited in a cave located 1000 feet below sea level. Through careful laboratory examination the manuscripts were assigned to the period 75-05 B.C., one of unusual turmoil, even for Palestine, climaxed by the Roman takeover.

Apolitical, and most scrupulous in their spiritual devotions, the Essenes were excused by Herod from taking a formal loyalty oath to him. Rumors were very strong at the time that Josephus, the famous Jewish chronicler and Commander of Galilee, who went over to the Romans in the first Jewish-Roman war (66-70 A.D.), had been reared as an Essene. John the Baptist was likewise considered to have been a member of the association since there were Essene chapters that subscribed to the rite of water baptism. Maturer reflection however, could hardly substantiate John's belonging to the order. If the prophet effected a rustic and wilderness existence, he did not, on the other hand, altogether seclude himself in a monastery but went out to minister among the general citizenry. The Essenes and their ascetic ideal perished in the tumultuous days of 66-70 A.D.

An interesting denomination of Judaism was composed of the Zealots, Josephus' "Fourth Philosophy," fourth, that is, after the Pharisees, Sadducees, and the Essenes. Zealots presumably split off from the Pharisees over the latter's apparent willingness to restrict their hostility toward the later Hasmoneans and the Herods to talk rather than engage them in open combat. The Zealots were the heirs of the Hasidic tradition of orthodoxy, militancy, and political separation when once it seemed that the Hasidims were about to be absorbed within the ranks of the Pharisees. Zealots were full covenanters. As the designation implies, they were jealous guardians of doctrinal soundness and eloquent proponents of the distinctiveness of Judaism and the Jews in the face of mounting pressure for compromise and accommodation with the evolving age. They hated Rome and the emergent world with its pleasures and temptations. The Sadducees were too upperclass and snobbish. The Pharisees stressed wisdom and the life of the mind at the expense of the emotions and action. The Essenes had isolated themselves while the Herodians sought fame and wealth.

Zealots maintained that a general awakening and period of divine judgment was to precede the advent of the Messiah. They intended to speed the day. A large portion of the apochryphal literature, with its theme of righteous rage, instinct for heroism, passion for rebellion, and sense of patriotism, was of Zealot inspiration. Self-styled tribunes of the people, such as Theudas, Judas the Galilean, and Hezekiah from Judea, burst forth from the company of Zealots, whom the staunch advocates of law and order dubbed "brigands". Constantly on the run, and aided in clandestine fashion by Jews who were not members of the organization, the Zealots were a costly problem to governors and rulers who had to deal with the situation, requiring on occasion nothing less than fullfledged military campaigns to root out the insurgents. Ardently messianic, and determined to preserve the distinctiveness of the Jews against all potential foes, the

Zealots were in the vanguard of the revolt of 66 A.D. They vanished to a man in their desperate last-ditch stand at Masada in 70 A.D.

Difficult to distinguish the Herodians, known also as the Boethusians, comprised a notable complement of Jewish society. Where entered in the New Testament (Matthew 12:13, 22:16; Mark 3:6), they are presented as joining with the Pharisees, in an attempt to trap Christ over the questions of sabbath healing and payment of taxes. The consensus of opinion is that the Herodians formed a political-social-economic grouping rather than a religious faction as such. They were probably the first citizens of prominence who adjudged Roman rule through the Herods the best of all possible arrangements short of independence itself which was unlikely. While one with the Sadducees in wealth and social standing, they were distinct from them in formulating the practical justification for Herod's right to be accepted as the legitimate ruler of Israel.

We complete our selective and summary survey of Jewish religious and cultural agencies with the scribes. Originally in use in Egypt and among the ancient Canaanite peoples in Palestine, scribes in Israel were from David's time on permanently attached to the government, administration, armed forces, and the temple. They labored as secretaries, technical writers, chroniclers, and in the general field of accounting. Court proceedings were recorded by them; they drafted legal papers, contracts and writs of divorce among them. Because of the nature of their work and the skills required, many scribes were in a position to advise kings, rulers, generals, managers of large estates, and local potentates. A highly respected undertaking, the career of the scribe carried with it very strict rules of conduct.

At some point in the development of the scribe as an avocation there arose the possibility of entrance into full time religious service. Scribes became proficient in the collecting, editing and codifying of religious utterances which were announced and offered to the reading and listening public as the Scriptures or the Torah. Baruch the scribe, son of Neriah, was the personal secretary of the prophet Jeremiah and perhaps his ministerial understudy as well. The renowned Ezra, whose exploits are covered in the Old Testament book which bears his name, who was a compiler and copyist of the Torah, hailed from the order of the Zadokites. He led a contingent of Jews from Babylonia back to Jerusalem (c.398-375 B.C.) and brought with him a codified version of the Mosaic Law. It was in the very nature of things that many scribes should also become teachers of the Scripture. Two centuries after Ezra, the scribe Ben Sira collected in Sirach the choicest aphorisms and moral insights he had delivered over the years to the students who had attended his school in Jerusalem. Most scribes, working as they did out of the synagogues and the academies, and as sturdy proponents of the entire Law, Written and Unwritten, were of the Pharisaical persuasion.

Having reviewed briefly the more outstanding and conspicuous of jewish religious and cultural organizations, we will now examine the major institutional developments. The senate or the sanhedrin had its antecedents in the remote past of Jewish history. From its earliest manifestations it was oligarchical in character, composed of the chief personalities, princes of the tribes, and heads of the families, through which Moses had intended to exercise leadership and execute divine commands. Cumbersome and unwieldy in numbers and appearance, Moses pared the assemblage to seventy, adherence restricted to the ruling elders and the more important of his subordinates. Although absorbed or rendered superfluous in the day of the indivdual judges and by the coming of Saul and his royal establishment, it managed to survive. The youthful and audacious David courted it after his conflict with Saul. Something along the lines of a national conclave was hurriedly summoned upon the death of Solomon, to determine the fitness of his son, Rehoboam, for the succession. Infuriated by his total lack of understanding of the grievances brought to his attention, those patricians and common folk from the ten northern tribes who had gathered at Shechem declared Rehoboam deposed before his reign had begun.

All this set an excellent precedent upon which to build. As the situation warranted these coming togethers became more frequent and routine, until an organ surfaced resembling a representative body. Its long evolutionary struggle for official recognition and permanent status was sealed in 150 B.C. in the renewal and the enlargement of the alliance Judas Maccabee had forged with Rome fifteen years before. The instrument of the pact was transmitted to Rome and Sparta in the name of "Jonathan the high priest, the senate of the nation, the priests, and the rest of the Jewish people." One should not think of the senate as a democratic instrument. It did not claim to be. There was much too intimate an association of the priesthood with the state, indicated by the fact that the overwhelming majority of the seventy-one members who normally composed the senate came from the camps of the Sadducees and the Pharisees. Moreover, it was the high priest who functioned as its executive officer during the two hundred years before the Christian Era, with the sessions of the senate convened in the temple. The senate was very jealous of the privileges it had won over the years. This could create a deadlock should a monarch decide to break with custom and to rule singlehandedly. Herod provoked much enmity when he ordered rebels to be exterminated without deferring to the senate which had jurisdictional right in all cases involving the death penalty. Herod Antipas, Herod's son, effected a reconciliation with the senate when he invited it to participate in the trial of Christ on Passover night in the palace of the High Priest Caiaphas.

A most imposing and venerable institution was the Jerusalem temple. From its embryonic form as the portable tabernacle during the wilderness journeys of the Israelites to its fixed location in the capital city, the temple, exercised an extraordinary fascination. It was the House of Yahweh, the meeting place of God and his Covenant People. It provided a patriotic and sentimental appeal for the Jews in much the same fashion as the Parthenon did for the Greeks and the Forum for the Romans. It was also a storehouse of grain, oil and wine which devotees brought to God. The stables and barns attached housed the animals to be sold and prepared for sacrifice. In its lifetime the temple was also used as a depository of funds. A steady source of revenue was provided by the so-called Temple Tax, amounting to ½ shekel, paid by the faithful Jew, and by the proceeds and donations derived from visits, tourism and jubilees. Huge sums of money were involved in offerings, currency exchange, interior furnishings and sacramental ornamentware. Jewish and non-Jewish rulers from Hezekiah to Antiochus IV periodically raided the temple treasury or lifted gold and silver vessels and utensils from the building to buy off potential foes, meet indemnity obligations to foreign powers as well as for personal use.

At the apex of the priestly hierarchy stood the high priest who overseed the entire operation of the temple and presided over the sacramental priests. The latter were in turn assisted by the ministering priests who were responsible for all of the preparations incidental to the religious activities carried out under the auspices of the temple. Membership in the three categories was based on family lineage. Although all of the priests hailed from the tribe of Levi, and all were therefore of the Levitical priesthood, a three-fold specialization and selection had taken place. From Aaron to Zadok, it was the descendants of the former who filled the seat of the high priest and the ritual and ceremonial priesthood. From Zadok on the candidates for the uppermost position were generally drawn from the sons of Zadok (Zadokites, later Sadducees), while the sacrificing priests, the Aaronides, who continued to be identified with the house of Aaron, and the Levites, strictly speaking, kept to their responsibilities as aids and helpers of the Aaronides. Socially and economically disadvantageously situated *vis à vis* the two higher orders, the Levites were to experience increasing hardships as they endeavored to fulfill their priestly vows. Some were to remain true to their original calling as best they could. Others made the most of the new avenues gradually opened up for service by the synagogues, academies, the rabbinate, and the rise of the Pharisees and the profession of the scribe. There were those who left the ranks of the priesthood and assumed secular pursuits.

The high priest chose most of the important subordinates; he functioned as the chairman of the senate. There were those who found the temptations for graft and venality too difficult to resist. In the books of Ezekiel and Malachi we have glimpses of how perilously close and frequently intermingled the sacred and the profane were in the temple. Rivalry and competition for the top post was keen and on occasion knew no religious bounds or moral restraints. So formidable and financially critical was the office of the high priest that the Maccabee-Hasmonean princes kept and fought to retain it for themselves. Herod was wise and flexible enough not to continue the practice. He exercised his right of selection, tapping Hananel, a foreign Jew, hoping thereby to placate the people, safeguard a measure of control for himself, while injecting just enough resentment among the priestly groups to make it extremely unlikely that they could discover the means of combining against him had they the desire to do so.

During the years just prior to Christianity, Judaism displayed much spiritual vigor as manifested by the several divisions within Judaism and considerable institutional innovation. When it met the test represented by Christianity, Judaism was in the early phase of transformation from Biblical to Rabbinical Judaism. Intimately involved in the fermentation was the appearance of synagogues and academies. The term "synagogue" was from the Greek, meaning "a bringing together," which later was ascribed to the meeting place itself. Synagogues and academies, the future *Yeshivot* of the medieval period, came into being among the Jews who had been dispersed abroad into areas under Babylonian and Persian control. Over the centuries the institutions spread to Syria, Asia Minor, Egypt, the West, and to the Holy Land. Challenged by their distance from Jerusalem and by their being deprived of the temple, Jews responded by congregating in halls within their reach. Determined to preserve what they could of their religion, local communities of Jews adopted prayer, praise, psalms, and textual exposition on the Law as a substitute for temple ritual and cultic offerings. If it is true that the Hellenistic age found animal sacrifice repugnant, it is also true that there were not lacking among the Jews those who questioned its intrinsic merits and general efficacy as a medium of atonement. This refinement of religious practices and beliefs was bolstered by the growing body of exegetical literature, appearing by 350 B.C. on the Torah (Law). By 450 A.D. this was to be accepted as the opening and main section of the Talmud ("Instruction," "Learning"). As a result adjacent to the Written Law and supplementary to it there was developed in readable form the Oral or Unwritten Law, consisting, in addition to the ancient popular customs a store of priestly reflections, rabbinical admonitions, judicial decisions and scribal observations.

The connection between the establishment of local houses of worship and the need for institutes or seminaries to train teachers and experts on the Law and the interested communicant is evident. Ezra in Babylon was a student and professor of the Law. As academies flourished and increased in number, extending themselves into Judea, Samaria, and Galilee, they produced on the eve of the Christian Era such early prototypes of the rabbi ("master," "teacher," "scholar") as Hillel the Elder, and his descendants the several Gamaliels, one of whom was reported to have been Paul's tutor in Judaism, and Shammai, Pallien, and Samaise to name several of the more illustrious. Hillel and Shammai were from Babylon. Formerly colleagues, they split and went their separate ways, each heading a rival academy. Hillel's school represented a conscious attempt to update Judaism through a more liberal application of the Oral Law and a more favorable disposition towards the contemporary scene, while Shammai's educational enterprise stoutly held the line against the use or infiltration of foreign and extraneous materials in the explanation and elucidation upon the Written Law. In spite of the opposition or reservations, the judicious and practical utilization of the Oral Law gained adherents and continued apace. By A.D. 200 the process of sorting and compiling the Mishna had been completed by Rabbi Judah Hanasi. Judaism now had an extra-Scriptural set of documents to range alongside the given law.

The combination of free synagogues and professional schools, with their spiritual guardians and mentors, had profound implications for the future of the Jewish religion. Ultimately, they were bound to undermine the religious leadership in Jerusalem. The reaction of the Jerusalem priesthood, particularly among the Sadducees, was to offer no major concessions to newer concepts and more modern ways but to confirm the superior merits of the Written Law and the compelling nature of temple ritual and sacramental ordinances. This is not to deny that there were those of the middle and upper clergy who discerned the signs of the time and cooperated with the synagogues and academies being founded. Conversely, there were many who subscribed to synagogues and academies but who still preferred and strongly advocated the temple approach to Yahweh. The events of 70 and 135 A.D. removed whatever obstacles the temple and the sacerdotal system may have been for the growth and spread of synagogues and learned institutes. Post-Jerusalem Judaism was to be characterized by a farflung network of synagogues and schools under the tutelage of the rabbi, the master of religious wisdom. In the process the dedicated layman had replaced the priest; an aristocracy based on blood had given way to an intellectual elite whose ranks were open to those who qualified through talent and motivation.

Concerning the scattering of the Jews, or the Diaspora it is to be admitted that many must have left Palestine voluntarily or because they thought they could make a better living elsewhere. Economic realities were harsh and discouraging. The natural resources were simply not available in kind or quantity to sustain anything but a scale of living modest by any standard of measurement. Even that was perpetually menaced by the political upheavals and military conflicts which put a blight on the entire area. Over 200 military campaigns were conducted in and across Palestine in the 260 years which separated the death of Alexander (323) from Pompey's seizure of Jerusalem (63 B.C.). The frightful loss of life, the devastation caused by armies constantly on the march had a very shattering effect.

Many of the enclaves of Jews in Italy and in Asia Minor cannot be explained except on the basis of self-generated emigration. When Lucine V. Flaccus, the former Roman governor of Asia, was brought to trial in Rome (59 B.C.) on the charge that he had embezzled, or at the least misappropriated, proceeds from the temple tax, it took nothing less than the prestige, legal maneuvers, and rhetorical skills of a Cicero to obtain an acquittal. In his defense of Flaccus, Cicero was constrained to point to the interventionist activity of Roman Jews in a manner which left no doubt about their numbers and ability to close ranks behind an issue which touched them deeply and to win the support of the general public. It is difficult to believe that the Jews in question were the same Jews whom Pompey had brought back with him in 63 B.C. as slaves, that they could have gained their freedom and have such an impact on Roman society all in a matter of four years.

The departure of the overwhelming majority of Jews from Palestine is not to be attributed to hard times, internal chaos, nor to military disturbances, but to the fact that they were forcibly removed. From the year 732 B.C., when Tiglath-Pileser III of Assyria captured several cities of northern Israel, to 132-135 A.D., the date of the final confrontation between Rome and the Palestinian Jews over the question of Jewish independence, an intermittent series of deportations were carried out. Frequently cities were emptied of their entire population. On other occasions a more selective procedure could be relied upon to produce the same effect. By taking hostages from the military, the political leadership, the nobility, priesthood, mercantile groups, artisan class, and by sacking key cities and villages, society was left in such a state of confusion and disrepair that the people who were allowed to stay were reduced to impotence for many years.

Many were the consequences of the end of independence and of captivity itself. Stunned by what had transpired, many of the exiled Jews organized on the outskirts of Babylonian and Persian societies where they indulged in a collective lament over the cruel fate which had struck them. The grief they shared and the nostalgia which overcame them is eloquently conveyed to us in the first four verses of the 137th Psalm:

1. By the waters of Babylon
   there we sat down and wept,
   when we remembered Zion.

2. On the willows there
   we hung up our lyres.

3. For there our captors
   required of us songs,

and our tormentors, mirth, saying,
"Sing us one of the songs of Zion!"

4. How shall we sing the Lord's song
   in a foreign land?

Most of the Jews quickly adapted themselves to the possibilities of their new surroundings. Their positive attitude was stimulated by the friendly tolerance practiced by the Babylonian and Persian kings in their own metropolitan states and by the opportunities provided in distant lands for new livelihoods in banking, commerce and administration. Such notable personalities as Daniel, Ezra, Jeshua, Sheshbazzar, and Zerubbabel in Babylonia, Nehemiah, Esther, and Mordecai in Pesepolis, capital of the Persian empire, or in Susa, winter residence of the Persian emperors, undertook a selective approach to their changing situation and its potentialities. They drew the line between their participation in business and civic affairs and their commitment to what was for them the overriding claims of their God. They did not isolate themselves. After all, had not Jeremiah dispatched a communication to them, urging them in the name of Yahweh, to "seek the welfare of the city where I have sent you into exile, and pray the Lord on its behalf, for in its welfare you will find your welfare" (29:7)?

More mindful than ever before of their Covenant obligations, and keenly aware that their faith, traditions, and existence as a people were being weighed in the balance, the dispersion Jews drew together in a very strong bond of unity, developing organs and agencies suitable to the maintenance of their identity. As the synagogue evolved, it not only served as a place for worship but also as a social hall, mutual aid headquarters, and the cultural center of its Jewish constituency. When under the enlightened and farsighted policy of the Persian Cyrus II (c.538 B.C.), confirmed during the reigns of Darius I (521-485), Artaxerxes I (464-423), and Artaxerxes II (404-358 B.C.), the temple was allowed to be rebuilt, the walls of Jerusalem repaired, and the restoration of a degree of national life achieved, the initiative did not arise from among the Jews who had remained behind but from those who had been driven into exile and their descendants.

If some Jews returned to Palestine when permitted, many stayed abroad. Eventually, they adopted the country of their exile as their new fatherland. Enjoying an unbroken communal existence extending over many centuries, the Babylonian Jews were to offer their singular contribution to Judaism and Jewish culture with the synagogues, academies, and the Baylonian Mishna or Gemora ("Completion"), an elaborate commentary on the Mishna of Palestinian origins. By the fifth century A.D. both Mishnas had come to form companion pieces and presented as such in the Talmud. To satisfy the spiritual hunger of the Jews in Alexandria, Egypt, who had adopted Greek and had lost the use of Hebrew, the Septuagint translation of the Old Testament was made available around 275 B.C. under the repeated promptings of Ptolmey II.

Against the specter of captivity, Jews were immediately drawn to re-evaluation. Reassessment was led by the prophets. Defeat, and the humiliation of exile could only be explained as divine punishment for disobedience, the turn to false gods and materialism. Kings, priests, and masses had defaulted on their Covenant responsibilities. If this God Yahweh was a stern and demanding God, he was also of the kind who could be importuned regarding his promises of deliverance. Out of this intensive cross-examination came the revelation that routine religion, formal compliance with its ritualistic aspects, was not enough. It was holiness, purity of motives, a humble spirit, intimate fellowship with God, in a word, personal salvation, which were the essentials of a religious experience. Along with this went the call for a conscience awakened and aroused to correct the ills of society. An initial concern for the poor, the deprived, and the innocent victims of misfortune was an inherent product of the Jewish mentality.

Unquestionably, a most magnificent piece of evidence of the broadening horizons resulting from captivity was the universalization of the message of renewal to incorporate the Gentiles and mankind in general. Due to the varied nature of their experience, many Jewish thinkers were being educated to read the divine will in terms of the greater accessibility of God to Jew and Gentile alike. Yahweh was above political and racial frontiers. The anticipation offered through Zechariah, whose ministry is dated 520-518 B.C., was that "Peoples shall yet come, . . . saying, 'Let us go at once to entreat the favor of the Lord, and to seek the Lord of Hosts" (8:20). The Messiah was to be the Redeemer of all. "A light to lighten the Gentiles and the hope of your people Israel," as Simeon expressed it in presenting the infant Christ child in the temple before God.

This enlarging of God's purpose to include Gentile believers was immediately or by implication reflected in the books of Job, Proverbs, Ecclesiastes, Ruth, Jonah, Esther, Micah, Zechariah, parts of Isaiah, the apocryphal entries Judith, Sirach, Tobit, all compiled between the sixth and second centuries B.C., and certain passages of the Pentateuch as well, wherein Yahweh was introduced as the willing God of all and the Gentiles treated as potential converts. The gradual disassociation of the idea of animal sacrifice from Judaism may have eliminated a major barrier. Faced by the problem of what to do with the people living in those areas of Palestine which had been seized and repopulated with strangers, the Jews, upon their return to the localities in question, felt they had no other recourse but to compel aliens to choose between Judaism or expulsion. We venture many preferred the former. Of the clerical orders, the Levites, from whose ranks were being drawn the temple aides, singers, instrumentalists, and guards, could conceivably have interpreted this opening toward the Gentiles as a legitimate extension of God's providential care. Many of the lower clergy will shift to the Pharisees, once their movement became operative, and prepare against tomorrow by installing themselves in sensitive posts in the synagogues and schools which the Pharisees were mobilizing as channels for the propagation of Judaism to all who would hearken irrespective of race and social derivations. The Pharisees did yeoman missionary labor among foreigners, especially among the Samaritans and Galileans. They devised the term "prosylete" to be accorded those aliens residing in Palestine who had embraced the Jewish religion and Jewish civic institutions.

Among those Jews who advocated a more direct approach to God by Jew and Gentile alike there were undoubtedly those who nurtured outright assimilationist sympathies. They were to be found in the priesthood and the landed gentry, the books of Ezra and Nehemiah provide many instances of marriages and agreements between aristocratic and priestly families of the Jews and prominent castes of other national groups. Backing them were sections of the intellectual and mercantile elements, urban dwellers in general, with the exception of the inhabitants of Jerusalem. This promising mutuality not only encouraged racial mingling, particularly in Samaria and Galilee, but also an incipient combining of different religious forms. Many in Judea readily attended the synagogues and visited the temple, participated and partook of their strikingly dissimilar services, without sensing any contradiction or incoherence in their devotions. Also engendered was the faint beginnings of a syncretist spirit, a blending or merging of diverse religious ideas and cultural modes, involving the Judaism of the post-exilic Jews and the beliefs brought in by non-Jewish immigrants. There were those who might accept Gentiles but not intermarriage because of prejudice, and the conviction that mixed marriages were a form of genocide.

A more generous and less restricted outlook was vigorously opposed by major sections of the Jerusalem-Judean religious hierarchy. Cast in close support was the populace of the holy city, the peasantry, and those of the nobles, merchants and intellectuals who wanted their people and their faith to remain uncontaminated. As separatists, the Zadokites, Sadducees, and Aaronides leaned heavily on the works of I, II Chronicles, Ezra, Nehemiah, the Psalms, those books which they thought underlined the original calling and peculiar fitness of the Jews. From their side came the writers who were responsible for the final codification of the Pentateuch with the addition of the traditions, the so-called "P" materials, which had been preserved by their priestly forbears. The Pentateuch as conclusively drafted was sure to document the fact that Judaism was a cultic religion of the Jewish people exclusively. It has been said that a major reason why the upper priesthood did not receive the apocryphal literature as divinely authored was because of the examples it set forth of reciprocity and good will between Jew and Gentile.

The temple constructed at about 400 B.C. on Mount Gerizim, the holy mountain of the Samaritans, located just thirty miles from Jerusalem and the Jewish temple, symbolized the resentment of the Samaritans against the hostility of the Jerusalem church establishment toward a broader disposition between Jews and Gentiles. Ethnic bias was a personal affront to the Samaritans since considerable intermarriage had occurred between aliens sent into Samaria by foreign potentates and Jews who had been left behind or who had been ejected and had later journeyed back. The Mount Gerizim temple was ordered razed by Alexander in 332 at the urgings of Judean Jews. Rebuilt, the Hasmonean ruler John Hyrcanus destroyed it in 110 B.C. in revenge. It was erected anew. The Samaritans also proceeded to compose their version of the Pentateuch which alone among the Old Testament Scriptures they adopted as authoritative. If the Samaritans limited the role of Moses and the prophets, they gave full coverage to the patriarchs, possibly because Abraham, Isaac, and Jacob accepted non-Jews within their circle of acquaintances, and to the awaited Messiah, as is attested by the exchanges between Christ and the woman of Sychar, a City of Samaria, recorded in John 4. This decisive parting of the ways is referred to as "the Samaritan split." Through their missionary endeavors among the Samaritans, the Pharisees may have succeeded in checking somewhat the hatred and bitterness between the Samaritan and the Judean Jews. Beyond that, their contacts must be inserted within the overall context set by the Jews and Gentiles at large. There the long-term trend appeared to be for selective compromise. The fact that a section of the Jerusalem temple (Court of Gentiles) was reserved for Gentile believers bears eloquent testimony both to the attraction radiated by Judaism and to the mood of cautious understanding which in spite of entrenched obstacles was gradually developing over the years.

Placing the relations between the Romans and the Jews under sharper perspective, one discovers that Rome emulated the Babylonians, Persians, and the Macedonians by according Judaism special considerations. Rome's protective air was an aspect of her grasp of imperial rule, and may also be held as evidence of the extent to which Jews in Italy were acculterated. It may have represented a measure of appreciation for the aid which Jews extended Julius Caesar in his duel with Pompey. The sentiment, moreover, underscored the respect which the Romans had for the Jews — an ancient race, a fabled and legendary people, whose history was a distillation of the experience and wisdom of the entire human family. Nor can we omit the awe which came over many a Roman when presented by the credentials of Judaism as a religion. Roman mythologies were shallow and superficial, unable to retain the allegiance of their communicants. Greek pagan cults offered a parade of capricious and self-indulgent deities who inspired within the individual no moral upliftment, who provided society with no example of righteous living. Those Middle Eastern cosmologies which were invading Italy ushered subscribers into long seances and interminable meditations which dulled their senses and paralyzed them into inactivity. By contrast, Judaism had a set of precepts, a body of authoritative documents, said to have been divinely authored. It demanded holiness. It featured a tough piety and a corresponding sober social ethic. Yahweh, the God of the Jews, spanned the centuries and the universe. He was the measure of all things. If the Greek pursued fulfillment in the realization of his individual genius, the Roman in patriotic attachment to the state, the Jew sought transcendence in communion with Yahweh and in his service. Yahweh was not a God to be taken lightly. He was invisible and yet everywhere at once. No graphic representation could be entertained of him. Mighty in rage and firm in justice, he was a God who brooked no interference and tolerated no rivalry with supernatural pretenders. Stern and severe he was, nevertheless, tender in concern and compassionate in forgiveness. As the Psalmist recorded of him, "as a father pities his children, so the lord pities those who fear him" (103:13).

Where the Romans are met in the Gospel narrative, the picture which emerges is that of a firm and disciplined people who were committed to the public welfare and who knew how to govern. Having denied them territorial independence, the Romans permitted the Jews a full chorus of religious beliefs, observance of traditions, and a moderate degree of political autonomy within an imperial framework. Centurions stationed in Palestine erected houses of worship for the Jews. They engaged in charitable works. One would have to say they did so on principle. Paul's *"Civis Romanus Sum* (I am a Roman Citizen)"* demonstrated pride and frank recognition of the many beneficial aspects of the Roman presence. Romans were reluctant to become involved in the trial of Christ. The performance of Pontius Pilate, Procurator of Judea (26-36 A.D.), was primarily that of a desperate official seeking the truth concerning the man before him, striving to harmonize his loyalty to Caesar with the desire to placate the people and still manage to set Christ at liberty. Many Jews refused or were hesitant to become embroiled in the Jewish-Roman Wars of 66-70 and 132-135 A.D. because of the reality of Roman power and for the fact that Roman occupation meant law, order, and a semblance of home rule. There were no other viable possibilities.

Jews took advantage of the opportunities offered to enter the Roman world. It is equally clear, however, that collaboration was drastically restricted by the incompatibility between the two constituencies. There were definite limits beyond which neither side could go in appeasing the other. There were Jews who surrendered their faith to the promises of the moment, who adopted pagan standards, attended the theater, the spectacular games, who undertook civil and military obligations in violation of religious scruples. They were in a minority. For most of the Jews there was always the realm in which they owed legitimate deference to earthly potentates and that other dominion of the spiritual whose mandates were paramount. The collision course in which the Roman Empire and Early Christianity found themselves was previewed in the potential deadlock existing between the Roman state and the Jews.

Full obedience and total conformity to the Law required the strong internal organization of the Jewish people. Sabbath keeping, the maintenance of pure food regulations, celebration of holy days, proper education, together with the practice of ethical monotheism, demanded constant attention. In age which neither understood nor honored separation of church and state, Jews had no choice but to appeal, as they had to Alexander, for the bestowal of special status. They petitioned the Romans for the right to live in accordance with their ancestral laws. This has been mistaken to mean that the Jews wanted all of the liberties and immunities of the average Roman or Greek citizen. This was not so. Jews could not request full civic privileges since the grant would have entailed the absolute endorsement of the state and its assumptions, something the devout Jew could not offer except at the penalty of his soul. Where, in fact, as in Alexandria, Egypt, and in several cities in Asia Minor, the Jews submitted for total political and juridical equality with the local populace, nativist elements sharply objected, protesting that the Jews were isolated from the mainstream of public life and too selective and discriminate in their approach to their responsibilities to the state.

The permission accorded the Jews to abide by their customs was an intelligent way of avoiding a fatal impasse. In safeguarding the position of the Jews, the Romans intervened when asked to arbitrate problems of sabbath court appearances and holy day observances, generally to the satisfaction of the Jews who pressed for governmental intercession. Having been implored by a Jewish delegation from Jerusalem, Emperor Tiberius Caesar politely censured Pilate and then ordered him to remove the Roman shields he had placed over the main entrance to the palace of the late Herod the Great (32-33 A.D.). Rome allowed the ½ shekel temple tax to be collected in Jewish communities and the proceeds sent to Jerusalem.

That the request of the Jews for extraordinary privileges bore with it the seeds of an anti-Jewish feeling among the majority of the indigenous population is true. Friction was unavoidable. The capacity of the Jews for diligence in their daily affairs, their solidarity, and their reputation as shrewd bargainers, reinforced the underlying suspicion caused by their achievements. Lacking an appreciation of the unusual conditions and distinctive features of Jewish life and culture, many Romans and Greeks were tempted to discern in the compactness characteristic of Jewish districts an anti-Roman or antistate orientation.

Anti-Semitism as a mental fixation and cultural style is ordinarily traced to the Egyptian priest, Manetho, who around 250 B.C. penned a history of his country in which Moses and the Jews were presented as a band of lepers who did not voluntarily leave but who had to be physically ejected. The pogrom or systematic massacre of the Jews, as occurred in Alexandria in 37 B.C., is chargeable to a hidden anti-Jewish bias. If nothing of the sort took place in Italy, Greece, and in the Greek and Roman cities of Asia Minor, the existence of separate and divided communities, against a background of Jewish assertiveness, strained the attitude of compromise and selective cooperation, and led to the promulgation of edicts, as happened in 19 and 49 A.D., ordering Jews to leave the center of Rome or to remove themselves altogether from Italy. Since these decrees and others could not apply to the Jews of the freedman class, were aimed also at numerous other ethnic groups, were shortly rescinded, or never fully enforced, many historians explain that the Romans were not motivated by racial prejudice or religious animus but out of apprehension over the many outsiders and exotic ideas invading Italy.

Concerning the responsibility for the death and crucifixation of Christ, it is time to put to rest certain misconceptions. The voice of prophecy foretold that everyone, Gentile as well as Jew, would turn his back on him. Moreover, Christ himself revealed, "no one takes it (life) from me, but I lay it down of my own accord" (John 10:18). Finally, it should be borne in mind that many of the Jews who rejected Christ and Christianity did so not because of a preference for some pagan deity or astral philosophy but in the name of Yahweh and Judaism, sincerely believing that in so doing they were maintaining full faith with their ancient Covenant relationship with God.

With the scattering of the Jews as a result of the second Jewish-Roman War, that of 132-135 A.D., the consecrated union of God, people, and the Palestinian land which had endured for many centuries was broken, until the establishment of the Israeli state in 1948. In the interim Israel had come to signify a cluster of beliefs and a set of practices embracing Yahweh and his people refined and preserved in the crucible of the dispersion, and gradually expanded and shaped anew to reflect the needs and spiritual aspirations of all mankind. In closing one would do well to recall what the Apostle Paul was to advise the Roman Christians, proud and perhaps all too haughty over their achievements and much too critical of the failures and shortcomings of the Jews. The Jews submitted Paul

> Are Israelites; to whom pertaineth the adoption, and the glory, and the covenants, and the giving of the law, and the service of God, and the promises; . . . . and of whom as concerning the flesh Christ came.

BIBLIOGRAPHY

Archeological Encyclopedia of the Holy Land. Ed. A. Negev. New York, 1973.
Baron, S. W., *A Social and Religious History of the Jews.* 2nd ed., 14 vols. New York, 1957-1969.
Bonsirven, J., *Le judaisme palestinien du temps du Jesus Christ.* 2 vols. Paris, 1924.
Brandon, S.G.F. *Jesus and the Zealots.* Manchester, 1967.
Bucher, A., *Types of Jewish-Palestinian Piety from 70 B.C.E. to 70 C.E.* London, 1922.
Burrows, M., *The Dead Sea Scrolls.* New York, 1956.
Busch, F.O., *The Five Herods.* Trans. E. W. Diches. London, 1958.
Charlesworth, M.P., *Trade-Routes and Commerce of the Roman Empire.* 2nd ed. Cambridge, Mass., 1926.
Daube, D., *The New Testament and Rabbinic Judaism.* London, 1956.
Davies, W. D., *Christian Origins and Judaism.* London, 1962.
Encyclopaedia Judaica. Ed. C. Roth. 16 vols. New York, 1972.
Finkelstein, L., *The Pharisees: the Sociological Background of their Faith.* 3rd ed. 2 vols. Phila., 1962.
Frank, T., *Roman Imperialism.* New York, 1921.
Grant, F.C., *The Economic Background of the Gospels.* London, 1926.
Hoehner, H.W., *Herod Antipas.* London, 1972.
Jones, A.H.M., *The Greek City from Alexander to Justinian.* London, 1940.
Josephus, F., *The Jewish War.* Trans. G. W. Williamson. Baltimore, 1957.
Lightly, J.W., *Jewish Sects and Parties in the Time of Christ.* London, 1925.
Magie, D., *Roman Rule in Asia Minor.* 2 vols. Princeton, 1950.
Mommsen, T., *The History of Rome.* 5 vols. Trans. Free Press, Glencoe, 1965.
Oxford Bible Atlas, Ed. H. G. May. London, 1962.
Radin, M., *The Jews among the Greeks and the Romans.* Phila., 1915.
Reinfenberg, A., *Israel's History in Coins.* London, 1953.
Rivkin, E., *The Shaping of Jewish History.* New York, 1971.
Rostovtzev, M.I., *The Social and Economic History of the Hellenestic World.* 3 vols. London, 1941.
The Social and Economic History of the Roman Empire. 2nd ed. 2 vols. London, 1957.
Roth, C., *The History of the Jews in Italy.* Phila., 1946.
Sanctis, G. de., *Storia dei Greci dalle origini alla fine del secolo V.* 5th ed. 3 vols. in 2. Florence, 1960.
Storia dei Romani. 5th ed. 4 vols. Florence, 1965.
Sandmel, S., *Herod: Profile of a Tyrant.* Phila., 1967.
Smith, M., *Palestinian Parties and Politics that Shaped the Old Testament.* New York, 1971.
Tcherikover, V., *Hellenistic Civilization and the Jews.* Trans. S. Applebaum. Phila., 1961.
The Bible: History and Culture of a People. New York, 1970.
The Oxford Annotated Bible With the Apocrypha. Revised Standard Version. Ed. H. G. May & B. M. Metzger. Imprimatur granted by Richard Cardinal Cushing, Archbishop of Boston. New York, 1965.
Zeitlin, S., *The Rise and Fall of the Judean State.* 2 vols. Phila., 1962-1967.

THE PAGAN GODS
OF GREECE AND ROME

James H. Steinel

James H. Steinel, Assistant Professor of History at St. John's University, received his doctorate from St. Louis University. Long interested in Church-State issues, he has published a series of articles on this subject including one on Church and State in Spain which appeared in *Studies in Modern History*.

The religion of the Ancient Greeks is known to many largely through the myths about Zeus and the other Olympian gods. These myths, however, are only one aspect of Greek religious thought and in some ways they have created a deceptive impression. Actually the Ancient Greeks had a very complex polytheistic religion that arose from several different sources, involved varying tendencies and underwent many changes in the course of time.

One of the problems involved in trying to study Ancient Greek religious thought arises from our familiarity with Christianity, a well-developed, sophisticated, monotheistic religion with a systematic theology as well as a clear link between religion and morality. Though later Greek religious thought shared some of these features, it was originally a very different system of beliefs. Greek religion presents many obvious contradictions if examined from a Christian, Jewish, or even a logical viewpoint. However, if we are to have some insight into the mind of the Ancient Greeks, as well as the impact of their thought on Western Civilization, it is necessary to focus on the origins and the message of their religion.

The complexity of early Greek religion was a result of the three different influences that initially molded it—Indo-European, Minoan, and Near Eastern. Many of the chief gods were clearly Indo-European so that the Greek Zeus had many similarities to the Italian Jupiter or the Germanic Thor. The primitive Indo-Europeans tended to worship vaguely-conceived sky-gods, personified forces of nature, and protective tribal gods. Initially, there seems to have been little mythology or real personification of the gods involved.

This changed, however, when the Greeks drifted down from the Danubian River area into the area of Aegean or Cretan civilization, in the Second Millenium before Christ. There they were deeply influenced by the far more advanced culture of the Cretans or Minoans. It is likely that some of the important Greek goddesses like Hera and Athena were Cretan in origin. It appears that when the Greeks conquered a district, they would either make the local goddess the wife of one of their gods or merge their characteristics into one deity. Because the Minoan deities tended to be earth goddesses, they were often easily paired with Greek sky-gods. Very likely some of the mythology and the process of personalizing the gods may be due to Cretan influence.

The Near Eastern influences came both through the Cretans and through direct contact with Asiatic peoples. The Greek conception of the afterlife, the concept of demi-gods, and Mycenaean burial customs show a striking similarity with contemporary religious practices in Mesopotamia and Egypt. In addition, some of the Greek gods like Aphrodite and Dionysius seem to have been at least partially Near Eastern in origin.

During the Mycenaean Period (1400-1100 B.C.) and the Dark Ages of Greece (1100-800 B.C.), these various influences merged and by the time of Homer (c.800 B.C.) the Olympian gods and the myths had attained their traditional forms. They are often called the "Homeric gods" since the form in which Homer presented them in the *Iliad* and the *Odyssey* became their generally accepted form.

To appreciate this development one must know how the early Greeks perceived their gods and the origin of the world. The Greek cosmology of the world was contained in the unpleasant myth that claimed that in the beginning Chaos produced Earth which in turn produced the Sky (Uranus) and together they produced Night and Day as well as some monsters like Misery, Murder, Hunger, and finally Cronos. Cronos eventually overthrew Uranus and became the Chief god. He then ate all of his sons except Zeus who overthrew him and the Titans. Zeus then forced Cronos to disgorge his still undigested sons and put him in chains in Tartarus (Hell).

Zeus and his wife Hera and his brothers and sisters, like Hades, Demeter, and Poseidon, and their children, like Apollo, form the Family of the Gods. They are also called the Great Gods of Olympus or the Olympian Gods because the Greeks believed that they lived on Mt. Olympus, the highest mountain in Greece. The Greeks conceived the gods as being human-like and having the vices of men; deception, fighting, cruelty, adultery, and pettiness were as common on Mt. Olympus as among mortals. The gods were basically eternal supermen and they often dealt with men in the same capricious, and often cruel way in which they dealt with each other. In the *Iliad*, the gods take sides in the war and personally kill mortals. The Greek gods are often pictured as basically hostile to man and fearful of him. In the Prometheus legend, Zeus tries to keep fire from man to prevent him from progressing. When Prometheus does give fire to man, Zeus punishes him cruelly by tying him to a rock where an eagle gnaws at his liver which continues to re-grow. Zeus and the other Olympian gods in this early period were considered to be subject to some ill-defined force, such as Fate or Destiny.

Below the great gods in this hierarchy there were a legion of minor deities: nymphs, satyrs, Muses, Graces, Furies, Sirens as well as personified qualities and ideas like Justice, Death, and Sleep. There were also numerous demi-gods or heroes like Achilles, Hercules, and Aeneas who had a god or goddess as one of their parents, but did not necessarily possess immortality.

There was no single standard myth that explained the origin of man. One of the myths has the Titan Prometheus or his children create man, but this legend only appears in written form quite late (4th Century). The legend of Pandora's box is linked with this version and the concept that woman was created to harass man seems to have had considerable acceptance. Some Greek peoples claimed separate origins, usually from the Earth. For example, the Thebans believed that the first Thebans were born from dragon's teeth sown in the earth. It is also possible that most Greeks assumed that Zeus was the creator since he was called "Father" even in the *Iliad*. One Greek myth also contains a story of the Flood.

The early Greeks believed in three types of afterlife. For most men it was a shadowy ghost-like existence in the caves of the Underworld. It was not the sort of existence that a Greek looked forward to. In the *Odyssey* when Odysseus visits the Underworld, Achilles tells him that he would rather be "a hired hand for a poverty-stricken farmer than king of all the ghosts down here." For those who had offended the gods or committed certain sins, there was a Hell called Tartarus. Typical among the inmates of Tartarus was Sisyphus, who eternally tried to push a huge rock over a hill in order to gain his release, but just as he neared the summit, the rock would get away from him and plunge back down the hill. For a few special heroes there was a pleasant place called the Elysian Fields or Isles of the Blest, full of green fields and agreeable companionship.

Another important aspect of Greek religion was the role of the oracles. The oracles' main purpose was to give religious advice, but they were most noted for their attempts to foretell the future. In the early period of Greek history the Oracle of Zeus at Dodona in northwestern Greece was the most popular. The sounds produced by the wind rustling through the leaves of a sacred oak tree were supposed to be the words of Zeus. However, the Oracle of Apollo at Delphi in north central Greece eventually became the most important oracle in the Greek world. Here, a prophetess sat on a tripod in a trance — probably from sulphur fumes — and muttered an answer which a priest below interpreted in verse.

How did these oracles continue to maintain their credibility for centuries? They seem to have collected as much information as they could on the situation and then couched their answers in ambiguous terms that covered several alternatives. One example of this ambiguity was the answer given to King Croesus of Lydia when he asked what would happen if he went to war with King Cyrus of Persia. The oracle replied that a great empire would fall. Croesus assumed that the empire meant by the oracle was Persia so he went to war and lost his throne. The oracle, however, was still right since a great empire, the Lydian Empire, had fallen. Typical, too, was the answer given to the Athenians when they asked how Athens should be defended against the Persians. The oracle replied that "wooden walls" would save Athens. Some Athenians interpreted the oracle to mean that they should defend the Acropolis since it once had wooden walls, but others urged — successfully as it turned out — that the city should be abandoned and reliance put on the wooden walls of their ships. Thus the oracle was covered whether the Athenians won or lost on either land or sea. Besides the oracles, the Greeks also used other methods of divination, such as observing the flights of birds or examining the entrails of sacrificed animals.

Another aspect of Greek religion was the festivals and games in honor of the gods. There were many local festivals and several important sets of games, such as the Delphic or Nemean Games. However, the most famous and important of the games were the Olympic Games held at Olympia in western Greece in honor of Zeus every four years after 776 B.C. These games involved some religious ceremonies, but they became in time mainly secular athletic contests with some cultural and mercantile aspects. Perhaps the most famous festival was that of Dionysius in Athens out of which Greek drama developed.

What was the attitude of the Greeks towards their gods and the myths? Did they really believe in these gods and their myths literally? Did they not see the absurdity and immorality in many of the myths? What was the purpose of Greek religious activities?

It does seem that the Greeks of this period believed in their gods, but not necessarily in the truth of all the myths. Some myths were simply folk-lore and probably considered as such. Others were traditional explanations which one might accept, doubt, or interpret symbolically. They were not a a scripture or dogma that had to be believed. As concerns the immorality of the myths, it did not matter since there was little link between religion and morality in this period and the gods were not considered as models for human conduct. Unquestionably the early Greeks tended to be less sophisticated and more tradition-bound than they were later. In addition, it should be noted that some of these stories did not set out to paint the gods as immoral, but it happened rather as a chance cumulative effect. For example, the many myths about Zeus' love affairs with different goddesses and mortal women were not a conscious attempt to make him the Don Juan of early Greece, but were due to the practice of linking a local goddess to a widely known god as a means of absorbing the local cult into a wider one. As this absorption of cults occurred many times, many myths of this type began to appear so that it seemed that Zeus' main occupation was chasing goddesses. Small wonder that later Greek thinkers were often repelled and offended by the immorality of the myths.

The basic purpose of religion in the eyes of the early Greeks was to seek the favor and avert the wrath of the gods by ritual, prayer, and sacrifice. Greek religion was oriented primarily towards obtaining the aid of the gods in this life rather than for the afterlife. Sacrifice was performed primarily by priests in a temple, often in a private chambers inside the building. Thus the Greek temple was not a church for general worship, but a place where usually only priests and priestesses entered and carried on the religious rites for the welfare of the state and not for individuals. The function of the priesthood was largely ritualistic and unlike the Christian priesthood they did not have much influence on Greek life. Greek religion was linked to the State and financially supported by the government.

Who were the gods that the Greeks worshipped in their temples and in their homes? They were primarily the great gods of Olympus, especially Zeus and Apollo; and also the special patron god of their particular cities, usually one of the Olympian gods. For example, Athena was the patron goddess and special guardian of Athens and Artemis (Diana) was the patron goddess of Ephesus in Asia Minor. Each occupation also had its special patron god or goddess, thus Apollo was the patron of shepherds and Hephestus (Vulcan) was the patron of craftsmen. The Greeks also worshipped some minor gods and in rare cases demi-gods like Hercules. In addition, the Greeks worshipped special family gods and their ancestors in special family or cult rites. Family cults were a very important aspect of religious worship in the early period and retained some significance even in the Classic period (800-323 B.C.); but they largely faded away in the following Hellenistic period.

Greek religion in the early period had only tenuous links with morality. Morality was based largely on tribal and family traditions and not on religion; and the myths formed an obstacle to basing morality on religion. Certain offenses that could not be handled by tribal law, such as perjury, had gradually been given a divine sanction; and men beyond tribal protection — travelers, guests, suppliants, and beggars — were considered to be under Zeus' special protection and thus had to be given hospitality and protection. Still, it was by no means a comprehensive morality if compared with contemporaneous Hebrew, Persian, or Egyptian concepts. Also some of the Greek concepts of sin seem rather harsh and unfair by Christian standards. The Greeks believed in the concept of formal sin — that if an objectively sinful act was committed unwittingly, it still deserved punishment from the gods. For example, Oedipus was punished for marrying his mother Jocasta without knowing that she was his mother. The Greeks also believed in inherited sin — that the gods would punish the descendents of a sinner. Thus the children of Oedipus, like Antigone, came to tragic ends because of Oedipus' sin.

The traditional Greek religion had many defects that eventually were to lead to its decline. However, in some respects it was superior to many other religions of its time. For example, in comparison with the Syrian gods, the Greek gods were organized in a more orderly hierarchy; there were fewer demon gods and they were not worshipped in Greece; there was less magic and idolatry; the rites were more dignified; and human sacrifice was quite rare.

Although the forms of Greek religion did not change very much, Greek religious thought moved in a number of new and important directions during the Classic or Hellenic period (800 — 323 B.C.). Among the chief trends were tendencies towards monotheism, increased linkage between religion and morality, more philosophical influences, the appearance of mystery religions and a more critical attitude towards the myths and to a lesser degree towards the traditional religion itself. The best way to understand these changes it to examine the works of the leading philosophers, playwrights, and poets.

The first important religious writer after Homer was Hesiod, who lived around 800 B.C. While much of Hesiod's religious writing was a recounting of the old myths without critical comment, he nevertheless strongly asserted his belief that Zeus was a just god who punished the wicked and protected the just. He claimed that the other gods also respected justice and punished man's misdeeds. Hesiod further emphasized the supremacy of Zeus claiming that Fate was the will of Zeus and not a blind force. Thus in Hesiod, the start of the tendencies towards morality and monotheism can be clearly seen. Another factor strengthening the link between religion and morality was the gradual acceptance of the concept that the extenal ritual purity required for sacrifice also implied an internal purity of soul. Xenophanes, a 6th Century Ionian philosopher wrote that there was only one God who knew and controlled all. He condemned the anthromorphic tendencies of Greek religion and claimed that God had a vastly different and superior nature.

Another important insight into Greek religious thought is found in the works of Aeschuylus (525-456 B.C.), the first great Athenian writer of tragedies. Aeschuylus emphasized the justice of both Zeus and of Fate, the power behind the gods. A benevolent Fate ruled both over gods and men in Aeschuylus' view. Also prominent in his plays was the role of the Furies who harassed sinners for crimes. The second of the great Athenian playwrights, Sophocles, often wrestled with moral problems in his plays and in his *Antigone*, he emphasized the primacy of conscience and of God's law over man's law. His plays expressed his belief that the gods would bring retribution for evil deeds.

The poetry of Pindar, the greatest lyric poet of the 5th Century, largely dealt with traditional myths and geneology. However, he strongly asserted that the gods were just and that a good man would be rewarded by a heaven-like afterlife in the Isles of the Blest. At the same time he also attacked Homer for telling false tales about the gods.

The attitude of Euripides, the third of the great tragedians of the Fifth Century B.C., towards the gods is a matter of some dispute. He held that God was a perfect and complete being, not just a superman; and that a god could do no wrong. He therefore condemned the myths for attributing immoral actions to the gods. However, in some of his plays, he did not treat the gods very favorably and some scholars feel that he was really a religious skeptic.

The next important milestones in the development of Greek religious thought were the ideas of Socrates and Plato. To accurately divide the thought and contribution of these two philosophers is difficult since Plato is our chief authority for Socrates and we cannot be certain whether some of the ideas that he ascribed to Socrates were Socrates' ideas or his own. It appears that Socrates emphasized the concept of the key role of conscience and the importance of virtue and a good life. Socrates also felt that he had a mission from God to help the Athenians find wisdom. He believed in a more real immortality for the soul than the shadowy existence of traditional Greek religion.

Plato (428-348 B.C.) constructed a philosophy in which the world was run by an eternal and all-perfect Divine Idea, the Good. This, he stressed, is the true reality and all the things in the world are imperfect reflections of the Good. To understand the nature of the Good was the aim of both philosophy and life. Though Plato did not distinctly link the idea of the Good with God, the characteristics of his idea of the Good had a similarity to the Judaeo-Christian concept of God, and he saw the universe as directed by God. Some of Plato's followers made the link clearer and late Platonic (or Neo-Platonic) thought was easily adaptable to Christian thought. Plato did mention the role of minor gods, but they were so inferior and subordinate to the Good that they did not mar his basic monotheism.

Plato also emphasized the moral dimension of life, seeing material things as unimportant and as a barrier to understanding the spiritual. This dualistic view, that the material and the spiritual are in opposition, has had considerable influence on later religious thought. In a moderate interpretation, it is similar to the Christian view that material things can often be an obstacle to religious growth. A more extreme form of Platonic dualism appeared in Gnosticism and Manicheism which both considered the material world intrinsically evil. Plato was among those Greeks who bitterly attacked the immorality of the myths. He condemned the poets for writing immoral stories about the gods and maintained that God cannot act from emotion or unjust motives. Plato considered the human soul to be immortal. However, unlike the traditional Greek or the Christian view, he believed that the soul went through a series of re-incarnations.

Though other interpretations can be made, the philosophical system of Aristotle (384-322 B.C.) was basically monotheistic. Aristotle looked upon God as the First Cause and Prime Mover of the Universe. He seems also to have accepted the concept of some form of immortality for the human soul. Thus the writers and philosophers of Greece made important contributions to the development of religious and ethical thought during the Classic Period.

Another important religious development in this period was the appearance of the "mystery religions." They arose to fulfill certain needs that were not met by the traditional State Greek religion of this period. Unlike the traditional religious forms, they did provide a personal relationship between an individual and a god, a promise of a meaningful immortality, a moral code, and emotional satisfaction.

One of the earliest forms of a "mystery religion" was the Eleusinian Mysteries celebrated at Eleusis near Athens. It involved the special worship of Demeter (the Roman Ceres), the goddess of the earth and crops. The ceremonies centered on the re-enactment of the myth of the return of Demeter's daughter Persephone from the Underworld. This was considered a symbol of the hope of a real immortality as was the rebirth of life in Spring caused by Demeter. To be a member of this cult, one had to be initiated and vow never to reveal the rites or doctrines to others. There were impressive and emotionally-oriented rites calculated to cause religious exaltation and ecstasy. The Eleusinians also went through rites of purification and the observance of a moral code was customary. A definitive reconstruction of Eleusinian beliefs is difficult because of the element of secrecy involved.

Even more widespread and important was the Orphic cult. It arose from the worship of Dionysius (Bacchus), the Thracian god of wine and to some extent of fertility. The original worship of Dionysius was rather debased, involving drunkenness, wild orgies and dancing, and the tearing apart of live animals and eating them raw. From this unpromising beginning the Orphic cult evolved into a mystery religion that called for its initiates to seek immortality by being purified from sin, leading virtuous lives, seeking a mystical union with the gods, and attending the Orphic rites. The central element of myth involved was a symbolic interpretation of the story of Dionysius that told of his being torn apart and then reborn. He was a symbol of man's rebirth after death. Also involved was the touching story of Orpheus, a Thracian minstrel who even went into the Underworld to rescue his wife Eurydice. Hades permitted her to leave on the condition that Orpheus would not look back at her until they were on the surface of the earth; but Orpheus was unable to resist his desire to see her and looked back. Eurydice was therefore forced to return to the Underworld, and Orpheus was later torn apart just as Dionysius had been. The Orphic cult had pantheistic tendencies (seeing God and the Universe as one) and believed in the re-incarnation of the soul. They emphasized the need for virtue and had an ascetic attitude, believing that virtue required self-control and a discipline of the desires of the body. Unlike the exclusively Greek Eleusinians, the Orphic cult saw all men as their brothers and actively sought non-Greek converts. It also differed from the Eleusinians because it was divorced from the State religion and its members were ardent missionaries of their ideas. One of the best developed religious and moral systems of Classical Greece, many of the tenets of Orphism were similar to those of Plato and the later Hellenistic philosophic religions.

The Pythagorean cult was in some ways a mystery religion, but was also a philosophic religion. Pythagoras, a Greek who lived in Italy near the end of the Sixth Century B.C., is best remembered for his mathematics; but he saw numbers as a key to religion, philosophy, and morality. From mathematics the Pythagoreans deduced a number of concepts, including one God in an ordered Universe; a dualism of body and soul; an ascetic approach to virtue; and a moral code. Like the Orphics, the Pythagoreans were organized in brotherhoods and sought to convert all men (even by waging war on neighboring Greek cities in Italy.) Pythagoras' ideas were also an important influence on Plato's thought.

Along with the constructive tendencies towards monotheism, morality, and the more developed religious ideas of the mystery religions, the Classic period in Greece also witnessed disintegrating tendencies in both religion and morality. Why? In part, because the criticism of elements of the traditional religion often led to confusion, disinterest, and even skepticism towards religion. Also the explanations of the world and the systems of philosophers like Heraclitus, Democritus, and Leucippus left little place for the gods in any meaningful sense. Even if the gods existed, they could have no significant effect on man in these systems of philosophy. The teaching of many of the Sophists like Protagoras were especially hostile to the traditional concepts of religion and morality. Protagoras, for example, held that there were no moral absolutes, that truth was relative, and that "man is the measure of all things." Greek morality had been based largely on the family, custom, the tribe, and the city-state; and certain social and political tendencies of this period, especially in the Fourth Century, tended to weaken these influences and institutions and thus weaken the moral foundations of the Greek people. In this period the loss of religious and moral roots mainly affected the intellectuals; but it was inevitable that it would later become more widespread.

Greek religion in the Hellenistic Period (323-133 B.C.) had four main tendencies: 1) the development of the great philosophic religions; 2) the continuing growth of mystery religions; 3) the accelerating decline of traditional religion and morality; 4) the widespread diffusion and influence of Greek religious ideas.

Philosophy in this period tended to be not just a series of abstract ideas, but rather an attempt to create a way of life; thus we have the appearance of schools of philosophy which were really philosophic religions. Pythagoreanism was somewhat like this, and near the end of the Classic Period another school of philosophy — called Cynicism — appeared. Its founder was Antisthenes, an Athenian disciple of Socrates. The Cynics believed that the aim of life and the way to happiness was solely the practice of virtue; nothing else mattered. Having an ascetic attitude, they stressed that bodily comforts, pleasures, and worldly goods were obstacles to virtue and peace of soul. The Cynics showed a great contempt for wealth, honors, and the conventions of society; and they often lived apart, and in rags, traveling about in pairs preaching their ideas.

Diogenes was perhaps the most famous Cynic. He is said to have gone about with a lighted lantern in the daytime looking in vain for an honest man. It is reported that when Alexander the Great met Diogenes and asked what he could do for him, Diogenes replied that Alexander could step to one side and stop blocking the sunlight. Though some of the Cynic's ideas were sound, their eccentric behavior and self-righteous attitudes precluded widespread acceptance. It should, perhaps, be noted in conclusion that the Ancient Cynic was not a "cynic" in the modern sense of being a disillusioned or skeptical person. Though the Cynics were skeptical about a number of things, they did have some positive aspects to their thought.

The most important and widespread of all the schools of philosophy was Stoicism. Its founder was Zeno, a Cypriot of Semitic origin who did most of his teaching in Athens around 300 B.C. Zeno accepted the basic Cynic concept that true happiness came from a virtuous life and detachment from material things and pleasures; but he applied it in a less bizarre fashion, adding many new concepts and an extensive philosophical rationale. To the Stoic, God was the supreme force in the Universe; he was just and reasonable and in His Providence watched over man and the world. Stoics emphasized that God works through the natural law, which works ultimately for the good of man; and even sickness and disasters are part of this Divine Plan, adding to one's strength of soul and character, and so they should be borne with patience and courage. Virtue was achieved by learning and conforming to this natural law, which was the will of God. God was best worshipped by a virtuous life and devotion to duty and this life of virtue led to peace of soul and true contentment. The Stoic moral code was more comprehensive than previous Greek ones and, in many respects, was similar to Christian concepts although there were significant differences in some matters such as suicide.

Stoicism was basically monotheistic, but there was also an element of

Pantheism and some Greek gods were admitted as subordinate beings like the Christian angels. Stoic philosophers such as Cleanthes identified God with Zeus, and all Stoics rejected the immorality of the myths, attempting to purify them by often highly imaginative allegorical and symbolic interpretations. Another key concept of the Stoics was their idea of the brotherhood of man. Unlike the Cynics, Stoics believed that living in an organized society was a good thing and that they had an obligation to aid and help their fellow-men. Early Stoicism did not have a belief in personal immortality since the soul was conceived of as a Divine spark that returned to God on death. Thus, in general, Stoicism represented the highest moral achievement of Greek civilization and had considerable influence on intellectuals of the Hellenistic world and, even more so on the Roman world. However, because of its lack of a personal relationship with God and its rather abstract philosophical thought, Stoicism was not a creed that satisfied the religious needs of the majority of men in the Ancient World.

The earlier mystery religions — Eleusinian and Orphic — continued to flourish in this period. Several new religions of oriental (especially Egyptian) origin, also appeared in the Hellenistic era. Among the new cults were those of Serapis, the patron of sailors, and of Isis, an Egyptian mother-goddess and goddess of love whose cult emphasized the promise of immortality to her followers. Another Oriental addition to Greek religion was the worship of kings as gods. However, this was more of a civic duty than any vital religious form. Also from the Orient came a great vogue of astrology and magical practices.

After the completion of Alexander the Great's conquests in 324 B.C. Greek rule and culture spread throughout the Near East and even to India and Greek cultural influence in the Western Mediterranean also increased. In theory, the Greek gods were now worshipped from France to India, but by this time the traditional Greek religion had been considerably eroded and its worship was largely formalistic. Greek rulers in the East often tried to assimilate and merge Greek and Eastern gods, such as Zeus with Amon-Re in Egypt, but they did not usually try to impose the Greek gods on their subjects. It was among the Greek ruling aristocracies and those natives seeking to join them that Greek religious ideas mainly spread, but in some areas like Rome, religion became thoroughly Hellenized. Even more important was the deep impact that the ideas of the Greek philosophers and the philosophic religions had on many Mediterranean peoples; and even those who, like the Jews, bitterly fought attempts to impose Greek rites on them, used Greek philosophical thought in systemizing and developing their theologies.

As already noted, traditional Greek religion and morals were showing serious signs of decline in the late Classic period; and, despite Stoicism and other similar beneficial influences, the decline accelerated in the Hellenistic era. Greek morality and religion had been linked to the family, tribe, and city-state. With the decline of the homogenity and power of these institutions after the great conquests of Alexander, religious and moral disorientation grew. The Hellenistic world was a cosmopolitan world of large states with the Greeks spread among many foreign peoples and the little parochial world that the Greek city-state had been was no more.

There was also a growing volume of philosophic and literary criticism which could not be suppressed by the State or public opinion because of the diversity of the Hellenistic world. Prominent among the critics of traditional religion and morality was the Epicurean school of philosophy. Epicurus, who taught at Athens about the same time as Zeno, maintained that the gods, even if they existed, had no care or interest in men and the only way to happiness thus was a selfish devotion to moderate intellectual and aesthetic pleasures as well as the avoidance of pain and other vexing human problems. Epicurus denied that man had any duty besides seeking his own pleasure which was in almost total opposition to the Stoic emphasis on virtue and duty. He bitterly attacked religion as various collections of evil superstitions which created fears that disturbed man's tranquility. It should be noted, however, that although Epicureanism was sometimes used as a mask for unrestrained hedonism, Epicurus felt that it was better to avoid sensual pleasures since they tended to upset man's tranquility of mind.

Another school of philosophy was that of the Cyrenaics, founded by Aristippus of Cyrene, who also considered the gods irrelevant to man's life and sought happiness through the enjoyment of sensual pleasures. The Cyrenaics' attitude could be contained in the maxim: "Eat, drink, and be merry, for tomorrow we die."

Skepticism towards religion was obviously widespread as well as diversified into many alternate schools of belief. The Academy, the school founded by Plato in 385 B.C., later in the same century fell under the control of Pyrrhon who denied that any real knowledge was possible about religion, morals, or philosophy. His followers, the Pyrrhonics or Academicians, continued to perpetuate his viewpoint. Yet another skeptic was Euhemerus of Messene who attacked the traditional gods as being merely men who lived in the distant past that tales had made into gods. Overall, the religious tendencies of the Hellenistic period had rather mixed results. On the one hand, they produced elevated philosophic religions like Stoicism; but, on the other, they led to religious confusion and the decay of moral codes both in Greece and in other countries affected by the Greeks.

The religion of the early Latins and Romans like that of the early Greeks was Indo-European in its origins. However, it retained many of its more primitive forms far longer than did Greek religion. For centuries and until about 650 B.C., Latin and Roman religion was basically animistic — that is, it centered around the belief that there are separate powerful spirits that cause different natural phenomena. Initially, the Roman gods were conceived of as impersonal powers (or numina) without human forms or attributes. Therefore, no temples or statues of their gods were necessary, nor were any myths. Originally each god was worshipped separately and little attempt was made to construct a family or hierarchy of gods. The early Romans saw religion as a ritual of prayer and sacrifice by which they would avert the wrath of their gods and secure their favor. The Roman attitude towards religion emphasized the contractual nature of the relationship between a god and men, and therefore precise performances of ritual were absolutely essential.

One of the most important and best-developed aspects of early Roman religion was the worship of the gods of the household and of the family. The chief gods of the household were Janus, the spirit of the door (often represented as having two faces) and Vesta, the goddess of the hearth or fireplace (a symbol of family solidarity). The Lar Familiaris was the particular god protecting that home and family and the Penates protected its storeroom. There were also many minor deities (often in pairs) that protected things like the hinges on doors and there was even a goddess who protected the sewers. There were other special gods for various aspects of life, such as birth and marriage.

The Roman family also worshipped the Genius of the family, originally conceived of as the male procreative force of the paterfamilias (the head of the household), but later considered as his spiritual double. At the same time the Romans worshipped the Manes, the spirits of their ancestors. They, like the Greeks, conceived of a ghost-like afterlife in the Underworld. However, they believed that on certain days of the year, the shades — or ghosts — of the dead revisited the earth and their families. On these days the Romans celebrated festivals in honor of their ancestors to commemorate them and to ward off any ill-effects from the departed. Various other religious festivals geared to the growth of the crops were also held. The paterfamilias was basically the priest of the family and carried on most of the special rites of the family although other members had some role. There were also particular gods of the clan who were worshipped by special clan rites.

The early Romans developed a strict moral code that was based on tradition and influenced all aspects of Roman life. The observance of this moral code had the effect of creating a conservative, well-disciplined people. Among the chief virtues that the Romans emphasized were: virtus — valor or fortitude; gravitas — seriousness of purpose; and pietas — loyalty to the state, the family, and the gods. The Romans also emphasized diligence in work, honesty, and truthfulness and they harshly punished adultery and other sexual offenses. While there was no direct link between religion and morality, the concept of obligation and duty that was involved in their contractual relations with the gods interacted with the moral concept of Pietas to help produce the Roman character. Since both religion and morality were part of their revered ancestral traditions, they were both integral parts of the Roman character and outlook. Thus, though indirect, the link between morality and religion among the early Romans was closer than among the early Greeks.

Rome probably first became an organized community and city-state in the 7th Century B.C. under Etruscan rule. Her State gods were developed not only from Roman and Latin gods, but also from Etruscan and even Greek sources since the Etruscans were strongly influenced by the Greeks. Janus, Vesta, and the Penates became important gods of the State. The Vestal Virgins, who took temporary vows of chastity, were formed to care for the temple of Vesta. There were also Latin gods linked to agriculture, such as Saturn, the god of sowing and planting, and Consus and Ops, the god and goddess of the harvest. The chief gods were Jupiter, a sky-god like the Greek Zeus and the guardian of the Roman State; Juno, his wife; Mars, the god of war; and Minerva, the patroness of craftsmen. Other significant goddesses were Diana, goddess of hunting, and Ceres, goddess of grain. Despite their Latin or Etruscan names, many of these state-gods were basically transplanted Greek gods; but their conception retained many distinctly Italian features. Some Greek gods, like Apollo and Hercules, were accepted with little or no change of name. In the earlier period, the Greek gods had come to Rome indirectly through the Greek-influenced Etruscans; but in the 5th and 4th Centuries B.C. the process became more direct with even more Greek gods, like Mercury (Hermes) and Libera (Persephone), being absorbed through contact with Greek merchants and by the conquest of Greek cities in Italy.

Another important Greek influence was the Sibylline Books, a group of oracular writings that were brought from the Greek city of Cumae and were thereafter consulted in times of crisis. It was during the Etruscan period that the Romans began to make statues and build temples, usually in Etruscan or Greek style, to their state-gods. Gradually, too, the Greek mythology was selectively absorbed into Roman religion and some Greek and Etruscan rites of worship also appeared at Rome. Thus, from about 650 to 264 B.C., Greek influences on Roman religion grew gradually and steadily. However, the assimilation process in this era was fairly smooth and somewhat selective and many Latin and Etruscan elements remained so that this process did not seriously disrupt either the religious feelings or the moral standards of the Roman people.

Etruscan influence was responsible for many of the organizational features of Roman religion. For instance, Roman religion was clearly a State religion, and part of the duty of consuls and other government officials was to offer sacrifice and preside at rites. The Romans considered religious observance to be a patriotic duty.

The organization of the priesthoods also reached its basic form in this period. The function of the priesthoods was to offer sacrifice to the gods on behalf of the State, not of individuals, and the priests were clearly servants of the State. The High Priest, or Pontifex Maximus, was an official elected for life who supervised religious observance to some extent; but there was not a true hierarchy. The priests were organized into a number of collegia or guilds. Among the most important were the pontiffs who supervised certain religious activities and kept not only records but the calendar as well. It was also part of their function to determine the numerous religious and legal holidays. The other important collegium was that of the augurs whose function was to take the auspices (attempts to tell the future by omens like the flight of birds or the examination of the entrails of birds). Roman law prescribed that the auspices must be taken before any important public act. There were also collegia that worshipped certain gods or performed special rites. Beyond the indirect political influence of augury and the calendar, the priesthoods had little general power outside of religious matters.

The many games and festivals, such as the Saturnalia, were an important feature of Roman religion. In this period they still retained a considerable amount of their religious purpose although they were now combined with more secular celebrations.

Until about 264 B.C. when the Punic Wars began, Roman religion, morality, and the resulting Roman character were a working synthesis that helps to explain the great success of Rome in this period. A number of diverse religious elements had been successfully absorbed and yet the Roman ideal of a simple, virtuous life was still largely a reality. However, after 264 B.C., the old Roman synthesis disintegrated under the stresses of a half-century of war, a great influx of wealth, radical economic and social changes, the spectacular rise of Roman power, and the uncontrolled flood of Hellenistic influence. By 200 B.C., the 12 chief Roman gods were identical with the chief Greek gods, and the Latin deities were largely fading away. In addition, Greek mythology was adopted in toto, and religious rites became mainly Greek. This headlong rush to Hellenism significantly weakened faith in traditional religion, especially since the moral weaknesses of the Greek gods made belief difficult for many Romans. The religious festivals were to a great extent replaced by secular games and the prestige of the priesthoods was notably decreased.

The appearance of some of the more debased Greek and Near Eastern rites caused considerable initial alarm. In the Second Century B.C., the censor, Cato the Elder, and the Senate attempted to ban the Dionysiac or Bacchanalian revels and the orgies connected with the worship of Cybele, the Great Mother of Pessinus, a goddess from Asia Minor. However, measures and attempts to enforce the old moral codes proved futile in the long run.

As in Greece, Roman religious and moral values were undermined by the spread of the anti-religious and amoral ideas of Greek thinkers like

Euhemerus, the Pyrrhonist skeptics, the Epicureans, and the Cyrenaics. Along with the cultural influence of the Greeks, there came the lack of moral principles so evident in Hellenistic Greece. In the absence of a vital religion, people turned more and more to astrology, magic, and other superstitious practices.

Social and economic conditions also helped to destroy the old Roman ethic. Great wealth, easily obtained, often replaced hard work and a simplicity of life with lazy and luxurious living. The ample opportunities for graft destroyed the traditional Roman honesty and made corruption an expected part of political life. A sturdy rural peasantry was uprooted from their lands by economic and political changes and forced into the morally degrading and rootless atmosphere of urban slums where they lived in poverty and idleness. Thus, by the end of the Republican era, Roman religion and morals were in a state of decline and confusion and the old Roman ideals and their sense of purpose was rapidly fading away.

Nonetheless, there were still Romans who continued to believe in and to live according to the old ideals while others retained an admiration for the old ways although it was often admiration from afar since they did not always live up to them. Near the end of the Republic a reaction to the moral confusion began to appear. This attitude shows clearly in the works of Cicero, who constantly pointed back to traditional values as the solution to the problems of his time and who led an honest and moral life in a time of great chaos and confusion. The historian Sallust, who in the earlier life had been an associate of Caesar's and enriched himself by dishonest politics, later changed his views and began the school of Roman historians that blamed the problems of Rome on its moral decadence.

A constructive religious and moral force in the later Republic was the Stoic philosophy, which was first introduced to Rome by Panaetius of Rhodes in the 2nd Century B.C. In its Roman form, Stoicism tended to have a belief in future immortality and to emphasize the brotherhood of man. It fitted in very well with the traditional Roman concepts of a strong sense of duty, strength of character, and seriousness of purpose. Stoicism impressed a considerable number of important Romans such as Cato the Younger and Cicero. In turn, Cicero was influential in popularizing Stoic concepts and identifying them with many traditional Roman values.

One of the chief policies of the first Roman emperor, Augustus (31 B.C. to 14 A.D.), was to try to revive and restore the traditional Roman religion and ethical values. He re-established some of the priesthoods that had dissolved, rebuilt temples that had fallen into disrepair, and constructed many new temples as well. He tried to encourage the revival of the Lares or family gods and he was initiated into the Eleusinian mysteries.

Augustus also added the new religious concept of an imperial cult, that is, the worship of the emperor or the State. He deified Julius Caesar and allowed the worship of his Genius or spiritual double during his life-time and colleges of priests appeared to conduct his worship. In Italy proper, though, he was more looked upon as the son of a god than as a god himself. Augustus also encouraged the cult of the goddess Roma, the personification of the Roman State. In many places the concept of worship of the Genius of Augustus was combined with the worship of the Roman State and temples were dedicated to "Roma et Augustus." The basic aim of this imperial cult was to join together patriotic and religious feeling as a unifying force in the diverse Roman world.

Augustus attempted to restore the earlier traditional Roman morals not only by laws and the moral tone of his own life, but also by influencing writers to expound upon his ideas. He passed laws against adultery and laws that tried to restore family life, favored fathers over bachelors, and penalized the unmarried and luxurious living. He and his family strove to live in a simple and traditional style. Augustus, as an influential patron of literature, expected his writers to inspire and then contribute to the growth of a religious revival. Virgil, the great Roman epic poet, in his portrayal of Aeneas emphasized the traditional virtues of faith and a sense of duty, treating religion with great reverence. Livy, in his histories of early Rome, followed much the same pattern.

The effectiveness of Augustus' attempts is hard to assess, but it was certainly an uphill battle. In the short term, the results were only partially successful as indicated by the conduct of Roman society in general and of Augustus' own family, in particular the scandalous conduct of his granddaughter Julia. However, in the long run Augustus' policies may have been an important causative factor in the shift of trends away from the dissolution of religion and ethical standards to the widespread revival of interest in both that appeared in the early Empire.

The Imperial period saw a continuation of the lives of luxury, of disregard of traditional moral standards, and of disinterest in religion by many Romans including emperors like Nero. Many Romans of the upper classes lived the life of feasting, orgies, and dissolute pleasures. And Epicureanism, hedonism, and skepticism still had many followers during the Imperial period.

However, the strongest trend of this period was towards an ever-increasing interest in religion and ethics. The growth of Christianity was indicative of this attitude, but the Greco-Roman pagan world also tended in the same direction. Many of the great writers of the Silver Age (14-100 A.D.), such as the historian Tacitus, the satirist Juvenal, and the dramatist Seneca, were stern moralists who condemned Roman moral laxness and blamed it for the troubles of the Empire. In the *Golden Ass* of Apuleius, we can see the mystical, orientel religious influences present in this period. A number of the emperors of the second Century like Trajan, Antoninus Pius, and Marcus Aurelius showed a keen and elevated moral sensitivity; and even in the chaotic Barrack Emperors' period of the Third Century, some of the emperors like Aurelian and Alexander Severus showed a considerable interest in religion.

The cult of the State gods and the worship of the emperor continued to be upheld by the Roman state and new cults were added and new temples built. The most pronouced tendencies in the official religion were towards syncretism, the equating of the gods of different religions, and towards a more monotheistic approach although this approach did not center consistently on any one of the traditional gods. The syncretic attitude led many persons to see that often the same one god was being worshipped under different names in different places. However, in this period as earlier, the most vital forces in religion and ethics were found not in the State cults but in the schools of philosophy and the mystery and Oriental religions.

The most influential school of philosophy in the early Empire was the Roman form of Stoicism. Three of the greatest Stoic philosophers — Seneca, a prime-minister and writer; Epictetus, a Phrygian slave; and Marcus Aurelius an emperor — lived during this era. In general, Roman Stoicism of the Imperial period had more of a religious flavor and a clearer monotheism than the earlier Hellenistic form. Epictetus and Seneca, in their writings, show a closer and more personal relationship with God than did the earlier and more Deistic and more intellectual forms of Stoicism. Some later Christian writers even felt that Seneca's ideas must have come from St. Paul. The emperor Marcus Aurelius is known as a Stoic, but other emperors like Trajan and Vespasian were also much influenced by Stoicism.

Another prominient philosophy was the Neo-Platonism of Plotinus and his disciple, Porphyry. Plotinus, who lived in the Third Century A.D., developed an elaborate philosophical theory; but its chief importance for religion was his explicit linking of the concept of the Good with an all-powerful God, which had only been implicit in Plato; and his linking of religious mysticism with Platonic philosophy. Plotinus saw a mystical, spiritual communion with God as the chief aim of life, and in moral ideas he followed and developed the Platonic dualism of the goodness of the spiritual and the baseness of material things. Neo-Platonism was popular among the intellectuals of the Late Empire and influenced prominent Christian writers like Origen and St. Augustine; but its concepts were too intellectual to have much influence among the masses.

Related to Neo-Platonism was Neo-Pythagoreanism, but its religious and moral aspects were emphasized more than its philosophic elements. It was monotheistic and saw God, the principle of good, fighting the evil effects of material things; and it recommended a strict asceticism — including vegetarianism and celibacy — as the means to moral virtue and to freedom from the evil influences of material things. Neo-Pythagoreanism interpreted the traditional gods, myths, and religious practices in largely symbolic terms. Capable of a wider acceptance than the more philosophic Neo-Platonism, Neo-Pythagoreanism was, on one hand, one of the chief forces opposing Christianity; but on the other, its similarity to some Christian beliefs also made it a bridge to Christianity for some.

The Greek mystery religions, both the Eleusinian and Orphic, had considerable influence in Rome; but some Oriental religions were even more prominent. One of the most popular of the Oriental mystery-type religions was the worship of Isis, the Mother of men, which was now linked with the cult of Serapis. Like the Greek mystery religions, the cult of Isis centered on a myth that symbolized rebirth. Impressive in its rites and strong in its belief in immortality, its moral beliefs, however, held a secondary importance to its rites and to emotional experience.

Despite opposition from Augustus, the worship of Cybele, the Great Mother goddess of Pessinus in Asia Minor, continued to grow in popularity. The cult had some similarities to that of Isis, but its rites were more orgiastic, including even mutilation, and culminated in a bath of blood symbolizing rebirth.

Mithradism was the last of the Eastern religions to come to Rome and was influential in the late Third and early Fourth Centuries. It was an adaptation of Zoroastrianism, the religion of Ancient Persia. Mithra was the unconquered sun-god, the god of battles, and the chief spiritual agent of the supreme God of good, Ahura-madza or Ormuzd. In its rites, the believers enacted the myth where Mithra, by slaying a bull, brought life and prosperity to man. Joined to the worship of Mithra was one of the strongest moral codes of the Ancient World. Mithradism portrayed life as a constant struggle between good and truth led by Mithra and evil. Though Mithra was called a god, he was clearly subordinate to Ormuzd and so the cult was basically monotheistic. It was very popular in the Roman army and among some emperors, but it also had many followers from other walks of life. Mithradism, however excluded women and lacked any real central organization or priesthood.

Similar to the worship of Mithra and sometimes joined to it was the worship of Sol Invicta, the unconquered sun-god. Originating from the worship of a Syrian sun-god, the cult of Sol Invicta developed along lines similar to Mithradism and eventually by the Fourth Century was partially fused with it. This basically monotheistic view eventually became the chief form of paganism. Some of the Third Century emperors, such as Aurelian, made it the State religion, and Constantine's father, Constantius, was probably an adherent. The last pagan emperor, Julian the Apostate (360-3), proclaimed his devotion to Sol Invicta and tried to replace Christianity with this cult.

Thus, by 312 A.D., though important and fundamental differences remained between paganism and Christianity, Christians found a large number of Romans sharing many of their basic concepts, including immortality, moral strictness, and the spiritual and monotheistic nature of God. They could also observe a widespread desire for religious satisfaction and a better moral code. While a Christian might ascribe this atmosphere to Divine Providence and a non-Christian to fortuitous chance, there is ample evidence that by the Fourth Century the Greco-Roman world had developed attitudes that made it ready to receive the Christian message.

Constantine's Edict of Milan in 313 A.D. and his subsequent favoring of Christianity brought a religious revolution within little more than a generation, a revolution that resulted in the decline and end of Ancient paganism. Thus, while Christians had been only about a minority of about 10% in 312, by 350 Christians formed a majority of the Empire's population, at least in the cities. Constantine, though he favored Christians, tolerated pagans and continued State support of pagan shrines and priests. His sons Constans and Constantius closed some temples and forbade public sacrifice, but did not seem to try to exclude pagans from public office. Julian the Apostate (360-3) made an attempt to restore paganism by initiating a number of anti-Christian measures. He also attempted to set up a monotheistic paganism and organize it along Christian lines. Julian's reign, however, was short; and on his death Christian emperors succeeded. Paganism did, however, retain some strength among the upper classes, in the Senate at Rome, and in the schools of Greece during the Fourth Century. There were still important pagan writers in the period, such as Ammianus Marcellinus, a historian, and Symmachus, a rhetorician and senator. Paganism also continued in many of the outlying rural areas or pagi. This persistence in the rural pagi gave it the name "paganism."

After 382, Gratian and Theodosius the Great renewed the persecution of paganism by closing temples, ending State support and the Olympic Games, and making pagan worship a crime. Christian persecution of the pagans seems to have been somewhat sporadic as had been the earlier pagan persecution of the Christians. There was even one brief and futile attempt to revive paganism at Rome under Eugenius in 391. Some paganism persisted into the Sixth Century in the same areas as earlier (Rome, Greece and the outlying rural areas), but its political and social influence was rather slight. In 529, the Emperor Justinian the Great closed the last pagan schools of Athens and launched a more systematic persecution. After this we hear little more of widespread Greco-Roman paganism.

Still, some pockets of paganism continued to exist in remote rural areas, partially because the Christian Church in this period lacked an effective rural parish system. One pocket of Greek paganism has persisted until the present day in a most unlikely place — Afghanistan. Here the White Khaffirs, descendants of the Bactrian Greeks who ruled the area for several centuries after Alexander's conquests, clung to some of their Greek religious beliefs. They continued to survive and keep their identity although they were surrounded by the Moslem world and under Moslem rule for many centuries. These White Khaffirs were fairly numerous until recently, but now there remain only villages that continues to practice rites resembling Ancient Greek paganism.

How can one explain the rapid collapse of a religious system that had lasted almost 1500 years and dominated the Western civilized world for almost 600 years? Three basic causes present themselves: the superiority of Christianity, the internal weaknesses of Ancient paganism, and the suppressive policies of later Roman Emperors.

Obviously, the hostility and later persecutions of the Christian emperors were important in the decline of paganism. These persecutions, however, were no worse than those survived by the Christians; and a truly vital faith would not have succumbed so quickly. Even while there was still toleration in the Fourth Century, paganism waned. Thus, deeper causes for its collapse need to be examined.

One of these underlying causes is the fact that Christianity had a degree of unity of belief and a church organization that not one of the many pagan cults or outlooks could duplicate. It was also a more all-encompassing religion than any of the pagan cults. Christianity had impressive rites, a rational justification, emotional satisfaction, a missionary spirit that sought to embrace all mankind, a high and comprehensive moral code, a strong faith in immortality, a personal one-to-one relationship with God, a fairly well-developed and functional theology, and an organized and hierarchical priesthood. While most pagan cults and philosophies had some of these qualities, no one had all of them. For instance, the cult of Isis had rites, emotional satisfaction, a personal relationship with its own goddess, and a belief in immortality; but it had little reasoned theology and down-played its moral code. Stoicism contained a high moral sense and reasoned theology; but it was weak on emotional satisfaction and lacked rites, a structure, and a priesthood.

Christianity, on the other hand, far better fulfilled the longings and tendencies of the Roman world for monotheism, immortality, a higher morality and a personal relationship with God than did the Greco-Roman pagan cults. Furthermore, the fact that pagan cults such as Mithradism and philosophies such as Neo-Platonism had so many concepts in common with Christianity made the transition to Christianity logical and comfortable for many Romans. Christianity also had the added advantage that Christ practiced the moral code that he preached, thus presenting an untarnished model for a religious person to imitate. There was no need for Christians to resort to elaborate symbolic justifications as the pagans had to do to avoid charges of immorality in the myths and actions of their gods.

Finally, the State cults by their very nature were so dependent on the State that individual cults had little chance of survival once the State disowned them and ceased to finance them. The pagan priesthoods were traditionally servants of the State and had no independent organization outside of the State to turn to for support. In a sense, the superiority of Christianity was unwittingly acknowledged by Fourth Century pagans themselves, since their alternate pagan religions began to look more and more like Christianity. For example — the Emperor Julian's paganism almost perfectly resembled Christianity — but without a Christ.

It is ironic, but true, that the trend of pagan religious thought in the Roman Empire led almost logically and inevitably to Christianity, and thus to its own demise.

BIBLIOGRAPHY

Altheim, F. *History of Roman Religion*. London,1938.
Bailey, C. *Phases in the Religion of Greece and Rome*. Berkeley,1932.
Cumont, F. *Oriental Religions in Roman Paganism*. New York,1956.
Dodds, E.R. *Pagan and Christian in the Age of Anxiety*. London,1965.
Edelstein, L. *The Meaning of Stoicism*. Cambridge, Mass.,1966.
Festugiere, A.J. *Personal Religion among the Greeks and Romans*. Berkeley,1960.
Fowler, W.W. *Roman Ideas of the Deity in the Last Century before the Christian Era*. London,1914.
Grant, F.C. *Hellenistic Religions: Age of Syncretism*. New York,1953.
Guthrie, W.K.C. *The Greeks and their Gods*. Boston,1955.
Hick, Robert Drew. *Stoic and Epicurean*. New York,1962.
Hus, Alain. *Greek and Roman Religion*. New York,1962.
Hyde, W.W. *Paganism and Christianity in the Roman Empire*. Philadelphia,1946.
Nillson, M.P. *History of Greek Religion*. New York,1964.
Ogilvie, R.M. *The Romans and their Gods in the Age of Augustus*. New York,1970.
Rose. H.J. *Astrology and Religion among the Greeks and Romans*. Gloucester, Mass.,1960.

THE INVESTITURE CONTEST

Glenn W. Olsen

Glenn W. Olsen, Associate Professor of History at the University of Utah, received his doctorate from the University of Wisconsin. A Fulbright Scholar, his areas of scholarly research and publication lie in medieval ecclesiastical, intellectual and legal history, and he has published in such journals as *Studia Gratiana, Traditio*, and *Explorations in Economic History*.

The Investiture Contest was a struggle over what the respective positions of the royal and priestly powers should be in a Christian society. Although the most visible aspect of this Contest was the struggle over lay investiture between Pope Gregory VII (1073-85) and the German Emperor Henry IV (1056-1106), the attempt to determine the proper areas of competence and jurisdiction of the various ecclesiastical and civil offices occurred at all levels of society, and remained a problem long after the deaths of both great protagonists.

Especially since the conversion of the Roman Emperor Constantine (312-37) to Christianity, the history of the Church had been filled with conflicts over the proper claims of the ecclesiastical and secular powers in regard to each other and to the individual Christian. However, the Investiture Contest of the eleventh century brought the opposed claims of the contending parties to a level of theoretical definition and actual warfare not earlier experienced in the history of the Latin West. The reasons for this seem fairly clear. By the eleventh century the continuing missionary activity of the early Middle Ages had been so successful that much of continental Europe had accepted the Christian view of the world. Although many lacked profound insight into the truths of Christianity, themselves often being only a few generations removed from paganism, most men believed in the basic teachings of Christianity. God the Creator had sent his Son to redeem fallen man, and at the end of time would judge all men. The sacraments had been given to the Catholic Church to help each man in his pilgrimage through this life, and the government of this Church had been granted to the priesthood, at the head of which stands the bishop of Rome.

Since almost all men accepted this view of the world, men did not think of themselves as members of two distinct institutions, the Church and the State. Rather they were all members of a single Christian society, in which there were two authorities, one ecclesiastical and one royal. Whereas the Christians of the first centuries of the history of the Church had lived in a world hostile to the Christian claims, the eleventh century man lived in a society in which there was general agreement as to the truths of Christianity. Therefore, whereas the early Christian had always been tempted to withdraw from his society in order to find Christian perfection, some men in the eleventh century came to conceive of the possibility of reforming society itself after the Christian ideal. Christians had always asked the question of what Christian perfection is for the individual, that is, of what things in life should be preferred and what things abandoned. Now in the eleventh century one could ask what the right order of society itself should be, and from one perspective the Investiture Contest was an attempt to order more perfectly Christendom after Christian principles.

Kings and Popes had long thought that they ruled by the grace of God for the end of leading men to heaven. However, in general from the eighth to the eleventh centuries certain secular rulers, first the Carolingians and then the German emperors after Otto I (962-73), had been much more powerful than the Papacy, and had presumed that the leadership of Christian society had been given to the royal power. These rulers conceived of themselves after the pattern of the kings of the Old Testament. They tended to look upon the Church and its properties as their own, or as a trust given by God to be managed by themselves. These theocratic monarchs were sometimes very pious men, and strove for the moral reform of the Church, but never did it occur to them that in principle the papal office was more important than their own in terms of the actual leadership of Christendom. The Papacy and the priesthood were competent in matters of doctrine and the performance of the sacraments, but the theocratic monarch presumed that the royal power ought actually to lead and govern society. A theocratic monarch such as Henry III of Germany (1039-56) could even desire a pure and influential papacy without doubting that the papacy and the emperor could achieve a kind of cooperation based on the defense of the Papacy by the protector and ruler of Christendom, the German Emperor.

One of the results of the period of theocratic monarchy was that at all levels of Church government the clergy tended to be dependent on secular political figures. Bishops and abbots often were chosen by kings, both because they helped in the governance of the realm, and because the king believed that it was the royal duty to lead the Church in his realm. From the period of the decline of the Roman Empire in the Latin West, most bishops of necessity had taken over functions which earlier would have been performed by secular officials. Throughout the early Middle Ages the political importance of the episcopate tended to increase, both because of the absence of strongly centralized governments, and because the clergy as a whole was the best educated segment of society and therefore a necessary instrument of government. With the rapid development of feudalism after the death of Charlemagne (768-814), bishops and abbots as well as nobles became members of the feudal hierarchy, and were granted or invested with lands in the form of fiefs or benefices by kings in return for the performance of governmental and even military functions. Since all episcopates already had lands attached to them, either received from pious donors or inherited from Roman times, it was not necessary for many generations to pass before the distinctions between the various properties and functions of the bishops became blurred. All over Europe, but particularly in Germany, bishops performed both civil and ecclesiastical duties. According to the law of the Church, as religious officials they owed their episcopal offices and sacramental powers to the ecclesiastical hierarchy, but as secular office-holders they owed much of their property to lay investiture by their feudal lord, whether king or emperor. Although by origins the granting of an episcopal office was completely distinct from investiture as a vassal in a fief, with the passage of time it came to seem that the bishop received the episcopal office from the fact that he was a vassal of the royal power. This point of view was reinforced by the fact that kings naturally chose men to be bishops who were loyal to them, and excluded those men who could not be trusted unreservedly to pursue royal policy. Although the canon law always maintained that the election of bishops pertained to the clergy, it came to seem that episcopal office was received through lay investiture, especially because the sacred symbols of the ring and staff were given in the lay investiture. When the eleventh century reformers came to reflect upon the nature of right order in a Christian society, the practice of lay investiture of bishops seemed the most obvious example of the way in which the royal power had illegitimately deprived the Church of the freedom to govern herself and to lead all men to salvation.

Just as the bishops were dependent on the secular power, so also were the lower clergy. Parish priests often were selected not by the ecclesiastical hierarchy but by the lord of the manor in which their parish Church was located. And just as the king chose bishops on the basis of their loyalty and governmental abilities, as well as sometimes their spiritual qualities, so the local lord often chose the parish priest not because of his abilities as a pastor but because he was a good financial steward. For just as the king looked upon the Church in his realm as his property, so the lord of the manor considered the parish church to be part of his property, to be a source of revenue through the collection of tithes and offerings. This arrangement, called the system of the proprietary Church, of course tended to give the clergy themselves interests and points of view not very different from those of laymen, and accounts somewhat for the frequently formal and superficial practice of religion found in these centuries. However, in the hands of pious laymen the system sometimes was used to great good, and in many areas the country-dwellers first came in contact with Christianity precisely because a layman used some of his lands to found and endow a parish church or monastery.

Nevertheless, many men searching for a more meaningful Christianity found the effects of the system of theocratic monarchy and the proprietary church unsatisfactory, and throughout the eighth to eleventh centuries various movements appeared seeking more adequate forms of Christian life. Until toward the middle of the eleventh century, these movements did not usually attack the social institutions based on theocratic monarchy and the proprietary system. They rather concentrated on moral reform and the search for perfection within the existing forms of society. This attitude of seeking primarily the reform of the individual rather than the reform of society was most clearly expressed in the reform movements within monasticism, the traditional mode of the search for perfection in the early middle ages.

Even during periods of general decadence and chaos, many monks had never lost sight of the final end of man, reformation in the image of God, and especially from the ninth century Europe was influenced by great reform movements within monasticism. Cluny, founded in 910, was the most famous of these, and sent reformers from Burgundy throughout Europe. However, there were many other reform movements, some stimulated by Cluny, and some of independent origins. The goal of Cluny was to restore the Benedictine rule, and indeed from Cluny there spread a great enthusiasm for the religious life lived in a community centered around the liturgy of the Church.

Return to this practice of the common life was, although the most influential form of monastic reform, only one among several patterns of reform. Especially common in Italy, but found all over Europe, were small congregations which had kept alive the hermit traditions of Eastern monasticism. Peter Damian, perhaps the most important of the mid-eleventh century reformers, had himself been the head of a small group of hermits at Fonte Avellana. With these small groups, a rather different emphasis was found than that which characterized the Cluniacs, for they were much more concerned with the practice of poverty, aesceticism, and the mortification of the flesh than were most of the followers of Cluny.

In some ways the Italian eremitical movements more directly formed the program of the Gregorian Reformers than did Cluny, for such Gregorian demands as that of the absolute prohibition of all private property for all monks and regular clergy were closely related to the emphasis on poverty and purity found among the Italian reformers. But this is not to minimize the role of Cluny. Cluny had found favor with many ruling houses in Europe, and Cluniac monks had done much to form the piety which several of the German emperors were noted for, the greatest of whom was Henry III, himself the initiator of many of the changes which were to issue in the Investiture Contest.

The reforms of monasticism up to the mid-eleventh century give evidence of a very widespread search for a more adequate appropriation of Christianity. Not all of this religious enthusiasm was channelled into the monastic life, and in the years immediately preceding the Gregorian reform, programs for the reform of the clergy also frequently began to appear. Since patristic times the urban clergy or canons had been formed into chapters around their bishops, and certain of the fathers, such as St. Augustine and St. Gregory the Great, had encouraged their clergy to adopt a life lived in common without private property. Although this form of life was not very commonly found perfectly followed, in the ninth century a council at Aachen (817) had considered and then rejected as too severe the proposal to demand that all the cathedral and collegiate clergy give up their private property and live in common. This ideal was again taken up by the generation of reformers immediately preceding the pontificate of Gregory VII, and especially Peter Damian argued that all regular clergy should live the full common life without private property so that, not being attached to the things of this world, they would be better able to preach the gospel. Before himself becoming Pope, Hildebrand (Gregory VII) had propsed at a synod held in Rome in 1059 that where possible the clergy adopt the full common life, living in community without private property. Again this proposal was considered too radical to be made mandatory, but at this and several succeeding councils it was approved as being a more perfect form of the Christian life.

The resistance to the reform of the canonical clergy was of course intense, since many of the clergy had wives or concubines, and most of them posessed private property and did not live in community. These abuses, which stemmed from the proprietary system, were not to be rooted out before the end of the Middle Ages. Although by the end of the Investiture Contest enthusiasm for the reformed regular canons was growing, at every stage of the reform of the clergy, popes and bishops had to fight deep-seated local opposition to any change in long standing practices. By the time of the death of Gregory VII it was clear that the papacy had committed itself to a policy of mandating the common life for all monks and regular clergy, the reform of the clergy had advanced little.

Not all enthusiasm for reform was directed toward the monastic and clerical vocations, and especially in the eleventh century lay reform movements became fairly frequent. These movements usually attempted to accommodate some form of the common life, based on the practice of poverty, to the laity. Perhaps the most famous of these movements during the period of the Gregorian reform itself was that of the Patarenes in Milan. Like most lay movements, the Patarenes gained much of their cohesiveness by opposition to corrupt and simonical clergy. One of the results of the period of theocratic monarchy was the common custom of giving a payment upon the reception of an ecclesiastical office, usually as a part of the practice of investiture by a layman. This practice, called simony, was against the law of the Church and of course tended to award spiritual offices to those who could pay the most, rather than to those most qualified to hold them. The laity naturally blamed much of the spiritual degeneration of the Church on the fact that this practice produced unworthy clergy, and as their own remedy for this abuse often proposed not to receive the sacraments from such clergy. Seen in context it seems fairly clear that many of these lay movements were also in part protests by the poor against the new wealth produced by the growing towns of the eleventh century. They were therefore potentially dangerous to the order of society, and indeed many of them in time adopted both religiously heretical and politically revolutionary programs. Nevertheless, the fact that Gregory VII actually encouraged the Patarenes to refuse the sacraments from unworthy clergy shows how desperately limited the means were by which reform could be advanced. Where the higher clergy would not reform themselves, as in Milan, Gregory felt he had no alternative but than to support these potentially revolutionary lay movements against the corrupt clergy.

It is clear from the foregoing that by the middle of the eleventh century the need for the reform of Church and society was widely felt. Although each of the above drives to reform played its part in preparing the way for the Investiture Contest, from the middle of the eleventh century reform came to center on the attempt to purify and restore the Papacy itself. For generations the Papacy had been dominated by local Roman and Italian aristocratic factions. Not strong enough to maintain itself above Italian politics, the Papacy had tended to degenerate into a political prize sought for by contending parties. Many of the Popes had received and used the papal office for political advantage, and their private lives had been no purer than those of the great laymen who dominated the Papacy. Without a strong secular defender, army, or territorial base, the Papacy was powerless to extricate itself from this position, although especially in the early eleventh century some of the Popes had made tentative attempts at reform.

Feeling this situation intolerable, in the 1040's the pious and capable German Emperor Henry III began to act to restore the Papacy. Himself deeply touched by the reforms of the Cluniacs, over a period of time Henry created conditions at Rome which finally permitted the capturing of the Papacy by indigenous Roman reform groups led by the future Gregory VII. Although these Roman reformers eventually went far beyond the reforms envisaged by Henry, they at the beginning fully supported the German intervention in Rome. The intervention was occasioned by the scandalous conditions resulting from the reign of Benedict IX (1032-48). In 1044 one of the Roman aristocratic factions drove Benedict from Rome and installed as his successor Sylvester III (1045). When Benedict's faction returned to power, he was restored, but almost immediately he granted the Papacy to a wealthy archpriest, apparently in return for the payment of a sum of money, who took the name Gregory VI (1045-46). Ironically, Gregory seems genuinely to have been interested in reform, and for this reason had committed simony in order to obtain the Papacy. Benedict IX soon decided that he after all still wanted to be Pope, and there followed a period of rioting and fighting in the streets of Rome as the supporters of each of the three papal claimants strove to determine the issue. Henry now intervened, and after calling three councils deposed all three claimants and nominated a reformed German bishop to become Clement II (1046-47). The following three Popes, all of whom had short pontificates, were also nominated by Henry.

Henry III's third nominee to the Papacy was his cousin, who took the name Leo IX (1049-54), and who refused to become Pope simply because of his imperial nomination, but submitted his nomination to the clergy and people of Rome in order to follow the canon law. Hildebrand, who had gone into exile with Gregory VI, was apparently impressed with Leo from the first, and when Leo stopped at Cluny, where Hildebrand was staying, on the way to Rome, Hildebrand joined him. From this time until he himself became Pope, Hildebrand was always active in the government of the Church at Rome. Leo's pontificate marks the beginning of the restoration of papal influence in the north of Europe, and Leo spent much of his reign travelling throughout France, Germany, and the Low Countries holding synods for the purpose of condemning and rooting out the various abuses so pervasive among the clergy. Leo also entered into negotiations with the Greek Orthodox Church for reunion with Rome, but in 1054 these negotiations led to the mutual excommunication of Pope and Patriarch. Leo had asserted the papal supremacy over the Greek Church, and the Patriarch of Constantinople had rejected this claim. Finally, Leo sought for some political arrangement to free the Papacy from domination by Roman factions. He first tried to establish a temporal state in Southern Italy. However, in 1053 the Norman army badly defeated the papal army at Civitate, and from this time the Papacy turned to the attempt to form a defensive alliance with other Italian states.

During the pontificate of Stephen IX (1057-58), cardinal Humbert of Silva Candida composed his *Libri adversus simoniacos*, which for the first time formulated the central demands of the Hildebrandine party. In the third book of this work, centering his attack on the idea of theocratic monarchy, Humbert argued that kings are simply laymen, and should have no right to interfere in the government of the Church because of their royal office. Bishops should be elected according to the norms of canon law, and not by kings. Laymen ought not invest bishops with the sacred symbols of ring and staff, because this implies that the grace of the episcopal office comes from lay investiture, a thing in fact impossible. Humbert, certainly the most gifted theologian of the Hildebrandine Party, had penetrated to the main issues soon to be involved in the Investiture Contest. Whereas most of the reformers, including Hildebrand himself, were men of action rather than speculative thinkers, Humbert was both, and his book, finished in 1058, had a great influence on subsequent events. It certainly lay behind the principles involved in the decree on the election of a Pope issued by Nicholas II (1059-61) the following year, and described below. And at the Lateran Synod of 1059 Hildebrand himself attacked theocratic monarchy in a fashion completely in accord with Humbert's arguments. Hildebrand stated that the Roman order, which had been corrupted since the government of the Church had passsed under the goverament of the Germans (meaning here since the time of the Carolinglans and the foundation of theocratic monarchy), must be restored by returning to the practices of the ancient Church. In sum, by 1059 the principles of the specifically Hilde-brandine program of reform had become clear. The reforms which had been envisaged by Henry III were considered not to go far enough, for Henry, while desiring moral and monastic reform, as well as a purified clergy, had wanted to retain control of the Church, and indeed to use a restored Papacy to strengthen his hand in Italian politics. Whereas the Cluniacs generally consented to this continuing pattern of theocratic monarchy, the ideal of the Hildebrandine party was a Church, led by a restored Papacy and a reformed hierarchy, completely free from secular control. Humbert had penetrated to the root issue of what right order is in a society organized according to Catholic principles.

Nicholas II was the first Pope fully in sympathy with this criticism of theocratic monarchy. Elected because the defensive alliance sought for by Leo IX finally bore fruit when Tuscany helped secure Nicholas' election free from domination by any of the Roman factions, Nicholas immediately added an alliance with the Normans to that with Tuscany. In return for the recognition of the Pope as the temporal overlord of southern Italy, Robert Guiscard (1059-85) was recognized by the Papacy as the duke of Apulia and Calabria and the future duke of Sicily. But the most important contribu-tion of the reign of Nicholas to the growth of the papal power was the papal election decree, promulgated at the Lateran Synod of 1059. For the first time in the history of the Church, this decree attempted to establish a precise method for the election of a Pope. Recent history had shown Nicholas that without such a method, the Papacy would inevitably be dominated by either secular rulers such as Henry III or the Roman factions. And so Nicholas devised a procedure to keep the election of a Pope as free from these external pressures as possible. Henceforth, Popes were to be elected only by the cardinals. This decision manifests the radical advance made in the program of the reform party under Humbert's influence, for the Hildebrandine·Party had now made the goal of free elections an explicit part of its program along with the insistence that the Church should be independent of all imperial control, even if that control should be in the hands of a man as good as the lately deceased Henry III.

During the peaceful reign of Alexander II (1061-73), the gains already made by the Papacy were consolidated. Henry IV of Germany was still a minor, and political conflict with the Empire was unlikely unless provoked. The ideal of a restored Papacy involved not only ecclesiastical freedom from secular control, but also the strengthening of the papal position within the Church, and Alexander devoted much of his energy to this later problem. Slowly the Church became more centralized through such methods as the use of papal legates to deal with local affairs in the name of the Pope, and the permission of the appeal of cases from local ecclesiastical courts to the Roman curia.

Alexander also exerted moral leadership over Christendom, several times intervening to reprimand and correct rulers whose conduct had become scandalous. The idea of the primacy of Rome had been taught in the ancient Church, and during the early Middle Ages the idea that the Pope is the universal Ordinary for all Christendom had occasionally been expressed. According to this teaching, the Pope stands to the Church as each bishop stands to his diocese. Just as the spiritual governance of all souls within his diocese is given to each bishop, so the government of the universal Church is given to the Pope. From the time of Leo IX the reformed Popes had tried to give some content to this claim to be universal Ordinary. Neither Alexander nor any of the other Popes ever thought of replacing theocratic monarchy with some kind of papal theocracy, in which the clergy would govern the daily affairs of Christendom. All the Popes presumed that there would always be a secular power, and that the respective functions of the priesthood and the royal power would be kept relatively distinct. What the Popes after Leo IX tended more and more to claim was a general right of supervision over all Christians, and over all offices within Christendom. In the concrete what this meant was that the Pope had the right to intervene in any serious moral or doctrinal case because all Christians were under his supervision as universal Ordinary. This should be seen as the background for the various claims of Gregory VII against Henry IV. Gregory felt he had the right and obligation to intervene in matters involving the salvation of souls, even if his intervention had political repercussions. Should the German Emperor flout the canon law in regard to episcopal elections and simony, the Pope, because he had the spiritual supervision of all souls, could reprimand and even depose the Emperor. This power derived from the inherent superiority of the papal office to all secular offices. Although relatively autonomous within his own sphere of activity, the Emperor only possessed his office on the presumption that he was a Catholic in good standing in the Church. Without this presumption, an authority that was subordinate in terms of the final end of man would be able to subvert the Church and lead men to damnation rather than aiding them to their salvation. That is, without the acknowledgement that in principle the royal office was subordinate to the papal office, right order in society could not be achieved, for the office in charge of the merely temporal aspects of man would be able to dominate the office in charge of the eternal end of man. The lower would govern the higher. This idea of right order, clearly present in the thought of Humbert, came to fruition in the reign of Alexander's successor, Gregory VII.

When Hildebrand became Pope in 1073, he had been the leading protagonist of reform at the Curia for more than twenty years. A man consumed by the vision of what the Church might be if freed to perform her earthly task, Gregory was willing to use any legitimate means to further this goal. Although personally overwhelmed with the obligations laid by God on the papal office, and with a full sense of his own limitations, when pursuing the interests of the Church Gregory manifested a realism founded on the shrewdest calculation. Living in a century that would not recognize the modern separation of religious and political matters, Gregory was a man willing to use political means to achieve religious goals. If force and political manipulation should be necessary to restore right order, they would be used for a legitimate end.

Granted this point of view, the Investiture Contest became inevitable, for Gregory was determined to gain the freedom of the Church, and this he realized would necessitate the prohibition of simony and lay investiture. Since in large measure the Empire was governed by the bishops, who held great fiefs from the Emperor, to prohibit lay investiture as an illegitimate limitation on the freedom of the Church would destroy the Emperor's control over his great office-holders. If the Emperor could not determine that only bishops favorable to him and his policy would be elected, then the Empire would disintegrate and fall prey to the territorial ambitions of the German nobility. Since the Emperor could hardly be expected to tolerate losing the loyalty of his great officers, conflict over the issue of lay investiture was implicit in the papal search for right order. The only reply that the Emperor could make to the theoretical claims of the Papacy was an appeal to tradition, since even the supporters of the Emperor assented to the general premises on which the Gregorian idea of the Papacy was built. The supporters of the Emperor could, for instance, hardly deny that the final end of man was salvation, and that the purpose of the sacraments and the clergy was to lead men to that end.

The Investiture Contest began in 1075 when Gregory issued a decree prohibiting lay investiture. The young Henry IV, who was faced at this time with a serious rebellion in Saxony, had been docile towards the Pope because of his political troubles in Germany. When in June 1075 Henry defeated the rebels, his actions toward the Papacy changed. He ignored earlier promises to stop the practice of simony and lay investiture. Legates were sent to Germany to threaten Henry privately with excommunication, and in response to this Henry summoned a synod to meet at Worms early in 1076. When the German bishops met they proved their loyalty to Henry by renouncing their obedience to the Pope. To this Henry added a letter deposing the Pope. In response to this action Gregory excommunicated Henry and all the German bishops who had sided with him. Beyond this, Henry was deposed and all his subjects freed from their fealty to him. This caused a rebellion to break out in Germany, for the German nobles were always ready for an excuse to limit the power of the Emperor, and thus to increase their own powers. Just as most of the bishops in Germany supported the Emperor, most of the nobility supported the Pope. The nobles declared that Henry was no longer Emperor, and that a council at Augsburg the following year would elect a new Emperor, with Gregory personally present and presiding. Gregory left Rome, and by January of 1077 was at Canossa in Tuscany. Henry, knowing that if the council at Augsburg was held his deposition would be enforced, left for Italy to meet the Pope before he could cross the Alps. At Canossa occurred the famous confrontation between the two men, with Henry presenting himself as a simple penitent whom the Pope by his priestly office was bound to absolve. By recognizing Gregory as Pope and receiving his absolution, Henry had avoided his deposition.

In Germany, however, the rebellion continued, and the nobles elected a new king. Gregory now made a claim that none of his predecessors had made, namely that he had the right to judge between the two rivals for the German throne. He of course decided against Henry, and in 1080 excommunicated Henry a second time for not recognizing the papal decision. Henry proved tenacious, however, and within the year had defeated his rival, deposed Gregory for the second time, and elected an antipope. Then, to end the conflict decisively, Henry invaded Italy and in 1084 took Rome. In desperation Gregory called for aid from his Norman vassal, Robert Guiscard. Henry withdrew before the Normans, who proceeded to pillage Rome. With the Romans enraged because of this, Gregory had no choice but to retire to Salerno with the Normans when they departed. He shortly fell sick and died in exile in 1085.

For a decade following Gregory's death Henry's political fortunes improved, until his eldest son Conrad revolted and by 1097 had forced Henry to abandon Italian politics altogether in favor of restoring his position in Germany. After the death of Conrad, Henry's next eldest son, Henry, revolted in 1104, and by the death of Henry IV the imperial government had disintegrated to such a degree that Germany was never to recover a strong central government in the Middle Ages. Looked at from a political perspective, one of the continuing results of the Investiture Contest was that at a critical period in her constitutional development the strength of the German nobility against the German Emperor was increased to such a degree that centralization became impossible, thus giving Germany a very different national development from England or France.

Henry V (1106-25) continued the struggle over investiture, which had never been resolved by his father. Paschal II (1099-1118) offered a disarmingly simple solution of the Contest, in proposing that in return for the emperor giving up lay investiture the Church would give up all lands which it held by feudal tenure. This proposal, which bears some similarity to the later Spiritual Franciscan vision of the Church as a purely spiritual society possessing no property (altough Paschal exempted the temporal possessions of the Papacy from the proposal), of course raised up against itself overwhelming opposition. It would have betrayed the German nobility, who had generally supported the Papacy, into the hands of the Emperor, who would have received vast amounts of land. And of course it would have deprived the bishops of most of their revenues. The unsteady Paschal backed down from his proposal, only to more gravely offend the Gregorian Party by formally approving lay investiture. The Gregorian reform had obviously fallen on bad days, and some talked of deposing Paschal as an heretic. But at least Paschal's proposals had performed the function of convincing most men that any solution of the Investiture Contest that attempted to change radically the existing practice of episcopal election was doomed to failure. When the Contest was formally resolved, the compromise achieved did little more than preserve existing practice, falling far short of the Gregorian hope for a free Church.

The resolution of the Investiture Contest was based on the principles already evolved in the settlement of the problem of investiture in England in 1107. According to these principles, it was necessary to recognize that the offices of bishop and abbot had a double nature. All compromise must be based on the premise that the obligations of the bishop within the ecclesiastical hierarchy must be fulfilled, and that the bishop or abbot must faithfully perform whatever duties are owed the secular authority because of the status of vassalage. The actual compromise was formed by Calixtus II (1119-24), who in 1122 negotiated the Concordat of Worms with Henry V. Although there were further settlements and negotiations after this Concordat, which suggests that the Concordat was not as decisive in ending the Contest in the minds of contemporaries as it has been for some modern historians, the principles embodied in the Concordat represented a compromise that could be tolerated by all parties involved. The Concordat first of all satisfied the procedure of the canon law by stating that bishops and abbots were only to be elected by respectively the clergy or the monks. However, much of the force was taken out of this concession by the provision that in Germany the elections had to take place in the presence of the Emperor, who had the right to decide a disputed election. Moreover, in Germany, after election the bishop or abbot was to be invested first with the *regalia*, the temporal rights and possessions held from the Emperor. Only then could he be invested with the *spiritualia* by his ecclesiastical superior, the sign of which investiture was to be for the bishop the giving of the ring and staff. In Italy and Burgundy, and this was simply a recognition of the relatively more independent position of Italy and Burgundy within the Empire, investiture with the *spiritualia* could occur immediately after election, and investiture with the *regalia* was to follow automatically within six months.

On first glance it might seem that after half a century of disturbance and warfare the procedure sanctioned by the Concordat did not differ very much from conditions before the outbreak of the Investiture Contest. It has often been noted that periods of revolutionary change tend merely to hasten trends already present in a society, and that after rapid change societies tend to return to previously existing patterns of life. In many ways this was true of the Investiture Contest, and perhaps this shows that the Gregorian search for right order implied a restructuring of society beyond that which has ever been accomplished by revolution. Christopher Dawson has remarked that even in those periods in which European society has been most unified, there has been deep-lying division between religious and temporal authority, and that in no age has the spiritual authority been able long to dominate the temporal authority. However, this is not all that can be said. The Investiture Contest did certainly cause some permanent changes. The period before 1050 had been dominated by theocratic monarchy, and though the secular power was far from broken, by 1122 the Church had gained a degree of independence unknown during the theocratic period. Although from the thirteenth century the old pretensions of secular rulers to dominate the Church were to be pressed with increasing vigor, it is not too much to claim that much of the vitality of the twelfth and thirteenth century Church was stimulated by the program of the Gregorian Reformation. From this point of view, the Investiture Contest must be counted a victory for the Papacy. Although falling far short of the goals desired by the Gregorians — reform for instance had hardly touched the proprietary system and the lower offices of the Church, the Contest had renewed Christendom and brought into public consideration some of the most basic issues involved in appropriating the Christian message.

The remote effects of the Investiture Contest are difficult to assess, but the following suggestions might be made. Within Germany, the imperial power was seriously injured, while the power of the nobility was greatly enhanced. All the monarchs of Europe for centuries to come would have to take the papal claims more seriously than they had been taken for centuries past. Beyond this, as the result of the Investiture Contest, in the twelfth and thirteenth centuries the Papacy was to play a role in European diplomacy far greater than any influence she had had before. This role went far beyond the actual material resources of the Papacy, and testifies to the presumed moral leadership that the reformed Papacy had won for itself. Although the continuing struggle between the spiritual and temporal powers, which in the later period fastened on issues other than investiture, was in the long run, due to the growth of the monarchical national state, to rob the Church of most of her independence of action, in the thirteenth century the fate of nations was often influenced by the temporal ramifications of papal policy.

Within the Church itself, the Investiture Contest had just as striking effects. During the period of theocratic monarchy, the Pope had had little influence in European life, and where effective ecclesiastical power was yielded it was at the episcopal level. The bishop of Rome had not stood above the other bishops of Europe, except in terms of the general respect paid the papal primacy. Ecclesiastical policy generally did not come from Rome, but was determined by national councils of bishops. As a result the bishops of each country tended to reflect national attitudes and the will of their kings more than devotion to the Church universal. The Investiture Contest made significant inroads on all these practices. More and more the Pope as universal Ordinary came to interfere in local matters in the name of the universal Church. Although it often appeared that the Popes were trying to strengthen their own powers by reducing those of the bishops, this perspective is somewhat misleading. The Popes desired to strengthen both the episcopal and papal offices, but only on the presumption that these offices would be held by men whose first interest was the comon good of the whole Church. Where this was not the case, and it often was not, the Papacy naturally had to attack the traditional prerogatives of the bishops as a means of removing the bishops from the influence of the theocratic patterns of life. In sum, the Investiture Contest engendered a struggle within the Church between the claims of the national churches and the Church universal. Although again in the later Middle Ages the old pattern of episcopalism tended to reemerge, the Investiture Contest had brought the papal office to a position far greater than it had held before.

Beyond all these considerations, Gerd Tellenbach has argued that Gregory stands at the greatest turning point in the history of the Church. Christians had always hesitated over what their relationship should be to the World, to the culture in which they found themselves. The predominant response of the Latin Church before Gregory had been to withdraw from the World. Now from the pontificate of Gregory the Papacy had committed the Church to the conversion of the World. The Church was no longer in its main emphasis to retire from the World, but rather to draw the World into Itself. This did not mean simply the conversion of all men to Christianity, but rather the permeation of society with Christian principles. Implicit in this was the task of reorganizing society according to Christian priorities. This search, in a society acknowledging the Christian view of the final end of man, meant that for right order to obtain in Christendom the superiority of the papal office to all other offices in Christendom must be recognized. As Tellenbach has summarized the matter, "Gregory's real service was to leaven the earthly lump with the principles of Catholicism, and to make the latter, in a manner hitherto undreamed of, a really decisive force in politics. His aim was to bring the kingdom of God on earth, as he saw it in his mind, nearer to realisation . . .".

BIBLIOGRAPHY

For general histories and bibliographies of the Investiture Contest see: Robert S. Hoyt, *Europe in the Middle Ages*, 2nd ed. (New York 1966); Schafer Williams, *The Gregorian Epoch: Reformation, Revolution, Reaction?* (Problems in European Civilization; Boston 1964); Geoffrey Harraclough, *The origins of Modern Germany*, 2nd ed. (Oxford 1962); *Handbook of Church History, The Church in the Age of Feudalism* (New York 1969).

The great work of synthesis on this period is Gerd Tellenbach, *Church State and Christian Society at the Time of the Investiture Contest* (Oxford 1959), but the following books will also be found to be extremely useful: Christopher Dawson, *Religion and the Rise of Western Culture* (New York 1950); R.W. Southern, *The Making of the Middle Ages* (New Haven 1953); J.P. Whitney, *Hildebrandine Essays* (Cambridge 1932).

On the monastic and spiritual background of the period see: Gerhart B. Ladner, *The Idea of Reform: Its Impact on Christian Thought and Action in the Age of the Fathers*, rev. ed. (New York 1967); M.H. Vicaire, *The Apostolic Life* (Chicago 1966); Jean Leclercq, *The Life of Perfection*, tr. Leonard Doyle (Collegeville, Minnesota 1961); Pierre Mandonnet, *St. Dominic and His Work*, ed. M.H. Vicaire and R. Ladner, tr. Mary Larkin (St. Louis 1944); David Knowles, *The Monastic Order in England*, 2nd ed. (Cambridge 1963). On the regular canons see John Dickinson, *The Origins of the Austin Canons and their Introduction into England* (London 1950), and on lay and heretical movements during this period Jeffrey Russell, *Dissent and Reform in the Early Middle Ages* (Berkeley and Los Angeles 1965). The effects of the proprietary system are treated in considerable detail by Catherine Boyd, *Tithes and Parishes in Medieval Italy: The Historical Roots of a Modern Problem* (Ithaca, New York 1952).

Some of the most important documents concerning the political theory of the eleventh century may be found in Brian Tierney, *The Crisis of Church and State 1050-1300* (Englewood Cliffs, N.J. 1964). For interpretations of the political thought of the Investiture Contest see: Walter Ullmann, *The Growth of Papal Government in the Middle Ages: A study in the ideological relation of clerical to lay power*, 2nd ed. (London 1962); R. W. and A.J. Carlyle, *History of Mediaeval Political Theory in the West*, vol. 4 (Edinburgh and London 1922); Ernst Kantorowicz, *The King's Two Bodies: A Study in Mediaeval Political Theology* (Princeton 1957). An excellent study of the legal problems involved in the Investiture Contest may be found in Robert L. Benson, *The Bishop-Elect: A Study in Medieval Ecclesiastical Office* (Princeton 1968).

For bibliography on the continuation of reform into the twelfth century see Glenn Olsen, "The Idea of the *Ecclesia Primitiva* in the Writings of the Twelfth-Century Canonists," *Traditio* 25 (1969).

CONSCIENCE, CONFLICT AND THE CRUSADES

Walter W. Willigan

Walter L. Willigan, Professor of History at St. John's University, received his doctorate from Fordham University. Interested in religion and sociology as well as history, he was President of the American Catholic Sociological Society and is presently President of the Queens County Historical Society. He has produced a number of books including *Social Order*.

To review the course of world history during the Middle Ages is to recall to mind a period of historic change such as men have rarely known. "God wills it" became the clarion call for thousands of Europeans in 1095 to undertake the long arduous trek to the East for the purpose of freeing the Holy Sepulcher in Jerusalem and, if possible, converting the infidel to Christianity.

The Crusades represented a unique blending of Christian idealism and savage warfare. For two centuries after 1095, thousands of Europeans-nobles, serfs and selfseeking adventurers were impelled to leave Europe and venture into the Near East. Sewing the sign of the Cross on their clothing, they were known as Crusaders or "wearers of the Cross." There were eight major Crusades: two achieved some success, the others ended in inglorious failure. What conditions in Europe caused this all-pervading ideal to seize the minds and hearts of Europeans? What motives impelled them to leave their homes and undertake the hardships and dangers of a venture into the unknown? What, moreover, did two centuries of such effort achieve?

Europeans believed in the Supremacy of two universal institutions: the Holy Roman Catholic Church and the Holy Roman Empire. This empire was created as a successor of the Old Roman Empire under which most of Europe had been united politically. The Pope, perceiving that Rome could no longer defend the West, placed a crown on Charlemagne's head on Christmas day 800 A.D. and the Holy Roman Empire was born.

This coronation was a recognition of the superior power of the Franks. Charlemagne's empire was short lived, for it was torn apart by civil wars and by invasions of pagan peoples beyond its borders.

During the ninth and tenth centuries a new pattern of social and political life emerged called feudalism. The major cohesive force in this society was a relationship of mutual loyalty between individual lords and their vassals. A feudal warrior's conception of loyalty was simple. A man fought for his lord. To end civil strife in Europe, Pope Urban II hoped to channel this loyalty to the benefit of the church. How could a man show his devotion to God better than by fighting for Him against His enemies, the infidels who had defiled Christ's sepulcher. The Crusader believed that God had called him to arms through His representative, the Pope, and he gladly answered this call.

Throughout Europe there were nobles more powerful than their sovereigns. The Godwins ruled England until their chief, Harold, was slain by the invading Normans. El Cid was the true monarch of Spain. In Germany, the Child Henry IV was buffeted among the dukes and bishops. In France many lords were stronger than their feeble kings. This century, however, was dominated by the Normans. In fact, all the great events which this age saw, all the mighty movements which swayed it, centered about this ambitious and energetic race. Feudalism with its rule of the barons reached its fullest development because the Norman Franks adopted it. Its system was peculiarily fitted to the haughty Norman's sense of equality among themselves, and of contempt for the subject races beneath them. The old viking blood stirred within them and they scattered through all of Europe, conquering and plundering and spreading their institutions and ideals along their path.

As shrewd and crafty as they were fierce and strong, they analyzed life with a merchant's eye to profit, and sold their swords or turned them against the buyers, with equal readiness. They matched their wits against every antagonist east and west, and were successful everywhere. William seized England, Robert Guiscard held southern Italy and Roger Hauteville became king of Sicily. Norman bands invaded Greece and threatened Constantinople. The establishment of barbarian kingdoms in the Western world and the subsequent growth of feudalism created new problems for the Papacy.

Pope Gregory VII led the Papacy into the first great Church-State confrontation. The Age of the Barons was a major threat to the Church because of the growing feudalism. As the Church acquired more and more land in Europe, the feudal barons attempted to bring the Church under their domination. This dispute often termed the "Investure conflict" was motivated by the pope's condemnation of an existing practice whereby kings and emperors appointed bishops and "invested" them with the symbols of spiritual office — the episcopal ring and staff.

Clerical immorality, the buying and selling of spiritual office (termed simony), as well as the sale of indulgences had to be corrected. A reform program which had begun in the French monastery of Cluny, now developed throughout the tenth century into a powerful surge of reforming vitality which charged all of western Christendom. The ascetic idealism of Saint Benedict and the theocratic reforms of Gregory the Great were pursued by a series of militant popes.

Serious plagues and famines induced many of the common people to turn toward religion as a bulwark against death and suffering. There ensued a widespread church building program as a community enterprise. The Church during this period was the great arbiter of human destiny. She guided the fusion of Greek, Roman and German elements in society. The influence of the Christian Church pervaded everywhere, for she gave medieval society its dimensions, its essential characteristics, its goals and its inner meaning. All men were born, lived and died under the protection of the church.

The time span for the Middle Ages in Western Europe extended from the fifth to the fifteenth century. The Middle Ages, however, were motivated by an idealism quite different from what had gone before or was to come after. This idealism was religious. To the medieval man, the life of the monk was the only truly religious life. Medieval folk were deeply conscious of sin; feared eternal damnation and believed in the necessity of doing some act of voluntary suffering as atonement for sin. Many did penance by going on a pilgrimage to the Holy places. From the fourth to the seventh century there developed in the West a fad for these journeys. Large numbers of pious or adventurous pilgrims of both sexes had made their way to the Holy Land. They traveled in small groups and apparently did not bear arms for self-defense. These small bands were eventually supplemented by larger enterprises, numbering several hundred to several thousand participants. Once he had become the temporal leader of the West, Charlemagne established a protectorate over the Christians of Palestine — a protectorate which lasted longer than his dynasty itself, and which for two centuries made pilgrimages to the Holy Land feasible. The Crusades were in essence super-pilgrimages.

Church leaders also attempted to limit feudal warfare and humanize conflict, through the Peace of God and the Truce of God which limited the days Christians could spend fighting. Both religious and lay leaders were well aware that there were too many fighting men abroad in the land, too many men and not enough land. It would be an aid to law and order in Europe if the brutal valor of these semi-barbaric Christians could be channeled elsewhere in the name of a higher cause. Better they burn and slay infidels, ravaging other fields than those at home, plundering and perhaps converting non-believers.

On May 29, 1459, another emperor, the last of a score of rulers of the Byzantine Empire, met death in battle as the victorious Turks put an end to an empire that had stood as the successor of Roman sovereignty and Greek culture in the east. This was the fate of a civilization that stood as an outpost of Europe, facing a hostile and barbarous East and protecting an unappreciative West that was itself slowly arising out of barbarism to new cultural heights. This empire preserved for later generations the Greek language and learning, it perpetuated the Roman imperial system and codified Roman law; it introduced into Europe the finest feature of Moslem culture through contacts which it made with the East. The Byzantine Empire, moreover, fused Greek and Oriental art and dedicated the new creations to the glorification of the Christian religion.

Constantinople stood as a crossroad of East and West. For over a thousand years the Eastern empire was the most splendid civilization the Middle Ages knew. Its wealth excited the envy and greed of all other peoples, especially the Turks in the East and the Italians in the West. The destruction of the empire was inevitable when its military and naval power became sufficiently weakened. Moslem and Slav countries lay as a meanacing ring about Christian Europe to the sourth, east, and north. For centuries the great Moslem states dominated the Mediterranean, firmly planted in Spain, Sicily, North Africa and the Middle East.

After the death of Mohammed in 632, the Moslem faith had spread along the north coast of Africa, up the eastern and western fringes of the Mediterranean world. The Moslem governors had been enlightened rulers and had permitted Christians to visit their holy shrines. At the beginning of the eleventh century, the death of the Turkish sultan threw the entire Turkish empire into civil war and anarchy. At the same time, decay set in the Byzantine empire. An aggressive aristocracy gained much power in the provinces, the Eastern Catholic Church was constantly absorbing land for monastic purposes.

External dangers also became more pressing. Venice became increasingly powerful in the West and took over control of the Adriatic region; in the East a counter-offensive was launched by the barbaric Seljukian Turks who eventually captured Jersualem and the shoreline opposite Constantinople in 1070. The following year the Turks defeated the Eastern Emperor at the battle of Manzikert in which the Byzantine army of one hundred thousand men was annihilated. Visitation rights for Christian pilgrims to the Holy places were denied.

The pressure of the Normans threatened Byzantine power as the former carved out possessions for themselves in southern Italy. By 1080 Byzantine power on the Italian mainland and in Sicily was smashed. Constantinople was threatened with encirclement. She faced the same problems which confronted the old Roman empire. Waves of nomads, the Patzinaks along with the Huns and Magyards marched up the Danube valley into the heartland of the Balkans. Asia Minor, the recruiting ground for the Byzantine soldiery and the granary of the empire was in dire danger of absorption.

In the following year, Alexius Comnenus gained the Byzantine throne as the result of a coup d'etat. He restored order and imperial prestige. However the Turkish counter-offensive became so menacing that the Byzantine emperor appealed to Pope Urban II to save the Eastern Christian empire as well as recovering the Holy Land. This request came at an opportune time. Pope Urban II, a former Cluniac monk had an all consuming desire to reunite the Roman and Eastern orthodox churches as well as advancing the power and prestige of the Papacy.

The vigorous nations of Western Europe were Christian, and they were determined to own the Holy City of Jerusalem. It was considered a horrible profanation that people of another race and religion, the Mohammedans, should possess the city of Christ and even prohibit Christians to visit it. Great armies of iron clad nobles and European peasants were destined to march eastward against the infidel. The fighting forces of Europe were organized to participate in a holy war. The frontiers of Christendom were to expand.

A council of the church gathered at Clermont in southern France in 1095 and Pope Urban II made a celebrated speech to the assembled multitude. He told them of the cruelty of the Arabs, and the wealth of the Holy Land, and reminded them of the poverty of their own country. When at last, he urged them to march in a body and restore to Christian hands the possession of the Sepulcher of Christ, a wave of religious ardor swept over his hearers, and with one voice they cried, "God wills it!" "Ay, God wills it!" exclaimed the Pope, catching at the words, "Let that be your battle cry, and the Cross your standard!"

Urban's plan for the first crusade provided that the birthplace of Christ was to be recovered and preserved from the defiling hands of the infidels. This was the motive which fired enthusiasm throughout the West. The crusaders were bound to take vows to complete their pilgrimage to Jerusalem. Their destination was the Holy Sepulcher. In his discourse at Clermont, Urban II aroused sympathy for the eastern Christians who were so sorely oppressed by the Turks. He moreover, urged the peoples of the West to go to the assistance of the eastern Christians as a religious duty. Some believe that Urban hoped to bring a reunion of the Greek and Roman churches. The Pope had a definite plan in mind as how the crusade was to be conducted. The crusaders were under the direct command of an ecclesiastical leader, Bishop Adhemar of Puy who was to keep harmony among the various lords. Furthermore, those unfit for crusading were to stay home. He explicitly eliminated old men, women without their husbands and children. Permission to go on a crusade was to be obtained from the local priest.

July 15, 1096 was the date set for the First Crusade to leave Europe for the Holy Land. This was a religious war against the Infidel in which all Christians, Greek or Latin, could unite. The Pope had placed a match to a tinder box. All Europe was roused. Through France the enthusiasm swept like fire. Men everywhere and of all ranks joined the crusade. They sewed the red cross on their shoulders, they carved it on their naked breasts, they branded it upon themselves with burning irons.

In their enthusiasm a large body of ignorant common people, set out for the Holy Land under the inspired leadership of Peter the Hermit. They waited for nothing, neither preparations nor provisions. As they plodded through Germany many of the peasants there caught the infection and joined them. As each new city loomed upon the horizon the duller ones would point and cheer, and cry "Is that Jerusalem?"

They swept across the Hungarian and Byzantine Empires like a devastating storm, plundering as they went. Less than half reached Constantinople whose Emperor hastened to transport them over the Bosphorus Strait into Asia. At last in the world of hunger as well as the sword of the Sultan of Asia Minor, only a few hundred survived to tell their story. More than five premature expeditions, collectively termed the peasants crusades, took place.

The pilgrim tradition reinforced by the deep enthusiasm roused by itinerant preachers, overwhelmed Urban's attempts to limit participation in the crusades. Both the clergy and other noncombatants, participating in the peasants crusade stressed the idea that the Holy Land was not to be won by force of arms alone. The power of the Word was greater than the power of the Sword. Moreover, the righteousness of the crusading cause was a sure protection.

Meanwhile, the French lords, who understood what a military expedition of this size and length entailed, were busy with their preparations for the first crusade. Four armies were gathered in different areas, and marched separately to unite at Constantinople. The army from the south of France was commanded by Count Raymond of Toulouse, mightiest of the lords of the South. It was he who had been the first of the nobles to enter the crusade. His wife and small son accompanied him, for Raymond had given his possessions to his heirs and vowed never to return from the East.

The army of Northern France was led by Hugh, the brother of the French king. In Italy an army gathered under the powerful knight, Bohemond. The fourth army composed of Germanic and French elements came from Burgundy, Lorraine, Luxemburg, and Flanders. This host was led by Godfrey of Boulogne, chief leader and hero of the First crusade.

Among these crusading leaders there was not one king. This great movement was the people's war, the baron's crusade. The four armies numbered six-hundred thousand men. Emperor Alexius of Constantinople asked for aid and the Pope sent it. The former was suprised at the religious fervor of the crusaders as well as by the great number of people who had enlisted in the Pope's armies. Surprise turned to fear of such a horde of fierce semi-barbarians, who were gathering in his land. He met them with alternate threats, prayers and trickery. The Norman leader, Bohemond wanted to sack Constantinople before they ventured into Asia Minor. But Godfrey of Bouillon refused because of the agreement, which the crusade leaders had made with Emperor Alexius, that all cities and territories which had been previously held by the empire were to be returned to Alexius. In return the Emperor was to supply the crusaders with supplies and transport over the Bosphorus, which he did with all haste in order to be rid of them, as he had also done for the members of the peasants crusades.

Antioch, the great capital of Northern Syria was reached at last, and the crusading army besieged it for seven months. The city was finally captured through the intrigues of Bohemond. The Christian army was admitted to the city and a terrible massacre of the defenders ensued. The crusaders' store of provisions was exhausted. They had hoped to replenish their stock by the capture of the city, but found the seven-months siege had reduced the defenders to more desperate straits even than they. Three days after Antioch fell, the entire army before it, and the Christians found themselves in turn besieged within its walls. Horrible were its sufferings! In their despair they even offered to surrender Antioch if permitted to depart peacefully.

Count Raymond of Toulouse came to the rescue. Legend says it was announced that one of his followers had seen a vision from which he had learned where the spear that had pierced the side of the Redeemer, was hidden in Antioch, and that if the crusaders charged out with that spear at their head, they would truimph over the infidels. Raymond himself led a procession, which found a spear in the place indicated; and the crusaders, fired with religious transport, clamored to be led to battle.

They burst forth from Antioch, a tragic and terrible spectre army, gaunt with hunger, staggering and swooning with disease. The Turks mocked them as they came. But a frenzy seized the Christians when they confronted the infidels, their strength returned, their mad charge was irresistible, and after a brave resistance, the whole Turkish host was driven in headlong flight. In the captured camp, the conquerors found food and wealth. As a result, the power of the Turks was broken at Antioch.

On June 10, 1099, the crusading army its number reduced to an estimated fifty thousand arrived within sight of Jerusalem. After a seige of five weeks, the Christians forced great towers against the walls and from them burst into the city, with Godfrey and Raymond at their head on July 15, 1099. The lust of blood was upon them, the remembrance of countless insults unavenged, hence they slew without mercy. Seventy thousand were massacred say the Arab writers.

A sudden reaction followed. The work of bloodshed was checked. The crusaders now reentered Jerusalem as pilgrims, barefooted, with

bowed heads, and singing psalms. Godfrey was selected as the ruler of
Jerusalem, with the title of Defender and Baron of the Holy Sepulcher. The
work of the first crusade was accomplished. Many departed for their
homes. Four little kingdons were formed; Godfrey's kingdom of Jerusalem,
Bohemond's dominion of Tripolis and Godfrey's brother, Baldwin's kingdom on the Euphrates River.

The First Crusade was a success in that it liberated the Holy Places and
created an organized Christian kingdom of Jerusalem as well as lesser
crusader states in the East. Pope Urban died two weeks after the capture of
Jerusalem, of which he never heard. Peter the Hermit became an object of
scorn and finally spent his declining years in a monastery in the south of
France. Legend and romance have been embroidered liberally into the
tale. Godfrey earned the title of saint and hero — the central figure of the
First Crusade. The real leaders, however, were Bohemond, the crafty
Norman and the old man, Raymond of Toulouse. The quarrels and mutual
jealousies of these two interfered with the success of each. As for
Jerusalem, neither of them wanted it, foreseeing well that in spite of
whoever might govern there, the city would remain really the property of
its priests.

Many factors threatened to break down the force of the original ideas
which Urban had about the crusades. First the ambition to make conquests
for themselves tended to produce factions which threatened to break up
the unity of the crusade. Second, the attitude of friendliness toward Eastern
Christians began to weaken. The Greeks did not get on well with their
Western allies, the "Franks" as they called them. They regarded the
Patriarch, or Bishop of Constantinople, as the head of the church, while the
Franks declared the Pope, or Bishop of Rome, the supreme ruler. Through
constant friction and irritation these two sects, both calling themselves
followers of Christ, grew to hate each other more than either hated the
Turks. Their unfortunate enmity did much to paralyze the crusade move-
ment; and thwart the union of Eastern and Western Christianity.

From the end of the eleventh century to the end of the thirteenth there
were eight distinct crusades as well as other movements of people who
went to the Holy Land. These crusades were full of paradoxes. Mingled
with the sincere and simple minded knights in the First Crusade were the
shrewd Norman adventurers and the profiteering merchants and shipow-
ners of Genoa, Pisa, and Venice. The cynical and heretical Emperor,
Frederick II, was more successful in his crusade than the Saintly King Louis.
Frequently, the materialist and bargain-hunting Italian merchants
achieved more immediate benefits than the devout pilgrims who gave their
lives that the Holy Sepulcher might be rescued from the Infidel.

Bernard of Clairvaux preached for a second crusade in 1144 because
the city of Jerusalem was again threatened. Louis VII of France and the
Emperor Conrad III joined forces. Suffering many misfortunes on route to

the near East their crusade ended in failure. A failure produced because of King Louis's pride and the weakness and the folly of his wife, Elinor. She was the heiress of Aquitaine and spent her life in idle frivolity. She decided to accompany Louis on this crusade, so all her glittering court attendants went also.

As the army advanced through the Turkish lands, the queen traveled with the advance guards. Louis had commanded his vanguard to hold certain rocky heights for the protection of his army. Queen Elinor preferred the pleasant shady valleys beyond, to the hot and barren hillside. So the courteous commander abandoned the hillside which the Turks seized and there ambushed the major segment of Louis's army. As further progress along the coast grew more and more difficult the King took ship with his best troops and sailed to Antioch. Vessels enough could not be found for the great body of crusaders so the wounded and all the host of common people as well as unarmed pilgrims were left behind. Some saved themselves by turning Mohammedan, the remainder starved, or were seized and sold among the Turks. Never was an undertaking so heralded and so pompously begun to result in failure more complete and shameful.

Several factors rose to the surface during the Second Crusade. First, the relations between the Byzantine Empire and Catholic Europe became more and more embittered. The Norman knights of the First Crusade held the land they conquered for themselves instead of honoring their pledge to Emperor Alexius. Relationships were further embittered by commercial privileges awarded by the Emperor, first to Venice in 1082, and then to Genoa and Pisa. Italian merchants were allowed to establish their own quarters under the jurisdiction of their own laws and at the same time pay lower taxes to the Byzantine merchants.

Another factor which was not clearly comprehended was the mounting Moslem "Counter-Crusade." The success of the First Crusade occurred at a time when the Islamic world was weakened by factionalism. The twelfth century witnessed a revival of the Moslem counter-crusade. Christian Edessa was captured in 1144 and Christian Jerusalem was subdued in 1187. These events evoked a military response from the West.

The next crusade (1189) was not under French leadership, as the earlier had been; it was led by the great German Emperor, Frederick Barbarossa. Under him marched Philip Augustus of France and Richard I of England. Barbarossa managed his crusade with consummate skill. He checked the bickerings of the rival kings; he made friends with the nations whose lands he crossed; and he advanced with the success of a great general through the wilds of Asia Minor, where so many thousands of earlier crusaders had perished. Then an accident caused his death. He was drowned crossing a river. His sorrowing troops returned home with his body. The crusade was left to King Philip and King Richard who ruined it by their repeated quarrels. Philip Augustus of France returned home and

Richard signed a three year truce with Saladin giving the Christian pilgrims permission to visit Jerusalem. This crusade did save Europe from a Mohammedan invasion, but with regard to its avowed object, the recovery of the Holy Sepulcher, it was almost as complete failure as its predecessor.

The thirteenth century which opened with the pontificate of Innocent III might have been expected to produce some successful crusades. However, the efforts of the Christians during the thirteenth century were a travesty of the traditional objective cherished by Urban IV. Historians usually recognize eight crusades in all, although those which intervened between the Third Crusade and the final efforts of Louis XI are confused in number; they seemed not even to have aimed to reconquer the Holy Land, and were either content with the smaller object of preserving the remaining Christian cities along the Palestine coast, or else they degenerated into mere plundering expeditions. Some crusades were preached against enemies inside the Catholic European community and against heretics or monarchs deemed a menace to European peace.

The Normans and the Venetians engaged in the Fourth Crusade (1203-04). They sailed from Venice not to attack Moslem Egypt or Syria but to capture Christian Zara and sack Constantinople. In its place they set up a Norman kingdom which survived for fifty six years when it was overthrown by the Greeks. Rather than liberating Jerusalem, they subjected Zara to the profit of the Venetians. Rather than restoring Western rule permanently in the East, they ravaged the Byzantine Empire.

The later crusades were no more successful than the first four. In 1212 the ill fated childrens crusade resulted in thousands of young people being sold into slavery by the merchants of Marseilles. The fifth crusade was a total failure and the sixth crusade (1228), through Frederick II, gained more privileges for Christian pilgrims than all previous attempts at slaughter, pillage and robbery, and recovered Jerusalem by negotiation.

Jerusalem fell to the Turks in 1244. Louis IX's deep religious spirit motivated him to undertake another crusade to rescue the Holy city. No one wanted Louis to go crusading. His barons entreated him not to; his mother warned him solemnly of his folly; even the Pope argued against Louis' leaving Europe. The young king, however, clung to his purpose.

It was characteristic of Louis that, despite his deep respect for religion, he refused to be dominated even by the Pope. He was sure of the purport of his own vow, and in the end all objections gave way before him. In this the Seventh Crusade, the heroism and saintliness of Louis IX shone forth at the expense of his reputation as a general. We see him in the enthusiasm of the mystic, combined with the headlong valor of an ancient Frank. However, the mastery over men displayed by Godfrey and the warlike skill of a Bohemond, are conspicuous by their absence.

Louis aimed his armament not against Palestine, but against Egypt, since there lay the capital of the Sultan of the East, and the chief power of the Mohammedans. Jerusalem itself was at the moment but a mound of ruins. The crusaders landed at Damietta, (1248) at the mouth of the Nile, and Louis, leaping recklessly into the water, led the way in a wild dash against the Saracen troops who lined the shore. These fled in disarray before the furious charge, and the strong city of Damietta was captured.

And there ended the crusader's triumph. The pleasures and plunder of Damietta sapped their eagerness to advance. Disease, ever the most fatal foe of the Northerners in those torrid climes, decimated the army. Five months later the army marched forward; enfeebled and despondent, ultimately to be massacred by the Moslems. The Christian army harassed from every side, retreated. The crusaders could find no rest. Men dropped of exhaustion in the ranks. Louis remained fighting with the rearguard until he, too, fainted from exhaustion and was captured by the Moslems. Not even a remnant of the wretched army escaped back to Damietta.

Great was the triumph of the Saracens over the utter annihilation of the invading army, and their capture of the renowned "King of the Franks". They slew all common soldiers and retained only such captives as they hoped to ransom. In exchange for Louis they demanded the surrender of Damietta and a million bezants of gold (about two million dollars).

The whole of France was scraped bare by his mother to collect the enormous sum demanded for his freedom. Following his ransom, Louis refused to return home. True to his vow to fight for Jerusalem, he sailed with a handful of comrades to the Holy Land. Here he remained for years warring against the Mohammedans, hoping against hope, that his example would arouse Europe to its former fervor and that other crusaders would flock to join him.

In 1256, he returned home after his mother's death in order to restore order in France. Again, in 1270 he undertook, in the face of universal protest, another crusade, the last of them all. Louis died of fever on the journey — a saint's and hero's death. This final expedition came to a disastrous end. The last stronghold of Christianity, Acre, fell in 1291.

Two centuries of struggle to keep the infidel out of the Holy Land ended in dismal failure. The primary effort of the Crusades was crushed, although the spirit continued for a time. Small Christian countries ejected the Moors from the Spanish peninsula and the tide of Moslem invasion was held back from Europe during the sixteenth century. The attempt to restore the obedience of the eastern church to Rome failed. The hope of the Byzantine emperors to recover their lands in Asia with the aid of European military power came to nothing. The forces which militated against the original aims of the Crusades was the growing hostility between Catholic Europe and the Orthodox Byzantine Empire; the emergence in Egypt of a new and aggressive Moslem power; as well as the independence and strength displayed by new forms of associations in Europe such as towns and monarchies which would win men's loyalties away from the universal church.

Papal authority was harassed by four major thrusts in Medieval society: (1) the growing national states which arose to replace the decaying Holy Roman Empire as opponents of the temporal power of the Papacy; (2) the local clergy who joined with the nobles in opposing papal interference in internal matters and who favored general church councils to curb the power of the Pope; (3) reformers who had seen the medieval reformation and the crusades transformed from their original high purposes to suit personal ambitions both lay and ecclesiastical; (4) the growing opposition of the middle class throughout Europe, whose attitudes toward life had been undergoing some severe changes because of the growth of trade, the exchange of ideas among all classes of people, and a growing feeling of national patriotism and religious self-reliance.

The church domination of the Medieval world depended upon the continuance of the medieval world order, but the fore-mentioned forces were at work, slowly undermining every aspect of that order.

The Crusades had much to do with the revival of individuality for the people developed a passion for travel and a knowledge of other lands and peoples. Contact with Moslem culture, the new observation of nature, the harkening back to classical ideals, the development of vernacular languages which replaced medieval Latin, the desire of the artist to be untrammeled by medieval patterns — these factors were instrumental in fostering the ideal of individuality among men. The lawlessness and confusion of the Italian Renaissance was due in no small part to the prevailing view that every man was a law unto himself.

This long series of crusades, from the end of the eleventh century until the sixteenth century, channeled off surplus manpower and energy into a Western counter offensive in all the directions from which the West had formerly been hard pressed; up along the Baltic and south across the Pyrenees, east into the Balkans, into Syria, even into Egypt. As men poured out of Europe, riches began to pour in, both as loot and merchandise. The Mediterranean, which for centuries past had been a Moslem lake, turned into a great highway once more. Italy revived and so did European trade. And the world was given the first inkling of the trends of Western expansion.

The reviving commerce between Europe and the East meant the growth of cities and betokened an advance in civilization. The Crusades hastened the revival of intercourse between East and West. Venice, Genoa, and Pisa, conveniently located, were called upon to furnish the crusaders with transportation and supplies. The Crusades not only enabled Italian merchants to bring Eastern commodities to the West; they increased the demand for such commodities. Spices added zest to the European diet. The Venetians obtained pepper from the Sultan of Egypt, to whom it was brought from the pepper vines of Ceylon, Sumatra, and western India.

From the same sources came cinnamon bark, ginger, cloves and allspice. Persia, India and Ceylon produced diamonds, rubies and pearls to satisfy the vanity of wealthy Europeans. The East was also the factory for damask, linen, chinaware, Persian rugs as well as cashmere shawls.

Such were the results of the Crusades. The Crusades were the grandest enterprise of medieval feudalism. In their blending of Christian idealism and barbarous warfare, they are the perfect examples of the fusion of widely disparate elements so characteristic of the Middle Ages.

BIBLIOGRAPHY

Atiys, A.S. *Crusade, Commerce and Culture*. Bloomington,Ind.,1962.
_____. *The Crusades: Historiography and Bibliography*. Bloomington, Ind.,1962.
Brundage, James (ed.). *The Crusades: Motives and Achievements*. Boston, 1964.
Coulton, G.G. *Five Centuries of Religion*. Cambridge,1927.
Haskins, C.H. *The Normans in European History*. Boston, 1915.
Lamb, H. The Crusades, *Iron Men and Saints*. New York,1962.
Memoirs of the Crusades. New York,1933.
Munro, Dana C. *Kingdom of the Crusaders*. New York,1936.
Oman, C. *The Art of War in the Middle Ages*. Ithaca,N.Y.,1951.
Runciman, Steven. *A History of the Crusades*. 3vv. Cambridge,1956.
Setton, Kenneth (ed.). *History of the Crusades*. 2vv. Philadephia,1955.
Small, R.C. *Crusading Warfare*. Cambridge,1956.
Thompson, James W. *An Economic and Social History of the Middle Ages*. New York,1928.

RELIGION
AND THE
EXPANSION OF EUROPE

William D. Griffin

William D. Griffin, Associate Professor of History at St. John's University, received his
doctorate from Fordham University. The recipient of a National Endowment for the
Humanities Research Grant, he is Associate Editor of *Studies on Burke and His Time*. He has
written several books as well as articles in such journals as *The Bulletin of the Institute of
Historical Research*, the *Journal of the Military History of Ireland* and *History Today*.

During the sixteenth century, Europe discovered America and re-
discovered Asia, while Christianity, hitherto primarily a Mediterranean
religion, spread throughout the world. The great era of European "reconnaissance" was also the golden age of missionary enterprise, and the
inextricable involvement of religious motives in the expansionist impulse
finds its expression in the classic phrase "God, Gold, and Glory". Greedy
for wealth and power though they were, the adventurers who undertook
such incredible journeys, and the rulers who dispatched them and reaped
the rewards of their toil, were motivated by spiritual considerations as well.
They hoped to bring the light of the Gospel into unknown lands, to spread
the true Faith among heathen peoples, and to make contact with those long
lost Christians who, according to legend, lay isolated somewhere in the
heart of Asia. But the very prominence of the missionary factor in European
expansion made it inevitable that the Church would share in the frustra-
tions and failures, as well as the dazzling successes, of that great outward
movement of Western Civilization.

From the middle of the fifteenth century Portugal had taken the lead in
seeking a water route to Asia, and the Holy See had confirmed her right to
rule the pagan lands discovered along the way. By 1497 Vasco da Gama
had rounded the southern tip of Africa and completed the perilous voyage
to India. But five years earlier, Columbus, striking out boldly across the

Atlantic, had planted the banner of Castile on the outlying islands of a vast new continent: Portugal's Iberian neighbor had become an aggressive rival demanding a share of the imperial spoils.

It was the task of the supra-national Papacy to arbitrate these conflicting claims. The Spanish-born Alexander VI, though scarcely indifferent to the claims of his countrymen, could not ignore the commitments made to Portugal by his predecessors. Like Solomon, he resolved the dispute by dividing the prize. To Spain he accorded the exclusive right of trade (by which the Europeans also understood conquest) in all lands lying west of the Azores. Spain would enjoy the same rights and privileges in this sphere as had previously been granted to Portugal, and received a similar mandate "to bring to the Christian Faith the people who inhabit the islands and the main land . . . . and to send wise, upright, God-fearing and virtuous men who will be capable of instructing in the indigenous peoples in good morals and in the Catholic Faith". To Portugal went confirmation of her rights east of the Pope's imaginary line. This papal decision was ratified by the Iberian powers in the Treaty of Tordesillas (1494), which moved the line farther westward so that Brazil (discovered in 1500) was subsequently included with Africa and the lands around the Indian Ocean in Portugal's, sphere, while the rest of America (still thought at that time to be part of Asia) fell to Spain.

The Pope seemed to have arrived at an admirable commpromise. But the rapidly changing circumstances of the coming century were soon to render it obsolete. The discovery of the Pacific raised the question of whether the Tordesillas line should be extended round the globe (favoring Spanish claims in the Far East) or limited to the Atlantic (thus protecting Portugese claims to the Spice Islands in modern day Indonesia). Furthermore, the King of France took a dim view of Pope Alexander's partition, remarking that he was unaware of any clause in Adam's will dividing the world between Spain and Portugal. Before long, not only Catholic France, but the newly Protestant maritime states of England and Holland would be disrupting the papal scheme. And finally, Rome would in time discover that her recognition of Iberian ecclesiastical as well as political sovereignty over the larger part of the earth was neither to her advantage nor to that of the non-European peoples so casually surrendered to royal patronage.

Sixteenth century Popes, preoccupied with European affairs, preferred to let the Spanish and the Portugese monarchs bear the burden of evangelizing the non-European world. The ecclesiastical rights, privileges, and duties of the Portugese crown in immense stretches of Africa, Asia and America were summed up under the designation *Padroado Real*, or royal patronage of the Church overseas. They were limited only by the similar *Patronato Real* in Spanish America confirmed to the Castilian crown in the early 1500's.

Across much of the globe — from Brazil to Japan — no bishop could be appointed, no new diocese created, no missionary dispatched, without the assent of the King of Portugal. The Crown could treat overseas clergy as government functionaries, employing and instructing them without reference to Rome. It could collect all ecclesiastical dues and tithes, disposing of them as it saw fit. It could advance or retard the cause of religion in the far corners of the Earth. It is hardly suprising, given these opportunities and considering the prevailing mentality of the day, that the Portugese Crown treated the Church of the *Padroado* as an arm of the State. One contemporary records that "the Kings of Portugal always aimed in this conquest of the East at so uniting the two powers, spiritual and temporal, that the one should never be exercised without the other." A later chronicler adds that "the two swords of the civil and ecclesiastical power were always so close together in the conquest of the East we seldom find one being used without the other; for the weapons only conquered through the might that the preaching of the Gospel gave to them, and the preaching was only of some use when it was accompanied and protected by the weapons."

It is perhaps the supreme irony of the Portugese Enterprise in the Orient that the Central Asian "mighty Christian kingdon" envisioned by medieval romances turned out to be neither wholly imaginery nor in any degree mighty. In 1500, fresh from his discovery of Brazil, Cabral landed in the south-western coast of India and encountered the so-called "Christians of St. Thomas." Claiming to have received the Faith from the apostle himself, these Indian Christians had been cut off from their fellow-Indians — as from their fellow-Christians — for centuries. While sharing some of the manners and customs of their neighbors, they had managed to avoid absorption into Hinduism and now numbered about 100,00 in Kerala. Far from being the strong allies against the march of Islam which the Westerners had hoped to find, this isolated community expected the Portugese to play the role of deliverer from Hindu tyranny and Muslim aggression. To this disappointment of practical hopes was soon added spiritual disillusionment. The Portugese, at first charmed by the apostolic simplicity of the "Thomas Christians", presently discovered that they were theologically unorthodox, and totally ignorant of papal supremacy. The Keralans, in turn, were alarmed to learn that their new-found friends had no intention of leaving them either political or religious autonomy.

Goa, the principal Portugese stronghold in India, had early become an ecclesiastical center as well, with a bishop subordinate to the nearest European prelate, thousands of miles away, in Madeira. By 1557, "Golden Goa" had become an archbishopric with dependent sees of its own, not only in India, but at Malacca in Malaya and Macao in China. The Archbishop of Goa, who was ultimately to be accorded the title "Patriarch of the Indies," thus presided over the whole of the Catholic Church throughout East Asia. The Thomas Christians could hardly expect to avoid his rule, yet they made vigorous efforts to do so. Their bishops were successively deposed for heresy, arrested, and banished, but they managed to survive until 1599, when a new and vigorous archbishop arrived, determined to reduce all to orthodoxy and obedience. The independence of the Church of St. Thomas was liquidated, and its adherents brought under Latin rites and practices. Three hundred years later Rome was to reverse these measures and to grant this ancient branch of Catholicism its own independent hierarchy: but by then the harm had been done, and Asian Christianity had become irretrievably identified with colonial arrogance.

While the fate of the Keralans was working itself out, the missionary role of Portugal in India had undergone its own evolution. Although Vasco da Gama had come to India "in search of Christianity and Spices," the latter had absorbed most of his successors' attention. Relatively few priests came to India during the first generation of Portugese rule, and their unimaginative efforts had produced a correspondingly small harvest of converts. Here, as elsewhere, a great change was to result from the coming of the Jesuits.

Formed in 1534 by the ex-soldier Iñigo de Loyola, his Basque compatriot Francisco Xavier, and five other enthusiasts, the Society of Jesus was to become the greatest of missionary organizations, a "militia of Christ," organized as an army for the conversion of pagans and heretics and the spreading of the Faith. Confirmed as a religious order by Papal decree in 1540, the rapidly growing Jesuit army was soon dispersed overseas, with Xavier himself arriving at Goa in 1542.

After initiating reform of the moral and missionary situation in that city, Xavier moved on to the Coromandel Coast, where thousands had received baptism in exchange for Portugese protection, but remained without instruction or pastoral care. In the words of one commentator, Xavier "arrived to find an untutored mob; he left behind him a Church in being." By the time this pioneer Jesuit had passed on to new work farther afield, his confreres were beginning to transform Portugese India. Setting much higher standards than their predecessors, the disciples of Loyola not only purged the Church in the East of laxity and negligence, but pressed the conversion of Asians in the neighborhood of Portugese settlements. Although forced conversions were forbidden, the Government, at the urging of the Jesuits, initiated a policy of favoring converts and discriminating against adherents of the old religions which facilitated the work of the missionaries. These tactics did not go without opposition from Portugese merchants and planters, who claimed that missionary "aggression" was driving away their domestic servants and farm laborers, and at times the authorities were obliged to publish renewed guaranties of tolerance in order to avoid a mass exodus of Hindus from Portugese territory. Despite these practical difficulties, Portugal remained fundamentally committed — like all European monarchies of the sixteenth century — to the concept of one ruler and one Faith, at home and abroad. And the Jesuits, while conceding that "induced" conversions were not the most desirable, knew that the later generations of new Christians would be sincere and docile adherents of the Faith.

Although Portuguese power in the East centered at Goa and its dependencies in Western India and lowland Ceylon, commerce and missionary activity had thrust into more distant regions. After the occupation of Malacca in 1511, the islands of the Indonesian archipelago had become the source of a lucrative trade in spices. But when Xavier visited the region in 1546, he found that the progress of Christianity had been minimal, and all the efforts of the Crown and clergy were unavailing against the firm allegiance of most of the islanders to Islam, and the need of merchants to avoid offending local Muslim Sultans.

Xavier, as Apostolic Nuncio in the Orient, had greater hopes of success in Japan. When he at last reached that remote Empire in 1549, he found the moment of his arrival propitious. Central authority had collapsed in a wave of political disorder, and effective power had passed into the hands of provincial magnates, who were displaying an unprecedented eagerness for Western contacts. Though the Japanese were primarily interested in initiating trade and obtaining firearms, Xavier and his fellow missionaries found them equally open to new ideas. "They are a people of very good will," the Jesuit wrote, "very sociable and very desirous of knowledge . . . They like to hear things propounded according to reason . . ." Gradually, Xavier came to modify his concept of the Christian approach to non-Christian peoples in a way which was to affect profoundly Jesuit mission tactics in the Far East. He had previously assumed that non-Christian social and cultural institutions were as valueless as non-Christian religions. But now, impressed by the nobler elements of Japanese civilization, he concluded that "while the Gospel must transform and refine, and recreate, it need not necessarily reject as worthless everything that has come before." Building upon the groundwork laid by Xavier, the Jesuits adapted themselves to local customs and concentrated their attention upon the provincial lords, who in turn influenced the conversion of their followers. By the end of the century, the Christian community numbered some 300,000, several Japanese noblemen had journeyed to Europe under Jesuit guidance to meet with King and Pope, and the first Japanese Jesuits had been ordained.

China had proved even more inaccessible to the Portugese than Japan, but, as in the island realm, the mutual advantages of trade had led to an accommodation, and by 1557 a European settlement had been established at Macao, near the mouth of the Canton River, Here, as in Japan, the King of Portugal's subjects were visitors rather than masters, and the *Padroado* could not guarantee missionaries more than a vague general support. Xavier had died in 1552 on an island off the coast, disappointed in his dream of evangelizing China. Portugese priests resident in Macao soon decided that conversion of the Chinese was indeed an impossible dream.

But in 1580, the Jesuit leadership chose a young priest who had been teaching in Goa to attempt the impossible. Matteo Ricci spent three years in Macao learning the language, absorbing the customs, and persuading the viceroy of the neighboring province to allow him entry to Chinese territory. After this initial concession had been granted, he slowly gained the trust and approval of the imperial officials by his prudent conduct and respectful attitude toward their civilization. Finally, in 1600, he was admitted to the Emperor's Court at Peking, where he won the favor of the monarch by his knowledge of Western techniques and his possession of such non-theological skills as map-making. It was only when he had procured such acceptance and had thoroughly acclimated himself to Chinese culture that he could hope to obtain a hearing for Christianity, which had to seem as little "foreign" as possible. By adopting the later view of Xavier that traditional culture must be respected and preserved if Christianity is to take root in new soil, Ricci won converts among highranking nobles and distinguished scholars, whose example in turn inspired others. At his death in 1610 there were some 2000 Christians in China, and his fellow missionaries looked forward to a rich harvest.

Pope Alexander's neat division of newly-discovered lands between Portugal and Spain did not survive Balboa's discovery of the Pacific in 1513. Within a few years, Cortez had conquered Mexico and established outposts on the great ocean's rim, and Magellan — a renegade Portugese navigator — had guided a Castilian squadron across it to the Philippines. These developments had all established a Spanish claim in Asia, which was reinforced by the theory of a globe-girdling Tordesillas line. The Portugese, however, had no intention of yielding the Spice Islands — the real goal of Spain's oriental ambitions — without a fight, and when the dispute was finally settled in 1529, by the Treaty of Saragossa, Spain had to content herself with the islands named after her great king, Philip II.

It was not until 1564 that the islands were formally occupied and Manila founded, but the Spanish Crown was not slow in asserting its *Patronato*. Mass had been celebrated as early as 1521 by priests of Magellan's expedition, and missionary activity was vigorously prosecuted by the Augustinians, who arrived in 1565, and other orders, including the Jesuits, who operated as readily in the Spanish sphere as in the Portugese. The lifeline to this mother country ran across the Pacific, not through the Indian Ocean, and the principal trade of the islands was the exchange of Oriental silks for American silver. Hence the bishopric of Manila, created in 1579, was dependent upon Mexico City, and religious developments tended to parallel those of America rather than Asia. There was no question here of dealing with a highly cultivated, ancient civilization. The simple tribesmen, aside from the fierce Muslim Moros, offered no serious resistance to political absorption and Christian enrollment, and within a century virtually the whole population was nominally Catholic. Established in

"Christian Villages" under the watchful eyes of Spanish priests, the Filipinos were allowed to retain their customs and languages, and, in a purely practical way, experienced little real loss from having passed under Spanish control. Yet the very ease of the civil and ecclesiastical conquest of the islands had its drawbacks. Cut off at a fairly primitive stage of their natural development, the Filipinos were deprived of any other cultural example than that of Spanish Christianity. The material advantages of this culture were largely denied them by the limited opportunities of obtaining a European-style education, and by the Castilian obsession with racial distinctions, while the paternalistic and overconfident attitude of missionaries whose converts were so easily won led to superficial Christianization. The ambiguities and distortions resulting from the sixteenth century conquests are still visible in the Philippines of the twentieth century.

The Philippine colonial experience, as has already been noted, tended to resemble that of America rather than that of Asia, and characteristics of sixteenth century Central and South America compelled a similarity of approach by Spaniards and Portugese in this part of the world which makes it more appropriate to consider Brazil apart from the other lands of the *Padroado*. Here again there was no need for the policy of restraint followed by Xavier, Ricci, and their colleagues in the Far East. As in the Philippines, the discoverers became conquerers, for they encountered neither highly developed civilizations nor formidable political and military entities. True, the Aztecs and the Incas, if not precisely civilized, had achieved a high level of barbarism; but both were brittle, aristocratic societies, unable to stand the strain of even the smallest European assult, and too oppressive for their overthrow to be lamented by the subject masses of Mexico and Peru. And here again, Christianity, introduced as an inevitable part of Iberian civilization was accepted with little resistance.

In contrast to the slow labor and the limited harvest of evangelization in the Orient, the spread of the Gospel throughout America corresponded to the rapidity and totality of the conquest itself.

Although Columbus had made his landfall only in 1492, the West Indies had been occupied by 1515, the Aztecs defeated and New Spain brought into being by 1521, and the whole Inca Empire annexed by the early 1530's. It required another generation to digest these rich acquisitions, but by 1580, the La Plata region had been explored and the Portugese had planted several flourishing towns along the Brazilian coast. The first bishopric west of the Atlantic — Santo Domingo — was created so early as 1511; within a decade there were half a dozen more, and by the end of the century a full-fledged diocesean structure had emerged in both Spanish and Portugese America.

There was, to be sure, opposition to the Church. Some natives proved less tractable than others, notably the Comanches and Apaches in the outlying provinces of New Spain which now constitute the southwestern

United States. Their resistance to Spanish conquest involved the massacre of many missionaries well down into the seventeenth century. The Arucanians of Southern Chile and the aborigines of the Amazon Basin likewise resisted domination or conversion. Almost as troublesome was the attitude of those colonists who regarded the red man as a ready-made slave labor force, to be exploited and brutalized at will. When reminded by a priest that the king had commanded his governors to care for, instruct, and uplift the pagan tribes, Pizarro, the conquerer of Peru, replied: "I have not come for any such reasons; I have come to take away from them their gold." Spaniards of the Pizarro School believed that the natives were "naturally lazy and vicious, melancholic, cowardly, and in general a lying shiftless people. Their marriages are not a sacrament but a sacrilege . . . . Their chief desire is to eat, drink, worship heathen idols, and commit bestial obscenities." Colonists who held such views were in constant conflict with the better sort of missionary, who constituted himself the protector as well as the teacher of the natives. One such was the Dominican Antonio de Montesinos, who demanded of the settlers in Hispaniola: "Tell me, by what right or justice do you keep these Indians in such cruel and horrible servitude? . . . Why do you keep them so oppressed and weary, not giving them enough to eat, not taking care of them in their illnesses? For with the excessive work you demand of them, they fall and die, or rather you kill them with your desire to extract and acquire gold every day . . . Are these not men? Have they not rational souls? Are you not bound to love them as you love yourselves?"

Far more renowned was Bartolomé de Las Casas (d. 1566), who devoted more than fifty years to the cause of the American Indian. In his enthusiasm he painted almost too idyllic a picture of the noble savage: "God created these simple without evil and without guile. They are most obedient and faithful to their natural lords, and to the Christians whom they serve. They are most submissive, patient, peaceful and virtuous. Nor are they quarrelsome, rancorous, querulous, or vengeful. They neither possess nor desire to possess worldly wealth. Surely these people would be the most blessed in the world if only they worshipped the true God." Las Casas angrily refuted those colonists who insisted that the redman was by nature a slave. No nation existed, he insisted, "no matter how rude, uncultivated, barbarous, gross, or almost brutal its people may be, which may not be persuaded and brought to a good order and way of life, and made domestic, mild and tractable, provided the method that is proper and natural to men is used; namely love, gentleness, and kindness." It was largely due to Las Casas' crusading zeal that the Spanish Crown promulgated the so-called New Laws in 1542, guaranteeing the human rights of the Indians and protecting them against enslavement.

As in the Philippines, both the Spanish and the Portugese governments in America conceded extensive jurisdiction over the native peoples to the clergy, while retaining the ultimate authority of the royal patronage, and using the missionaries, in effect, as a species of local civil service. "Christian villages" were formed in many districts under strict priestly management, where religious — and the rudiments of secular — instruction was imparted in the regional dialects. The most elaborate project of this sort was the celebrated mission territory of Paraguay, which by 1623 included twenty-three fortified settlements, populated by some 100,000 Guaranis. Here the Indians lived an orderly and contented life, albeit under almost military discipline imposed by the "soldiers" of Loyola, who were often obliged to lead their native militia against Brazilian slave raiders.

But if the missionaries succeeded in protecting their charges from enslavement, the need for mass labor to sustain the plantation economy of tropical America remained. Africa was to supply the manpower.

Portugal had made its first contact with the blacks of tropical Africa as far back as 1444, and had sent the first mission to the Congo in 1490. Some conversions were made, and in 1518 a Congolese prince named Henrique, who had spent some twenty years being educated in Lisbon, was consecrated bishop. It is not certain that he ever returned to the Congo, but in any case, the lack of priests, the death of influential Christian chieftains, and the indifference of the majority had led to the extinction of the West African Christian community by mid-sixteenth century. The same fate befell all subsequent Portugese attempts to evangelize West Africa. Temporary local successes were always followed by reversions to paganism. The Portugese conquests in Angola and Guinea extended the bounds of their effective control, but did not materially affect the success of the missions. Much the same was true of East Africa, where a Portugese colony in Mozambique, and less permanent outposts elsewhere in the region failed to produce more than temporary local conversions, usually inspired by some chief's desire to gain Portugese aid in war with his neighbors. The high mortality rate among missionaries in Africa, the lack of political stability and the constant feuding among the natives, the uncertainty and contradictions of Lisbon's African policy, all contributed to the failure of Christianity to take root among people whose traditions, culture, and even languages few Europeans had, in any case, troubled to study.

Even the redoubtable Jesuits in time became disillusioned with the prospect of painless conversion of the West African tribes. One, addressing the Portugese Crown in 1563, declared that his experience had convinced him that these were barbarous savages who could not be converted by the methods of peaceful persuasion used in Asia, but must be dealt with by harsher means. Another wrote from Angola in 1575: "Almost everybody is convinced that the conversion of these barbarians is not to be achieved through love, but only after they have been subdued by force of arms . . ." These opinions reflected the general views of Portugese clergy and laymen alike and the Dark Continent — for the time being at least — was abandoned to exploitation for material gain. The indigenous population, "un-redeemably evil and bestial", were declared legitimate prey for slave hunters.

The Church's concern over the fate of the American Indian was not matched by distress over the slave trade. Even Las Casas seems to have regarded the negroes as suitable substitutes for his proteges, though he later repented and declared that if it was unjust to enslave redmen, then it was equally unjust to enslave black men. With a few other exceptions, the Iberian clergy raised no objection to slavery as such, which was a normal practice in many parts of the world, including the Mediterranean countries. The Africans, it was argued, were not the subjects of the Kings of Spain or Portugal, as were the American Indians, but of their own "kings", who might sell prisoners or even their own tribesmen, at will, without any blame falling on the Europeans who transported these unfortunates to America. It was even suggested that by taking pagan (or Muslim) negroes away from their own country and placing them under Christian masters, they were given a chance for salvation. Such excuses were too specious to be taken seriously even at that time, and the Spanish Jesuit Antonio de Sandoval, one of those honorable few who fought the system, pointed out that the slave traders often incited tribal wars to increase the supply of slaves, rather than merely benefitting in an innocent way from the Africans' natural belligerency, and that, in practice, slave holders usually brutalized rather than Christianized their chattels. When the northern Protestant states, England and Holland, began building tropical Empires, they, too, occasionally experienced scruples over slavery. Yet Anglican and Calvinist theologians, like their Catholic counterparts, were overwhelmingly ready to ease tender consciences with sanctions drawn from the Bible and well-established precedent. The African slave trade flourished during the era of expansion because it was profitable — to the Portugese entrepreneurs and to the planters colonizing states; because its horrors were little known to most Europeans; and because it solved the problem of labor without burdening the American Indians, for whom the European Governments felt some degree of responsibility. The guilt for initiating this trade rests upon the European sovereigns who authorized it and the colonial Church which acquiesced in it. The consequences of their actions and acquiescence are all too evident in the twentieth century as Africa writhes in rage and confusion, torn between the "western" and the "non-western" worlds.

Whether one considers European expansion in the broadest sense, or totally in its religious aspect, the sixteenth century is the "Iberian Century". The Kings of Spain and Portugal had taken the initiative in exploration and in evangelization. The work of propagating Christianity had been left entirely to the diligence and generosity of royal patronage. The great missionary orders — notably the Jesuits, but with the Franciscans and

Dominicans not far behind — had enjoyed crown sponsorship and had ventured to the far corners of the earth in Spanish and Portugese vessels. In America, where conversion was practically universal within the area of effective government control, millions had been baptized. The Spanish dependencies comprised five archbishoprics and ten bishoprics, under whose jurisdiction a growing corps of parish clergy supplemented the labors of the religious orders. In Brazil though Bahia (given its first bishop in 1551) long remained the only diocese, the missionaries had rapidly extended their work south, north, and west, bringing European laws and government in the wake of the Gospel.

The Asian realms of the *Padroado* at the end of the sixteenth century reflected the limited nature of Portugese sovereignty and the greater resistance of the Oriental religions to Christian penetration. There were few converts in the Muslim and Muslim-dominated East African, South Arabian, and Persian Gulf sectors of Portugal's commercial empire, for Islam was almost impervious to evangelization, and even in the trading posts directly ruled by Lisbon, it was deemed prudent to avoid antagonizing neighboring princes. The coastal regions of India, especially around fortresses like Goa, had a Catholic population of between 150 and 200 thousand (exclusive of the "Thomas Christians"), Ceylon some 30,000, and Malacca, Siam, Burma, and Indochina together a few thousand more. Indonesia, again, offered Islamic opposition to missionary activity, and among its huge population there can have been no more than 20,000 Christian converts, concentrated in such Portugese strongholds as the Amboina and the Lesser Sunda Islands. Macao had perhaps 3000 Christians, but the work of Ricci and his colleagues in the interior of China was only beginning to bear fruit. The pride of the *Padroado* was, of course, Japan, where the quantity of conversions was matched by the quality of converts. The Christian community amounted to nearly 300,000 at the turn of the century, mainly in the districts around Nagasaki and Kyoto. Thus, there was no more than a million Christians at the end of the sixteenth century in the vast area stretching from East Africa to Japan — little enough when compared to the teeming millions who still adhered to their traditional faiths, or even to the multitudes baptized by the missioners in the New World. The Spanish enterprise in the Philippines belonged to the American sphere in the missionary as well as in the political sense, and the scorn felt by some of the aggressive clergy at Manila for Portugal's "business before the conversion" attitude is expressed by a Dominican writing in 1598: "It is certain that neither the Royal Crown nor the Faith will be greatly increased by the Portuguese, since they are quite satisfied with holding the ports which they already have, in order to secure the sea for their trade."

Yet, in the final analysis, the statistical record of Christians (whose numbers might easily increase or decrease with changing circumstances) is less significant in an evaluation of the "Iberian Century" than certain other characteristics of missionary labor and achievement in the 1500's. The semi-political connection of the Iberian clergy with their Government meant that they were often more involved in secular than in spiritual concerns, to say nothing of those whose opportunities to engage in trade or planting turned them into businessmen as well as civil functionaries. Even where these distractions and diversions of interest were surmounted, the missionaries remained essentially the representatives of a colonial Church structure, the dependent and inferior status of which was emphasized by the absence of a native clergy. Although a few Asians received ordination during the first century of European expansion, repeated decrees of the hierarchy in Latin America forbade the granting of Holy Orders to American Indians, negroes, and persons of mixed blood who had not "shown such qualities as would fit them for the dignity of the priesthood". Despite the shortage of clergy in many districts, there was no relaxation of this prejudice against an indigenous priesthood until the very end of the colonial era. Reluctance to confer the priestly office was matched by a widespread belief that the new Christians ought not to be admitted to the fullness of the sacraments until a long period of instruction and strengthening in the Faith had passed. The American Indian in particular was regarded as a second-class Catholic, with only those who had been most docile and regular in their duties being admitted to communion, and then only at Easter. In Asia, the survival of Christianity rested precariously upon the tolerance of local potentates, and the declining strength of the Portugese *Padroado*. In America, though conversion was well-nigh universal, it was a bold missioner indeed who dared speculate on the depth to which the new religion had penetrated.

The Iberian phase of Eurpoean expansion presents to the historian a baffling picture of grandeur mixed with squalor. The religious experience which accompanied that phase was no less contradictory and disturbing in its implications for the future.

The decline of Iberian predominance in Europe and overseas, accompanied by the recovery of France, the flowering of Elizabethan England, and the maritime exploits of the Dutch, was reflected in the diminished effectiveness of the Iberian missions. The Papacy, in its turn, had become both more sensitive to its obligations and bolder in asserting its primacy, now that the formidable Philip II was gone from the scene. In 1622 Pope Gregory XV acted to bring the missions under Rome's guidance and direction by creating the Congregation for the Propagation of the Faith.

Francesco Ingoli, who supervised the work of the Congregation from its founding until his death in 1649, was a shrewd and realistic ecclesiastical statesman, as well as an ardent champion of his Faith. Thoroughly informed about the state of the Church overseas, he committed the Congregation to a new approach in missionary activity. It included an end to the stranglehold of Spain and Portugal on the extra-European Church, an increase in the number of bishops and closer connections between them and Rome, growth in the number of parish clergy to balance the itinerant members of the religious orders, and the development of a native priesthood as soon as possible in every region. The Church, in Ingoli's view, must take an indigenous coloring in each nation, if it was ever to escape the "colonial" character of an alien importation. Xavier's and Ricci's ideas are more boldly and confidently expressed in the Congregation's instructions to its missionaries: "Do not regard it as your task, and do not bring any pressure to bear on the people to change their manners, customs and uses . . . . What could be more absurd than to transport France, Spain, Italy or some other European country to China? Do not introduce all that to them, but only the Faith, which does not despise or destroy the manners and customs of any people, always supposing they are not evil, but rather wishes to see them preserved unharmed . . . There is no stronger cause for alienation and hate than an attack on local customs, especially when these go back to a venerable antiquity . . . . especially . . . when an attempt is made to introduce the customs of another people in the place of those which have been abolished. Do not draw invidious contrasts between the customs of the peoples and those of Europe; do your utmost to adopt yourselves to them".

With regard to the development of secular clergy drawn largely from the non-European population, the Congregation's interest and sincerity was no less clearly evident in the pledge to "hasten the conversion of the heathen, not only by proclaiming the Gospel to them, but above all by preparing . . . and raising to ecclesiastical orders those of the new Christians . . . who are considered best suited to that holy state; in order to create in each country a clerical order and a hierarchy such as Jesus Christ and the apostles have appointed in the Church . . . That is the only way in which true religion can be established on a permanent footing . . . and priests of the country . . . will be able to bring their countries to the point at which they will no longer need help from abroad."

The creation of the Congregation itself had aroused suspicion and criticism on the part of Spain and Portugal. The plan to increase the number of dioceses overseas met with outraged protests that bishops could be created only by and with royal patronage. The Papacy thereupon circumvented the concession so incautiously made a century before by naming vicars apostolic, who were simply bishops under another name, without territorial titles, but duly consecrated and capable of exercising all episcopal duties within a given area. The appointment of these direct representatives of the Pope was deeply offensive to Spain and Portugal, and posed a dilemma for the missionaries, who could be stripped of their priestly functions if they refused to obey the vicars, or deprived of their financial support from the Crown if they took the oath of obedience. The disputes and hostilities arising from this issue did much to weaken the good effects of Rome's program in Asia.

While most of the vicars apostolic were Italians or Frenchmen, two appointments deserve special mention — that of Mateu de Castro, who, despite his name, was a convert from Hinduism, and Lo Wen-Tsao, a native of Fukien. Castro, who was named in 1637 to oversee the interior part of India (where the Portugese had accomplished little), was refused recognition by the Archbishop of Goa and bitterly opposed by the Jesuits, who regarded him as a troublemaker. There is little doubt that resistance to papal interference was in this case complicated by ethnic considerations, and after many trips back and forth to Rome and much correspondence, Castro had to resign his duties and leave his native land. Much the same obstacles were encountered by the first native-born Chinese bishop, whose appointment as vicar apostolic for northern China came only in 1674. No Spanish or Portugese bishop in the Far East was willing to consecrate him for fear of offending the Iberian governments, and it was years before the arrival of a new Italian vicar apostolic in the area enabled him to receive the consecration necessary to his spiritual office. During the brief remainder of his life, he was criticized by the Iberian missionaries for allowing Christians to retain too many of the traditional Chinese customs and practices. Rome's remarkable step of raising Asians to the episcopacy was not repeated during the colonial era. The threat which such an experiment posed to the European political and racial position in the Orient aroused too much controversy to suit later Popes. It would be well into the twentieth century before the Catholic Church vindicated its universality by appointing the next native bishops in India and China.

France had been slow to join the ranks of the European expansionists. To be sure, François I (whose sour remark about Adam's will has already been quoted) had sent Jacques Cartier to Canada, and in 1534 had defied Iberian hegemony by claiming that remote wilderness under the name of New France. Cartier recorded how his party knelt before a great wooden cross they had erected and "folded our hands and venerated the cross in the presence of a large number of savages, in order to show them — by the lifting up of our hands to Heaven — that our salvation depended only on the Cross." This elementary bit of mission work was pursued no further, however, for dynastic wars and civil strife preoccupied Francois' successors — some of whom were hard-put to retain their throne — for the remainder of the century. The only other French ventures into the Western Hemisphere during the 1500's — short-lived settlements in Brazil and Florida — were carried out by the Huguenots, whose ambiguous relationship with their own sovereign and constant skirmishing with the Iberian lords of America left little time for preaching the doctrines of Calvin among the aborigines.

It was not until the early seventeenth century that domestic peace and a lull in international rivalries permitted the newly-established House of Bourbon to develop serious colonial ambitions. Although France never received the sweeping concessions of Crown patronage made by the Renaissance Popes, the decline of the Iberian monarchies and the policy of Papal intervention in the mission fields permitted France, or at least subjects of the French king, to play a major role in the new era of Catholic expansion. The claim to New France became a reality within the expeditions of Champlain, and Mass was celebrated in Canada for the first time in 1615, on the site of Montreal. The evangelization of Hurons, Iroquois, and other savage inhabitants of this new frontier was eagerly undertaken by French Jesuits with the warm approval of their ruler, and by the early 1620's several groups of missionaries were at work in Canada. Their record of success was marred by such tragedies as the martyrdom of Father Issac Jogues and his colleagues in 1646-49, and the virtual annihilation of the Christianized Hurons by their hereditary and obstinately pagan enemies the Iroquois in 1650. In later years Paris was to view the Indians of New France and Louisiana primarily as a military resource, supplementing the sparse European population, and to court the wartime alliance or peacetime trade of the heathen tribes along the Great Lakes as more important than their conversion. The same policy would be reflected in the employment of Christian "mission Indians," such as the Abenaki of Maine, as irregular troops under command of their Jesuit mentors in raids against New England settlements. By the end of the century, the souls of the Indians had become less valuable than their skill in taking English scalps.

The era of Cardinal Richelieu's ascendancy as chief minister of France (1624-42) also saw the establishment of a French presence in the West Indies. St. Christopher was occupied in 1625; Guadeloupe, Martinique, and Tortuga soon followed, with a dozen lesser islands added during the 1640's and 1650's. Here the indigenous population had long since disappeared, to be replaced by a small European planter class, a somewhat larger element of free mulattoes and negroes, and a mass of African slaves — most of whom continued to profess under French rule the somewhat lax Catholicism that by now characterized the Spanish Caribbean.

Intimations of colonial adventures yet to come are afforded by the arrival of French missionaries in Indo-China and Madagascar during the seventeenth century, two hundred years before French political dominance was extended over these regions. Southeast Asia had produced few converts even during the active days of the *Padroado*: Buddhist Siam, for instance, had not yielded to the Jesuits' best endeavors. But between 1623 and 1630 the French priest Alexandre de Rhodes, who displayed an exceptional ability to master the local dialects, baptized some 6700 Vietnamese. After ten years of exile, he was again able to return to that country and to build up a flourishing Catholic community, which survived intermittent periods of persecution and his own rebanishment in 1645. Thanks to Rhodes' development of the catechist system, by which a lay brotherhood of converts maintained the community, and to his reduction of the Vietnamese language to the Latin alphabet as a medium of instruction, the Catholic population of Vietnam reached several hundred thousand within a few decades, and survived as a bulwark in Asian Christianity and an outpost of Western influence until the coming of the French in the 1880's.

A far different story comes out of the French attempt to annex and colonize Madagascar. In 1642 the French East India Company planted a colony on the great island in the Indian Ocean, and sent Carmelites and Lazarists to minister to the settlers. But all efforts to preach the Gospel to "the heathen" suffered from poor direction and from the mounting resentment of the tribes towards the colonists. At last, in 1674, the Malagasy rose against the interlopers, slew many, and forced the surviving French to flee. Although the Lazarists made two further short-lived expeditions to the island in the eighteenth century, their labors were wasted, and it was left to military conquest in the late nineteenth century to secure Madagascar to France and to secure new opportunities for Catholic missionaries.

Although their missionary activities belong most properly to a later age of European expansion, some mention should be made of Orthodox and Protestant Christianity. The rapid extension of the Muscovite state in the fifteenth and sixteenth century spread Russian sovereignty over the Tartar hordes on the European side of the Urals, the primitive tribesmen of Siberia and the nomads of Central Asia. By 1648 Russian explorers had reached the Pacific, and the time had come for the assimilation and Christianization of the vast areas and diverse peoples already conquered. As in so many aspects of Russian history, it was Peter the Great who initiated the enterprise. In 1700 he ordered a campaign of evangelization "for the strengthening and extension of the Orthodox Christian Faith and for the proclamation of the . . . Faith among the the idolatrous peoples; also in order to bring the . . . tributary peoples of the neighborhood of Tobolsk and the other towns of Siberia to Christian Faith and holy Baptism". But Peter's goals were as much political as religious, and throughout the history of the Russian missions the identification between Church and State remained so close that the spread of Orthodox doctrine was synonomous with the spread of Tsarist rule.

In the course of the eighteenth century, the Muscovite missionaries moved successively into West Siberia, China (where they won only a handful of converts), the Kalmuck steppe country, the Middle Volga region, East Siberia, Kamchatka, and the Aleutian Islands. The results in terms of numbers, to say nothing of sincerity of conversions, were often disappointing, but everywhere they went, the Orthodox clergy established a Russian presence — with all that this implied for the future — and furthered, even if in a tenuous form, the expansion of European civilization.

During the Reformation conflicts of the sixteenth century, the newly-born Protestant Churches obviously had little time to spare for missionary enterprise. Their sectarian rivalries prevented cooperation against Rome, much less joint evangelization overseas. Moreover, the Protestant areas of Europe, unlike Spain, Portugal, and France, were scarcely in contact with the wider world outside until the belated emergence of England and the Dutch Republic as maritime powers. When reproached by Catholic controversialists with the charge that despite their alleged apostolic fervor they had done nothing to spread Christianity among the heathen, certain Protestants insisted that missions were unnecessary and even undesirable. According to this point of view, Christ's command to preach the Gospel to all the world was intended only for the original apostles; those peoples who had not welcomed the first opportunity for salvation need not be offered a second chance. This rather unimpressive argument convinced many in Northern and Central Europe, and about the only efforts at spreading the Faith generated in those parts during the early Protestant era were King Gustav Vasa's mission (from 1559 on) to the pagan Lapps of sub-arctic Sweden, and a few unsuccessful attempts by German and Czech Lutherans during the late 1500's to distribute religious tracts in the Turkish-ruled Balkans.

The appearance of English and Dutch mariners upon the Seven Seas to dispute mastery of the non-European world with the Catholic powers, marks the true beginning of Protestant participation in the Western expansion. The Netherlands East India Company was founded in 1602 to carry Dutch trade into the Orient in defiance of the hated Spanish and their Portugese allies. Pressure from the Reformed Church to transform this into a religious as well as a commercial crusade led the company (whose monopoly made it, in effect, arbiter of all Dutch affairs in the East), to set up a seminary in 1622. From this Calvinist institution in Leyden missionaries went forth to Indonesia and Ceylon, which were wrested from the Portugese during the following decade. These clergymen were employees of the Company, charged primarily with caring for the Dutch colonists, but allowed a cash bonus for each convert baptized. Thus stimulated, the Dutch ministers preached unceasingly, and the special privileges promised by the Company to natives who joined the State Church won over not only the non-Christian, but the Catholic population in the tens of thousands. Taiwan (Formosa) was also snatched from Iberian domination in 1624, and during their tenure there the Dutch made numerous converts — a feat they could not duplicate when they later supplanted the Portugese as the only Western nation permitted to trade with Japan.

While the Dutch were able to make virtually a clean sweep of Portugal's dependencies in the Far East, they found themselves outclassed in the New World. Only a precarious foothold was gained in the Caribbean and South America against fierce Iberian opposition, and the New Netherlands territory (incorporating present day New York State) was held for only a single generation, scarcely long enough to make a deep impression, religious or otherwise, on the North American Indians. Holland's nemesis here was England, that newly-aggressive sea power which was soon to colonize most of the Atlantic coast, and, ultimately, to oust France, too, from the continent. English clergymen, unlike their German brethren, were convinced that the savages of America deserved a chance to hear the word of God, especially in its purified and reformed state. As early as 1583, the charter authorizing Sir Humphrey Gilbert's abortive venture in the New World spoke of the need to convert the "poor infidels, it seeming probable that God hath reserved these Gentiles to be introduced into Christian civility by the English nation."

But after the landing at Jamestown (1607) and Plymouth (1620) had finally set England on the road to empire, neither the Crown nor the Anglican Church displayed much interest in promoting either civility or Christianity. Most sustained attempts made to spread the Gospel during the seventeenth century were the personal projects of dedicated individuals like the Presbyterian John Eliot, pastor of Roxbury, Massachusetts, who imitated Catholic practice by gathering his converts into "praying towns." By the time of his death in 1690, there were several thousand Christian Indians, guided by twenty-four preachers carefully trained by Eliot from among his most promising disciples. But much of Eliot's work — and that of other missionaries in British America — was negated by incessant warfare between the Indians and the colonists. The founding, in 1701, of the Anglican Society for the Propagation of the Gospel in Foreign Parts led to an increasing concern during the eighteenth century with the spiritual and material state of the non-European peoples under English rule. But a hundred years of irresponsibility on the part of the Government and negligence on the part of the Church hierarchy had left little for the missioners to do but pick up the fragments of scattered tribes and cultures.

Unlike the Dutch, who ruthlessly destroyed everything the Portugese missioners had accomplished in Asia, the English (apart from a decade of fanaticism under Cromwell) displayed a tolerant indifference towards Catholics in the increasing domain of their East India Company. The Company, founded in 1600, had discouraged missionary work for fear of provoking Hindu resentment and thus jeopardizing its commercial interests. Hence Protestantism found no foothold in India during the seventeenth century. It was not until King Fredrick IV of Denmark was inspired to introduce the Gospel among the inhabitants of the tiny Danish trading post of Tranquebar that two Lutheran clergymen were commissioned to preach on the Coromandel Coast. They arrived in 1706, the first non-Catholic missionaries to reach India from Europe. The close cooperation between the two royal houses (Prince George of Denmark was Queen Anne's consort) and the proximity of the Danish and English colonies in India led to Anglican interest in this enterprise. A collaborative program ultimately developed, and through this early example of ecumenical endeavor the Orient was to be brought into contact with another facet of the European mind.

Just as Christianity had been inseparably woven into the fabric of Europe, so it was to form no inconsiderable part of Europe's contribution to the world at large. By the time the first great era of expansion had run its course, Christianity had ceased to be a purely European phenomenon. But it was still far from establishing itself as a universal religion.

The New World had undoubtedly become an extension of Christian and European Civilization. The aborigines had been unable to resist the overwhelming force of the conquerers' firearms and Faith. While the process would go further, and the new ways penetrate more deeply, in the North than in the South, America contained no viable cultural or religious alternative to the Western Heritage. The case was far different where ancient, non-Christian civilizations flourished. During the later seventeenth century, Christianity was violently extinguished in Japan and harassed by persecution in China. In India the higher castes, who were the guardians of the traditional culture, remained aloof, and even the lower caste converts were unstable. The Islamic lands had turned a deaf ear to the missionaries, and in Africa, Christianity was still the white man's religion.

After nearly two centuries of arduous labor and heroic self-sacrifice, during which Christianity had played a major role in the expansion of Western Civilization, the goal of universality seemed as far away as ever.

The reason for this lack of fulfillment lies precisely in the Church's involvement in and identification with European Imperialism. Despite the wise counsel of missionaries like Xavier and Ricci, and the well-intentioned experiments of Ingoli's Congregation, the Church had made no serious and consistent efforts to develop an indigenous priesthood or assume a "national" character in the newly-discovered regions. This might have been less important had Christianity displayed a truly supra-national character. But it invariably manifested itself to the non-Western peoples as a Western creed. Sometimes its clergy seemed no more than the mouthpieces of oppressive colonialism. At other moments, they appeared preoccupied by sectarian hatreds, quarrels between rival mission groups, or squabbles over patronage and jurisdiction. But always there was a foreign air about Christianity. Too often its avowed principles of compassion and brotherhood were negated by blatant displays of cultural chauvinism and racial arrogance. Whether among the nominally converted American Indian multitudes, the tradition-bound masses of Asia, or the hunted, defiant tribesmen of Africa, Christianity remained essentially part of the European way of life — to be met with suspicion, approached with caution, and accepted, if at all, only with the gravest reservations. The Christian Faith, like Western Civilization, had gained only a foothold in the non-Western world, and further progress would have to await another stage in their mutual history.

BIBLIOGRAPHY

Blake, J.W. *European Beginnings in West Africa, 1454-1578.* London, 1937.
Boxer, C.R. *The Christian Century in Japan, 1569-1650.* Berkeley,1951.
_____. *The Dutch Seaborne Empire.* New York, 1965.
_____. *The Portugese Seaborne Empire.* New York,1969.
Crouse, N.M. *French Pioneers in the West Indies, 1624-1664.* New York, 1940.
Hanke, L.V. *The Spanish Struggle for Justice in the Conquest of America.* Philadelphia,1949.
La Costa, H. De. *The Jesuits in the Philippines, 1581-1768.* Cambridge, Mass., 1961.
Latourette, K.S. *A History of the European Missions.* Vol. III. New York, 1940.
Maclagan, E.D. *The Jesuits and the Great Mogul.* London,1932.
Pannikar, K.M. *Asia and Western Dominance.* London,1953.
Parkman, F. *Pioneers of France in the New World.* Boston,1950.
Parry, J.H. *The Age of Reconnaissance.* New York, 1963.

POLITICS AND RELIGION IN RUSSIA: MOSCOW "THE THIRD ROME"

Stephen C. Feinstein

Stephen C. Feinstein, Assistant Professor of History at the University of Wisconsin, River Falls, received his doctorate from New York University. The State Director of the Annual University of Wisconsin Soviet Seminar, Dr. Feinstein has made several visits to the Soviet Union.

Until the Bolshevik Revolution of November, 1917, it was commonly held by most observers that the community of Russian Orthodox believers inside the Russian Empire was one of the most devout religious communities in the world. The success of the Bolsheviks, however, and the subsequent disestablishment of the Church and apparent lack of support from the population led to a reevaluation of the entire conception behind the religious-political foundation of the Russian State. In particular, the question may be raised, ''What did the Russian Revolution of 1917 signify in terms of the viability and relevance of the Orthodox Church?'' To answer this question properly, a brief survey of the history of Christianity in Russia is necessary in order to provide the understanding of the evolution and significance of the doctrine of the "Third Rome."

Christianity first came to Russia in 988 when Vladimir, Prince of Kiev converted from paganism to the Eastern Orthodox form of Christianity. The decision to accept Christianity over other religions had both political and religious significance. By the 980's, the newly emerging Kievan Rus State on the Dneiper was surrounded by nations which adhered to either Christianity, Judaism or the Islamic faiths. Most countries bordering on the west and south adhered to Christianity, while Kiev's proximate neighbors in the southeast, the Khazars, embraced Judaism. Further east were the Volga Bulgars, who were Mohammedans.

Because of Vladimir's position in the center of these three major religions, any decision to convert himself or the Slavic peoples of Kiev had to be interpreted as more than a religious symbol. Adherence to the "correct" religion had strong political overtones. Acceptance of Judaism might conceivably mean the establishment of a Jewish state from the Dneiper to the Caspian Sea. Conversion to Islam might make a political entity from the Dneiper to the Volga which certainly would loom as a threat to the Byzantine Empire. In the end, however, these two alternatives were pale compared to the appeal of Christianity. The Jews had no home-land (the conversion of the Khazars was a recent one), which gave the impression that God's grace was not theirs. Compared to Christianity, Islam did not offer the same religious intensity or political advantages.

In the end, Vladimir's choice came after his envoys had journeyed to Constantinople to observe the services in St. Sophia. They were deeply impressed and reported to Vladimir that they "knew not whether we were in heaven or on earth." This observation by the Kievan envoys to Byzan-tium was not the sole reason for the conversion, but rather capped a long series of events ending with Vladimir's conversion. Christianity had always been identified with the successful and rich empires of the west. Vladimir's grandmother, Olga, and various other leaders of early Kievan Rus had converted to Christianity. Finally, as the political horizons of Kiev widened during Vladimir's reign, the opportunities afforded by the west appeared to be more easily attainable through Christianity. Indeed, as the historian B.H. Sumner has written, "Byzantium brought to Russia five gifts: her religion, her law, her view of the world, her art and writing."

The political consequences of the appearance of Christianity were deep. Before 988, the basic authority of the Prince of Kiev had been derived from his position as foremost descendant of the Varangian Princes who had originally colonized the country in the ninth century. His duties as administrator were directly related to the economic foundations of Kievan Rus: he would protect trade, the Steppe trade routes, the overseas markets of the country and the population in case of invasion. With Christianity, however, a new aura of grandeur appeared to surround the position of Prince. From Byzantium came the concept that the sovereign ruler was appointed by God to establish and maintain domestic order. Adherence to this conception was a prelude to the full acceptance of the Byzantine concept of Caesaropapism.

The acceptance of what later came to be called Eastern Christianity led the people of Kiev and later Russia to accept what may be called "pure" types of orthodox practices. Orthodoxy in the Byzantine definition basically meant preserving what was "pure" and fixed, which in turn implied that theological and philosophical creativeness was not taboo, but on the other hand was not encouraged. Early Russian Christianity was characterized as having no monastic orders; and when monasticism was adopted, it was an oriental type which emphasized reclusion, imitation of ascetics, self-torture and other ascetic practices.

Outside the monastery, most of the people had been converted to the new faith, but possessed little subjective knowledge of the religion. Relapses into paganism were common, as well as the continuation of the practice of sorcery, magic and witchcraft. The famed stone carvings on the exterior of the Cathedral of St. Dimitri in Vladimir (1194-97) and Cathedral of St. George at the Yuriev-Polski Monastery (1230-34) are testimonies to the probable maintenance of some pagan traditions. These carvings possess an array of elements, including figures which mix both human and animal body parts together. The veneration of icons, in particular the strong affinity for particular saints and martyrs suggests that Christian icons were simply substituted for pagan figures, at least during this early period.

General enlightenment for both the clergy and population of Russia came slowly. At first this was due to the inability of the Greek and Byzantine missionaries to speak the Russian language. Even when the language problem was solved, the qualifications of teachers among the clergy did not seem to improve. Beyond the second generation of Russian priests, there appeared to be a lessening of piety among the clergy which was caused apparently by the Russians' turning away too rapidly from Byzantium. The Russian clergy found itself without sufficient means to replace their own ranks. A typical example of the persistence of such illiteracy is found in the fifteenth century complaint of the Archbishop of Novgorod on the ignorance of the peasants who sought ordination as deacons and priests.

The result of the lack of education among the priests themselves was a decisive factor in the gradual erosion of the theological and philosophical inquiries so common to early Eastern Christianity. The priests, as well as the people became accustomed to identifying the substance of the religion with its outer forms, even if those forms were incorrect because of bad teaching. This would have profound repercussions for the future church. As a general rule, if the Church ever became involved in political disputes, it would sacrifice some potential political-social role for changing society in exchange for preservation of the basic form of the religion.

The conquest of the Russian lands by the Mongols was a turning point for all aspects of Russian life, including that of the Church. For a while, there was a chance that the Mongols might embrace Christianity in some form, either Orthodox or Roman Catholic. By the beginning of the fourteenth century, however, these invaders moved toward Islam, which they received from the Volga Bulgars. Despite the acceptance of an antagonistic religion by the Khans, a general policy of toleration and exemption of the Church from taxation was inaugurated in Russia.

The acceptance of Islam, however, did not ease matters for the Russian people. In fact, it proved a useful propaganda device for gaining support for liberation of the Russian lands. Liberation of Russia, which had begun as a political struggle against a foreign invader now took on all the aspects of a crusade. Thus, it is in the very early stages of the Mongol domination that the beginnings of an alliance between the church and the Russian rulers can be seen. By 1480, when this struggle was successful, the Russians began to envision their emancipation as part of their newly won position as "the chosen people." In particular, this new label would apply more correctly to the Muscovites, who would lead the national liberation movement from the fourteenth through sixteenth centuries.

There is another aspect of church affairs during the Mongol period that deserves special mention. One of the striking characteristics of the Church during this period was the extension of monasticism. Between 1350 and 1500, more than one hundred and fifty new monasteries were opened in Muscovy alone. Most of this colonization, which occurred in wilderness areas, had several important features and consequences.

First of all, monastic expansion did not follow the initiative, but rather appeared as a pioneering movement toward the frontier regions of northern and eastern Russia. Eventually, the government would follow in the wake of the pioneering efforts by the Church. Secondly, most monasteries of this period were small colonies or brotherhoods, which recruited widely, from every class and every age group, who were inspired by the saintliness of a single personality. By the end of the fourteenth century, the monastery movement had become a strong vested interest group which could aid or deter the growth of the political state.

By the end of the fourteenth century too, the Russians had become attached to the idea of the church being linked to the ideal of universal monarchy. This principle of rule of state had antecedents in Biblical and contemporary historical epochs, especially in the development of the historical concept of the Roman-Christian Empire. As early as 1393, Anthony, Patriarch of Constantinople had asserted to the Muscovite Prince Vasily I that the position of the Emperor played an important part in the Christian world, more so than other civilizations: "it is impossible for Christians to have the Church without having the Emperor because the Empire and the Church constitute one unity and one community." In practice, the Muscovite attachment to this idea meant its continued recognition of Constantinople as the "New Rome" or logical successor to the Roman Empire in the West after the latter's collapse in 495 A.D.

Moscow's adherence to Constantinople during this period, however, was not to be defined as a position of clear-cut obedience. There was always the alternative of independence from Constantinople, as was the case with the Balkan Slavs who had broken away. The débâcle, from the Muscovite view, of the Council of Ferrara-Florence of 1438-39 set the tone for future Muscovite actions. At this council, the Eastern Church accepted unity with Rome (thus ending the schism which had existed since 1054) in order to repel the Turks from Europe. Vasily II, Grand Prince of Moscow, viewed this agreement as a betrayal of Orthodoxy. He dismissed the Metropolitan Isidore of Moscow for supporting the council and set himself up as champion of the Russian church. Thus, from this decision came the clear understanding that Moscow could remain faithful to the Eastern Church except when that institution was taken over by "heretical" elements.

In the meantime, the Russian Church itself developed from its ranks a series of remarkable personalities who were responsible ultimately for establishing the key position the Church would play in politics. The first of these was Sergius of Radonezh (1314-1392), one of the most popular Muscovite saints and perhaps the most important spiritual force of his age. He established the Troitsa-Sergeev Monastery which became the largest and richest in all of Russia. The symbolism of its proximity to Moscow could not be overlooked. Sergius generally shunned politics except for one occasion: in 1380, Prince Dmitry of Moscow made the decison to go on the military offensive against the Mongols. Before the Battle of Kulikovo Field, where the Muscovites would emerge victorious, Sergius blessed the troops and gave the Church's full support with the words, "Go against the godless boldly, without wavering and thou shalt conquer." The victory at Kulikovo seemed to affirm the earlier conviction that the struggle against the Mongols was part of the crusading movement.

During the same period when Sergius of Radonezh was going about his tasks, the position of the Church was reinforced through the additional work of Alexis, Metropolitan of Moscow (1300-1378), well known for his administrative ability which made him a central figure in the Muscovite government; in addition, Stephen of Perm (d.1396) paved the way for pioneering mission work in the north of Russia. The work of all three of these church fathers provided the basis for the eventual recognition of the autocephalous or self-governing Muscovite Church, independent of both Kiev and Constantinople.

By 1453, then, the date of the fall of Constantinople to the Turks, the Orthodox Church had managed to pull itself away from its early position of ignorance and had managed, through the national liberation struggle and through the work of its dedicated workers to achieve new prominence in Russian society. In fact, by the middle of the fifteenth century the Russians had taken the attitude that their Church represented something of a "purer" form of Christianity because of their reluctance to recognize the validity of the Council of Ferrera-Florence. The fall of the Eastern Empire in 1453 was viewed by the Muscovites to be "God's justice" for the "betrayal" of 1438.

Because the Eastern Churches had been founded on the principle of Caesaro-papism the question presented itself after 1453 as to whether the Muscovite Church could exist without the Empire. There were three possible alternatives which appeared during this period, and rapid answers were found for each. The first possibility was for the Muscovites to admit that the fall of Constantinople was not final, and that it might be emancipated by the Russians. The millenary cycle presented the answer here: 1492, equivalent to the year 7000 on the Julien calendar passed with no indication of emancipation. The second possibility was to recognize the supremacy of the Holy Roman Empire and the Pope as the logical successors of Byzantium, an impossibility because of negative predispositions by most Russians toward this alternative.

The last possibility, and the ultimate choice for the Russian Church was to set up Moscow as the successor, politically and religiously to the Eastern Empire. Indications of movement toward this position can be seen during the reign of Ivan III (1462-1505). Ivan began to use the title of "Tsar" (Caesar) rather than "Grand Prince," and received psychological support for this position because of his marriage to Zoe Palaeologus, niece of the last Byzantine emperor. He established diplomatic relations with the west, but did not recognize the Holy Roman Empire as a Christian Empire. By 1524, the idea of the Third Rome began to appear in Muscovite documents, as indicated in the Epistles of Philotheus of Pskov to Tsar Vasily III:

> And now, I say unto thee: take care and take heed pious Tsar; all the Empires of Christendom are united in thine, for two Romes have fallen and the third exists and there will not be a fourth; thy Christian Empire, according to the great theologian, will not pass to others . . . .

Philotheus' concern with the number "three," so symbolic in Christian traditions apparently echoed many Russian legends which emphasized similar themes. One legend, dating from the beginning of the thirteenth century told that Grand Duke Daniel Ivanovitch discovered a three-headed beast in a swamp. A Greek sage explained to Daniel that a large city would be built on the same spot. The symbolism here needs no extended interpretation: Moscow is the third head of the beast, the Third Rome.

Thus, by the middle of the sixteenth century, the Muscovite Church appeared to define itself as the logical successor to the Byzantine Church. But again, this progression was not totally religious, but had strong reinforcement from the political sphere because of the Tsar of Moscow. In 1547, Ivan IV was crowned "Tsar" for the first time and was recognized as "basileus" by the Eastern Church. In 1589, the Metropolitan of Moscow was raised to the position of Patriarch, ranked fifth behind Constantinople, Alexandria, Antioch and Jerusalem. This period in Russian history was one of Empire building facilitated by the Tsar's control of ecclesiastical affairs and the Patriarchate itself.

This seemingly rapid extension of the autocratic power over the Church was not strange nor accidental. The precise issue which led to the expansion of the powers of the Tsar was the issue of monasteries and the secularization of Church land. By the sixteenth century there was a considerable expansion of monastic lands, linked to the pioneering efforts of the early Church. However, with the growing power of the state, two issues came into focus regarding these lands: first, monasteries added little to the coffers of the state treasury because of tax exemptions. Secondly, with the necessary extension of the administrative duties of the state during the sixteenth century, land became a valuable commodity for use as reward for service to the Tsar. As such, monastic lands became the subject of secularization in connection with the new needs of the government.

The position of the Church itself over the issue of monastic lands was not clear. Nil Sorsky, a late fifteenth-century Church reformer adopted a position that the Church was being corrupted by its huge monastic holdings and should therefore divest itself of property in order to concentrate on the needs of the individual. In theory, Sorsky and the reformers should have been natural allies of the Tsar. However, because of their anti-authoritarian position in both Church and secular matters, plus their belief that the state should restrict its duties to the material realm, the reformers did not appear as practical allies.

The solution to the dilemma of monastic lands must be understood in terms of the power structure of the Muscovite state. As the Muscovite State grew in size, the Russian Princes and Tsars desired a commensurate extension of autocratic powers, free from the traditional restrictions which had been imposed by the boyars and the representative bodies of Russia, the Zemsky Sobor (Council of the Land) and the Boyar Duma. To obtain the desired end, autocracy had to have allies. Under these circumstances, the Church appeared as a likely candidate for this position, even though the position of the reformers was highly palatable to the Russian rulers because of their emphasis on a Church free from worldly taint.

The alliance that was eventually worked out, to the detriment of both reformers and boyars was that the Church would support the growth of absolutism while in return, the Grand Duke would keep his hands off the monastery lands. The supporters of this policy within the Church were the Josephites, or followers of Joseph of Volokolamsk (1439-1515) who supported the property principle on the grounds that monasteries proved their utility as training grounds for the Church hierarchy, and were therefore indispensable to the Church. In return the Grand Duke promised to help the Church defend itself against heretics and reformers.

While at the outset of this alliance there appeared to be balanced potential gains, in reality all such gains would accrue to the autocrat, at the expense of Church, reformers and boyars. For once autocracy would be built with firm power, no one group could effectively challenge it or resist the implementation of a policy defined to be in the interest of autocracy.

Before this conclusion came about, however, Joseph of Vol-okolamsk worked out a firm ideological position justifying the divine-right powers of the autocrat and clarifying his powers vis-à-vis the Church. For Joseph, the power of the ruler was given from God as his representative on earth. As God's representative, the ruler's main task was to preserve the faith and to be the highest judge in the land, in both secular and ecclesiastical matters. The ruler was to defend orthodoxy against any assaults, from both secular forces and heretics. For the defense of the religion, orthodoxy in turn would teach the principles of obedience to its followers— that is, obedience to the ruler with his divine powers. In practice, the Princes of Moscow simply carried the doctrine of obedience to its logical end in terms of pure power. In the long run too, Church lands would not remain sacred. Gradually, through the eighteenth century, the Church fell under taxation and eventually Catherine the Great would secularize all monastic holdings by 1764.

While it appeared that the Church played a subservient role to that of the autocrat in pre-seventeenth century Muscovy, it should nevertheless be pointed out that the office of Patriarch still possessed a tremendous potential for the acquisition of power. This fact became apparent during the Time of Troubles (1604-1613) when the Muscovite State was threatened from internal disunity and foreign invasion from Poland and Sweden. Among the many possibilities for major changes in the nature of the state came that of a foreign Tsar in the absence of a legitimate successor, plus the replacement of Catholicism (from Poland) or the Reformed Faith (from Sweden) for Orthodoxy. The real fears that were generated by the former possibility led to the assassination of the first "False Dmitry" in May, 1606, just before his coronation as Tsar and marriage to a Polish princess. This whole affair— the Polish forces in Moscow, a false pretender leaning toward Catholicism, the presence of the Jesuits — led to speculation that the faith and state were in great difficulty. Additional attempts by the Poles to place King Sigismund of Poland, his son Wladyslaw, or Charles IX of Sweden on the Muscovite throne seemed to verify the anxieties held by higher Church authorities about the dangers to the faith.

In 1611, after seven years of near-chaos for the country, Patriarch Germogen ordered the Muscovite people to mobilize for defense of both country and faith. This was the effective beginning of the national liberation movement to eliminate foreign rule and the apparent threats from the western religions. During this period, the main aim of the movement was to place an Orthodox Russian Tsar on the throne and thus eliminate all potential dangers to the continued existence of the state. This finally took place in February, 1612, when Mikhail Romanov was elected Tsar by the Zemsky Sobor (Council of the Land), an organization representative of the boyars, Church officials and various other classes. Mikhail's election with reaffirmation of autocratic powers led to the conclusion that the Tsar was needed for a least two vital functions: (1) to act as an arbiter among dissenting parties; and (2) to defend the faith.

Mikhail's reign, however, had significant repercussions for the position of Patriarch. Mikhail was sixteen years of age at the time of election. The presumption by the boyars was that he was a good choice because of the ease with which he might be manipulated. This policy, however, never came to fruition because of the return of Mikhail's father, Metropolitan Filaret (Nikita Romanov). Filaret had himself been a candidate for the throne in 1598 before losing out to Boris Godunov. Forced to become a monk, he rose in the Church hierarchy rapidly and was imprisoned by the Poles while on a diplomatic mission during the Time of Troubles.

Upon his return, Filaret was elected Patriarch by the Zemsky Sobor, on conditions which he laid out for himself and to which his son, the Tsar, expressed no objections. Filaret demanded and received the authority over both Church and state administration, as well as full economic support from all of the landed estates of the realm. He received the title of "Great Sovereign," the same title possessed by the Tsar, which was not to be taken lightly. Filaret considered himself co-Tsar and reinforced his conviction with an ideology. He adhered to the Byzantine doctrine of *Epanogoge*, worked out by Patriarch Photius in the ninth century, and made it a reality during his lifetime.

According to the *Epanogoge*, Jesus Christ was the supreme ruler over both Church and state. Administratively, on earth this power was divided between state and Church. The emperor was the supreme power in the secular realm, the enforcer of both secular and ecclesiastical laws. The emperor was the defender of the Church and its dogmas, but he himself must be submissive to these dogmas. The patriarch, on the other hand, had control of the "soul" of the Church, meaning the power to interpret the Church canons. In the long run, this doctrine boiled down to the basic realization that the community of believers could be directed only by a balanced and friendly relationship between the patriarch and emperor. For the case of Mikhail and Filaret, however, a new element was injected which led to ultimate submission of the former before the patriarch: Filaret was Mikhail's father, which in turn led to his adoption and effective utilization of the title of Great Sovereign. In terms of the "Third Rome" conception, this could be interpreted only as further evidence that Muscovy had become the true seat of orthodoxy after 1453.

Mikhail Romanov's overwhelming subservience to his father led the two men to work closely together to rebuild the Muscovite State after its near destruction. However, this father-son relationship, with its very unique qualities added to by ideology, was not the usual norm for Muscovy. Clearly, the relationship and the utilization of the *Epanogoge* worked because of the familial tie. It remained to be seen if such a relationshp could be established outside of a family tie between Tsar and patriarch.

This test came in 1652 when the Metropolitan of Novogorod, Nikon, was elected to the office of Patriarch. Nikon, of course, fully agreed with the Byzantine principle of Epanogoge which his precursors had followed. In addition, however, Nikon wanted to raise the position of the Patriarchate of Moscow above the fifth position it had been given when it was created in 1589. The new patriarch thought that in order to effect this transition in ranking, reforms would be needed.

In order to carry his program from thought to action, Nikon adhered to the program of a group known as the zealots. These men called attention to the discrepancies in translations of the Psalter (Bible) and various differences in ritual between the Greek and Russian churches. In the long run, however, Nikon would go far beyond the guidelines imposed by the zealots.

In the aftermath of his ascension to power, the patriarch passed laws, with the administrative support of Tsar Aleksei Mikhailovich, designed to revitalize the Muscovite Church. In an attempt to cope with the high incidence of alcoholism in the country, laws were passed limiting the sale of the beverage to one bottle per person, with prohibition on Church feasts and holidays. Attempts were also made to check the intermingling of non-baptized foreigners (into the Orthodox church) with Muscovites. All foreigners who fitted into this category were obliged to move outside of Moscow into a new area known as the German suburb. This reform presumed that the presence of foreigners was the cause of contemporary Church problems.

The brunt of the Nikonian reforms, however, came regarding Church art and ritual. Nikon objected to the utilization of western principles in icon painting, as well as the practice of many boyars of purchasing icons in the west and having them blessed by an Orthodox priest. The patriarch himself led an auto-da-fe on these "irreligious" icons. Among his many ritual changes, Nikon revised certain parts of the Psalter in order to bring it closer to the Greek model, he reduced the number of genuflexions during the Ephraim service of Lent, and finally, changed the method of the sign of the cross, from the use of two fingers to three.

The reforms, while on the surface seemed routine or insignificant, surprised everyone, including the zealots, and led to immediate and violent opposition. This opposition must be understood in terms of the traditions of the Russian Church. From its earliest days, the major concern of the Church had been with ritual, rather than content. Certain prescribed procedures, inherited from one generation to the next, were maintained and deemed "correct" even if the result of a mistranslation, transliteration error, or possible fabrication. In essence, because of the perpetuation in an illiterate community of believers, plus a clergy which itself showed no particular strength in this area, normal changes became crisis situations. Political intrigues, of course, were important during the crisis which ensued. Nikon began to wear costly and splendid garments and ordered a new palace built for the patriarch in the Kremlin near the Tsar's residence. The symbolism of his actions could not be ignored by those elements who saw the patriarch as a danger to themselves: as long as the patriarch stood for perpetuation of the doctrine of *Epanogoge* as defined by Patriarch Filaret, it meant the strengthening of autocracy against the designs of the boyars. Nikon made more enemies when he was left in control of the country during the Tsar's absence to the front of the Polish War. Rumor and conspiracy led to suspicions by the Tsar himself against his patriarch, and ultimately a demand for Nikon's resignation. Nikon, however, refused to resign, and held that even a Church council could not oust him from power.

The die, so to speak, was cast against the patriarch, for in the process of carrying out his Church reform and simply reinforcing the doctrines laid down in the past, he managed to rouse against him prelates, boyars and Tsar. The Church Council convened in 1666 convicted Nikon of many actions against the Tsar and dignity of the Church. He was removed from the position and became a monk. However, the same Church council also confirmed all of his reforms.

It would be the reforms and Patriarch Nikon and their confirmation by the Church Council of 1666 that would open the Great Schism in the Russian Orthodox Church. There was a large group of believers who refused to accept the textual and ritual changes in the religion. They became known collectively as the *raskolniki* or men of the schism, commonly called "Old Believers." By 1666, the movement against the reformed religion had become extremely widespread in northern Russia and in the region of Nizhi-Novgorod. The leader of this vocal opposition was Archbishop Avvakum, a powerful defender of the old faith.

That the Old Believers would come to the prominence that they did reflects some of the overall curious points about Russian Orthodoxy, plus the confluence of some chance happenings. Obviously, part of the reason for the schism was the early predilection of the Church for emphasis on form. Added to this, in obvious terms, was the political role which Nikon and other patriarchs had aspired to play and which led in turn to questioning of their devotion to the faith itself. Then other factors emerged: 1666, by virtue of the significance of the three sixes in the year was prophesized to be the end of the world, where the appearance of anti-Christ would herald Christ's imminent return to earth. Nikon, it turns out, and later Tsars Aleksei and Peter I became strongly identified, with the anti-Christ because of their adherence to the reforms of the 1650's plus their increased devotion to the secularization of Russian society.

In 1666, the Old Believers hoped that their own views would be reaccepted as the basis of the religion, especially after the removal of Nikon. This wish was not realized. For the same council in upholding Nikon's reforms was forced to defrock all of the priests who refused to acknowledge the proper changes, while the movement as a whole was condemned. While Avvakum was burned at the stake, the movement continued to spread and survive, mainly because the *raskolniki* alone believed that they were the only true Orthodox Christians, who maintained their beliefs in defiance of anti-Christ. It is at the same time that the idea of "Holy Russia" became popular, especially among the followers of the old faith: they rejected both emperor and state as being dominated by anti-Christ, but they did not reject "Holy Russia," the incarnation of the Third Rome. They maintained their ties with Russia for one major reason: two Romes had perished, Moscow was the third, after Moscow, nothing. The language of the seventeenth and eighteenth centuries came to reflect this dichotomy: *Rus* referred to the state inhabited by Orthodox, Christian believers. *Rossiia*, the political state, was dominated by the forces of evil. The Old Believers never used the latter word.

How important was the Old Believer movement? Undoubtedly of tremendous importance, given the timing of the Schism. The Old Believers, in addition to representing a difference in religious position, became the embodiment of political opposition towards the state. If the state was now in the hands of "evil" forces, oppositon could be justified. Thus, from this position, the defenders of the old faith rebelled against or escaped from the government. In 1668, the Soloievsky Monastery, on the White Sea, rebelled against the government in the name of the old faith; the insurrection lasted for over six years before the government forces emerged victorious. Others formed sects of their own, with some strange habits such as castration, self-immolation and the like. However, despite these habits, they survived (mainly through recruitment), always to loom as a possible threat capable of allying with other anti-government forces to become the mainstay of an outright rebellion. Peasant rebellions, especially the one led by Emile Pugachev in 1773 called for "restoration" of the rightful Tsar and the old faith.

Even greater significance, however, comes from the political bankruptcy which the Church found itself in after 1666. Clearly, the position of patriarch was discredited because of the position he had aspired to play in Russian society. At no time after this period would a patriarch ever assume the role of a Filaret or Nikon. In fact, the patriarchate was effectively abolished in 1700 when Peter the Great refused to appoint a successor to Patriarch Adrian. From the political point of view, the Schism was a disaster for future Russian history, for that society found itself without a "regulator:" the peasantry was enserfed as of 1649; the Zemsky Sobor and Boyar Duma were on the verge of extinction; and the Church itself lost its voice as an independent entity in Russian society. In essence this meant that from 1666 to 1917, the Church would be no more than an arm of the government, a means of enforcing obedience to autocracy. Finally, with a powerless Church, great cultural intrusions would have no elements to effectively stop their inroads. Thus, at the same time the Church collapsed as a major force in Russian society, "westernization" and "secularization" became the most important watchwords for Russia.

While Peter I (1682-1725) was beyond question an Orthodox believer, his interest was not in the traditional duty of the Tsar to defend the faith, but rather in modernization and maximization of cultural contacts with the west. By definition, however, contact with the west meant introduction of certain elements that would destroy the essence of the traditional Church. Peter's personally cutting the beards of the nobility has dramatic significance in this regard: the Orthodox believer had to have a beard in order to face God as an equal in the hereafter. Without a beard, he was placed in a hopeless situation. Smoking in public during the seventeenth century carried the penalty, supported by the Church, of having one's nostrils slit. Peter, on the other hand, would encourage smoking because of the potential for tax revenue. In an obvious sense, the plight of the Church may be understood from these two examples.

Beyond this, however, Peter understood that the Church possessed potential for promoting the moral and political reform of the Russian people, and he set about to use it in this respect. As early as the year 1700, with Peter's failure to name a new patriarch, one can discern the beginnings of anti-Orthodox legislation. In the following twenty-five years, Peter would increase the tax burden of the Church, disallow renewal of charters, confiscate property, prohibit land acquisitions, require submission of accounting books and even regulate the numbers and composition of the clergy.

After 1700, the duties of the patriarch were divided among the office of Metropolitan of Ryazan and an institution which had been in existence since 1649 known as the Monastery Prikaz. Originally, the latter institution had jurisdiction over all civil actions involving clerics. Both of these positions, however, were clearly controlled by the Tsar during this period. There was no possibility that either would come to rival the power of autocracy. By 1718, Peter, after some experimentation, found himself disposed to alter in a radical fashion the traditional administration of the Church. Having already adhered to the collegiate idea in civil government, he came to accept it as the basis for future administration of the Church.

Thus, with this background, it was somewhat predictable that the Orthodox Church would become a simple appendage of the state. The Ecclesiastical Regulation of 1721 made this a *fait accompli* by abolishing the patriarchate and transferring its power to a new institution called the Holy Synod. The Synod, furthermore, was staffed by laymen, and was watched over by an official authorized by Peter in 1722, the Chief Pro-curator, whose duty was to sit and observe and to make certain that no unusual delays crept into the fulfillment of everyday business. Therefore, by 1722, the Russian Orthodox Church found itself totally submissive to the state and in a real sense, controlled by it. Outwardly, of course, most of society was still "Holy Russia" — the community of believers, who were more or less oblivious to these substantial changes which had taken place in the administrative structure of the Church. For Peter, while he changed the administration of the church, was content to leave the question of a general reform of the clergy as a whole up in the air.

From the reign of Peter onwards, one can perceive the importance of the Church only in one regard — for political purposes and extension of the boundaries of the empire. Thus, in the 1760s, 1770s and 1780s, the issue of protection of Orthodox Christians in other countries became of prime concern to the Russian rulers. The hypocrisy of the issue as religious in substance could not be overlooked: the issue of protection of Orthodoxy was linked to Tsarist involvement in the affairs of neighboring countries both for offensive and defensive reasons. The issues. of the rights of the Uniates versus the rights of the Orthodox populations in Poland and Lithuania came to be a major cause of the first partition of Poland in 1772. A clause in the Treaty of Kuchuk-Kainarjii which ended the Russo-Turkish war in 1774 contained an important clause which guaranteed Russia the right to protect Orthodox Christians living within the boundaries of the Ottoman Empire. In precise terms, this meant a guarantee for Russian political involvement in the Crimea, the Danubian Principalities, the Bal-kans and the Middle East. The débacle of the Crimean War (1854-56) can be in a large measure traced to this utilization of religious issues for political purposes.

The war of 1812 against Napoleon has a double meaning when viewed from the context of religion. On one hand, it is important to comprehend that the defeat of Napoleon's invasion army was due to massive utilization of every device associated with patriotism. The Church, therefore, stood as an important defender of "Holy Russia," at least nominally since that term denoted the people rather than the poli-tical state. On the other hand, however, the "liberation" of France led to Russia becoming involved in more cultural cross currents than it had previously encountered — in particular interplay with a western, secular society which was toying with many different theories of change, among them liberalism and revolution. This led to the unique situation where the Church or Orthodoxy had to go on the defensive as soon as it had won the war over Napoleon, lest the vicious ideas of the west penetrate Russia and lead to further "deterioration" of faith and culture.

This xenophobic view of the west, while not initiated by the Church, corresponded to the views of Nicholas I, who became Emperor in 1825. Nicholas, faced at the outset of his reign with the Decembrist uprising, believed that this rebellion was due to infiltration of the evil ideas of the west. Russia, during his reign, was to be made secure against such penetration. To effect this, Nicholas' Minister of Education, S. Uvarov, devised an ideology, a comprehensive theory of state which depended heavily upon the conservative traditions of Russian Orthodoxy. This ideology was called "Official Nationality" and had as its basis an official trinity: "Autocracy, Orthodoxy and Nationality.

All three of these words are closely related, and the first two had roots deep in Russian history. Autocracy for Nicholas was the recognition of absolute, unlimited monarchy, a simple reiteration of divine right theory where the power of the Tsar was unlimited. The Tsar in this scheme was to be obeyed not out of fear, but of religious obedience. Thus Orthodoxy was the only true form of Christianity which had the purpose of teaching the moral obligations of the people toward the state. In addition, since Nicholas reaffirmed the close political tie between the ruler and religion, other "incorrect" forms of religious worship became suspect and the subject of intolerance. Thus, by the middle of the nineteenth century, other religious groups which had more or less flourished or survived as a result of the toleration policy emanating from Catherine the Great's enlightenment began to be objects of intolerance. The Jews, Old Believers, Catholics and Lutherans of the Empire began to feel the brunt of the state's capacity for oppression: the Jews, for example, were confined to a geographic area of western Russia called the "Pale of Settlement" and were prohibited from moving into Great Russia. In addition, other limitations, such as double taxation and occupational limitations were introduced because of their alleged murder of Christ. At a time when the Jews were receiving civil rights in the west, their position, as was the position of other groups in the empire, deteriorated.

The word nationality (*narodnost*) reflected upon the basic structure of the Russian empire after its expansion in the eighteenth century. Russia became a multi-national empire which held within its bounds cultures and languages quite distinct from Russian. To Nicholas, such differentiations were a potential danger to the state because they represented centrifugal forces which might be influenced by the west. Therefore, the word nationality effectively meant a policy of establishing intellectual dams to keep out negtive influences, such as liberalism, cosmopolitanism, western religions and languages. A positive feature of this policy meant purification of the Russian language. However, since Orthodoxy was an obvious component of this philosophy, it played what may be termed a keystone role: as the Church was responsible for building the moral fibre of the people and keeping the country culturally safe from the west, all education should come under its control. The presumption was that since other nationalities in the empire spoke different languages and practiced other religions, "Russification" of these people and their conversion to Orthodoxy would make Russia more secure. In practice, the attempts to implement this policy led to increased polarization among nationalities and reaffirmation of their cultural uniqueness in defiance of the Tsar.

Nevertheless, "Official Nationality" cannot be dismissed lightly. For in essence it remained the *modus operandi* of the empire until 1917. To be sure, certain parts of the doctrine deteriorated, while, on the other hand, certain articles were enhanced when the appropriate conditions manifested themselves in state politics. During the latter part of the nineteenth century the figure of Konstantin Pobedonostsev would embody the doctrine of "Official Nationality" at a time when the country was moving into modernity and was desperately searching for some device to impress autocracy with the need for constitutionalism.

Pobedonostsev was Procurator of the Holy Synod from 1880 until 1905. This office alone, however, does not express the expanse of his power. In addition to being lay head of the church, Pobedonostsev was the chief tutor and advisor to both Alexander III and the last Tsar, Nicholas II. In essence, he was the equivalent of the prime mininster and his presence was deeply felt.

Pobedonostsev's thought can generally be characterized as a traditionalist and pro-slavophil, which was combined with chauvinism, hatred of liberalism and hatred of abstract ideas. He stood as a first-rate defender of both autocracy and the position of the Church. To him, these two institutions were part of Russia's salvation from the evils found in the rest of the world. Pobedonostsev felt that the enlightenment had led in turn to deep negativism by intellectuals toward the Orthodox Church. He conceived to the Church as a devoted congregation of pious believers and a prime carrier of Russian national culture. The Church stood as the major support of autocracy, which in turn supported the Church. To Pobedonostsev, change in any sphere had to be slow and imperceptible. Only through conservative change could the state progress and maintain itself as a community of believers, uncomplicated by the erroneous teachings of the west.

The danger of Pobedonostsev's thought was not in its inherent qualities, but rather in the fact that it came in an environment where change was impossible and where the quality of life in Russia deteriorated sharply because of government action or inaction. In addition, Pobedonostsev's personal antagonisms seeped into official policies, with the result being that many national and non-Orthodox religious groups came under great attack: Jews, Armenians, Poles, Georgians and Ukrainians all suffered during the latter part of the nineteenth century. Outspoken critics of the government and church policy were silenced. The most tragic case noted was that of Leo Tolstoy who was excommunicated from the Church.

In short, by the beginning of the twentieth century, the Orthodox Church became so strongly identified with the forces of reaction that it could not construct any reasonable policy which would aid the plight of Russian society. Even the 1905 revolution, which led to a parliament being incorporated into the government structure, failed to produce a major reform of the Church's apparatus and outlook.

When the revolutions of 1917 came, the Church acted in a naive and self-centered manner. It declared its independence from the state by July, 1917; but on the other hand, it demanded from the Provisional Government the right to control schools, the right for compulsory religious education in schools, and the predominance of Orthodoxy over other religions. In short, the Church tried to assert its independence while at the same time preserving all of its advantages as a focus of potential political power. In this attempt it failed. The Provisional Government could not possibly recognize all of these demands, especially when that government aspired to represent a new form of democracy and toleration. As a result the Church labeled the Provisional Government anti-Christian.

On the eve of the Bolshevik seizure of power, with the fabric of the state torn apart, the Church concerned itself with re-establishment of the patriarchate. After the Bolshevik seizure, the Church openly supported the White forces as a means for its own salvation from the "Godless" Marxists. The result was a vicious reaction by the Bolshevik power designed to undermine the authority and influence of the Church. In December, 1917, the inevitable occurred: all Church land was nationalized and control of the schools was transferred to the new government. The Church was deprived of its right to register births and marriages. Finally, all state financial support for the Church, a key item in its long history, was discontinued. The Church which so long had been an appendage of the state lost its position.

Whatever the form of government established in 1917, assuming that autocracy had no chance of being resurrected, it would have clashed with the "Third Rome" conception. That notion could only flow from a union of Church and state, according to the Caesaropapist doctrines handed down from Byzantium. The Church since 1453 had acted as if it would never have to readjust to new political conditions. After all it was said "Two Romes have fallen, Moscow is the third, there shall not be another." The great irony of history is that this folk expression was essentially correct, and the Church played the part beautifully.

BIBLIOGRAPHY

Billington, J.H. *The Icon and the Axe*. New York, 1966.

Conybeare, F. *Russian Dissenters*. Cambridge, 1921.

Cracraft, J. *The Church Reform of Peter the Great*. Stanford, 1971.

Curtiss, John S. "Church and State," in Cyril Black (ed.). *The Transformation of Russian Society*. Cambridge, 1960.

Gorodetzky, Nadejda, "Training for the Priesthood in Eighteenth Century Russia," in S. Harcave. *Readings in Russian History*, I. New York, 1962.

Miliukov, Paul. *Religion and the Church in Russia*. New York, 1942.

Raeff, Marc. "An Early Theorist of Absolutism," in S. Harcave (ed.). *Readings in Russian History I*. New York, 1962.

Spinka, Matthew. "Patriarch Nikon and the Subjection of the Russian Church to the State," in S. Harcave (ed.). *Readings in Russian History I*. New York, 1962.

Stremooukhoff, Dimitri. "Moscow, the Third Rome: Sources of the Doctrine," in *Speculum*, January, 1953, pp. 84-101.

Timasheff, Nicholas. "The Inner Life of the Russian Orthodox Church," in Cyril Black (ed.). *The Transformation of Russian Society*. Cambridge, 1960.

Vernadsky, George. *Kieven Russia*. New Haven, 1948.

_____. *Russia at the Dawn of the Modern Age*. New Haven, 1959.

_____. *The Tsardom of Moscow: 1547-1682*. New Haven, 1969.

Zenkovsky, V.V. *Medieval Russia's Epics, Chronicles and Tales*. New York, 1963.

THE ITALIAN RENAISSANCE, THE TRADITIONAL RELIGION AND THE NEW MORALITY

Frank J. Coppa

Frank J. Coppa, Associate Professor of History at St. John's University, received his doctorate from the Catholic University of America. The author of several books including *Planning, Protectionism and Politics in Liberal Italy: Economics and Politics in the Giolittian Age* and *Camillo di Cavour* he has served as editor of several others. His articles have appeared in such journals as the *Catholic Historical Review*, the *Journal of Modern History*, the *Journal of Church and State* and the *Journal of Economic History* among others.

The term Renaissance was coined by those who looked upon the Middle Ages as a period of slumber and stagnation. Western Europe, it was believed, was awakened from its torpor by the classical culture of Rome and Greece which shone through the long, dark night of the barbaric centuries. It was Giogio Vasari, the biographer of artists and architects who employed the expression *rinascita* some two centuries after the notion had been born, but he used it to refer to the rebirth of art rather than a total civilization. Not all, however, accepted this view. Jacob Burckhardt in his celebrated *Civilization of the Renaissance in Italy* (1860) viewed the Renaissance as the first chapter of modern history as the Italians revolted against the authoritarianism and asceticism of the former age. Hence he rejected the idea that the new thought was spawned by antiquity, claiming instead that it was stimulated by a spirit which was in many ways unique.

Likewise there is some difference of opinion as to the dates of the movement — and more recently some have questioned if there was such a thing as the Renaissance at all — despite the conviction of some that it commenced in the 1300's and came to an end in the 1500's. In point of fact, there is a difference of opinion on almost every aspect of the Renaissance except that, whatever it was, it originated in Italy and reached its highest, or lowest, form there. Thus some prefer to employ the term *Rinascimento* to describe the period which in more ways than one ushered in the modern world.

Although not overtly anti-religious, the Renaissance's emphasis on man rather than God, its stress on this world rather than the next, its concern with form more than content, as well as its appreciation of art for arts sake, represented a radical departure from the sentiments of the Middle Ages. Previously events in Europe were viewed as an integral aspect of the history of the Church. Secular thought was then so rare, the influence of the Church so pervasive, that even those who railed against her influence sought to reform rather than remove her presence.

This is not to deny that Christian culture had come into contact with the rationalist, secular thought of the ancient world. Actually, as early as the twelfth century the work of Aristotle (384-322 B.C.), translated from Arab sources, had reached Western Europe provoking something of an intellectual crisis. Rather than emphasizing faith, the works of this great systematizer of human knowledge stressed the laws of logic and the tools of analysis.

A disastrous rift in the Christian community as well as a potential religious rebellion was avoided by the timely appearance of two scholar-philosophers who assimilated Aristotlean thought without abandoning Christian dogma. Albertus Magnus (1206-1280 A.D.) collected and commented upon the writings of Aristotle, while Thomas Aquinas (1225-1274) synthesized the logic of the pagan philosopher with Christian faith in his *Summa Theologica*. The Purpose and aim of this work must be seen in the context of the confrontation of Christianity with the secular thought of Greece. Since the Aristotlean system presupposed an ordered universe, Greek philosophy only strengthened the conviction of Christians that there was a prime mover and original architect.

Moving from philosophy to poetry, the Florentine Dante Alighieri (1265-1321) appropriately called Dante (the giver), paved the way for the return of the muses to Italy. The great Italian poet, one of the most talented figures mankind has produced, though inspired by Vergil (70-19 B.C.), the best known of Roman poets, reflected the religious climate of the Age of Faith in his masterpiece, *The Divine Comedy*. Adhering to the moral values and civic virtues of the Christian civilization which had developed in the past thousand years, he asserted that humanity would never know peace until it accepted the precepts, though not the temporal power of, the Church.

The role of education, Dante indicated, was to provide man with a knowledge of God, enabling him to fulfill the Divine Will as well as his own destiny. Only by preparing for the next life could one find true happiness in the present. These beliefs enabled the troubled author to cope with political disappointment, unrequited love, and banishment from his beloved Florence.

Even before Dante commenced his *Divine Comedy* the winds of change were sweeping over the Italian peninsula and slowly but steadily struck at the civilization and life-style which his work reflected. One important force for the alteration of the social and economic order south of the Alps was the steady growth of trade with the East by way of Byzantine Italy. In the *Mezzogiorno*, the Italian South, Bari became the center and capital of Byzantine activity. To the west, the three duchies of Amalfi, Naples, and Gaeta, though nominally subject to Constantinople, were practically free. They preserved their formal relation of alliance and allegiance with the Eastern Empire only for the commercial advantages they could draw from this connection. Thus assisted, Amalfi from the 10th to the 12th centuries held first place among the Tyrrhenian ports. Only later was she rivaled by Pisa and Genoa in the Mediterranean trade.

On the East Coast Venice emerged as the dominant maritime power in the Adriatic. While maintaining cordial relations with the West it continued its close collaboration with the Eastern Empire — obtaining advantages from both. By the end of the 11th century the Venetians enjoyed freedom of trade with the far-flung possessions of Byzantium and its extraordinary development had a profound impact upon the continent.

Among other things the development of international trade and the heightened commercial expansion encouraged the rise of a class of free artisans who found a ready market for their wares and services in the port cities or inland towns. In the interior these towns tended to develop alongside a major trade route or inland waterway. Ferrara, Mantua, Cremona, Piacenza, Milan as well as Florence all owe a good part of their prosperity and political importance to such waterways. In those areas where rivers and roads converged, urbanization was all the more rapid and social change the most marked.

Like most other far-reaching changes, this early urbanization provoked both unrest and protest as older social forms and relations were torn asunder by the introduction of new and aggressive elements. The overriding aim and ambition of the middle class landowners and merchants was to escape the intolerable restrictions of the feudal magnates. They were to succeed in their endeavor for by the 12th century, power in the towns passed from the aristocratic overlords or bishops to organized groups of citizens. Shortly thereafter the middle classes elected their own representatives who assumed control of the city and provided for its defense. This process, which led to the formulation of the commune, represented an important step in the secularization of the administration and the transformation of society.

The Crusades accentuated the trend. It is true that the first Crusade recruited most of its manpower in France, the Rhineland, and the Norman states, but the movement could not have succeeded without the assistance of the towns, almost all of them Italian, which had a long tradition of relations with the Byzantine world and a ready accumulation of capital. Thus the Italian towns not only provided transport craft and warships, seige guns and machines, but the funds to finance the venture as well.

For their contributions and collaboration they were rewarded with ample commercial concessions. The first Italian cities to profit from the conflict were Pisa and Genoa since the greatest number of crusaders hailed from Western Europe and not surprisingly turned to these Tyrrhenian ports for assistance. Initially the Venetians had been restrained from intervening in the Crusades due to their friendly relations with the Eastern Emperor who had but recently granted them entry and preferential treatment in all his ports of Europe and Asia. Nevertheless in 1100 they sent a fleet of two hundred vessels to Jaffa and received rich compensation from the Christian monarch of the Kingdom of Jerusalem.

Following their first naval expeditions Venice, Genoa and Pisa continued to facilitate the conquests of the western forces. With each victory came new and profitable concessions. Sometimes the Italians were granted an entire quarter of an eastern city, but more often simply a street where they conducted their business. What the Italians wanted most was an area under their control where they could load and unload their wares and freely buy and sell. To assure that their rights would not be impinged upon or in any way violated they demanded and received extraterritoriality — the right to be tried in all civil and commercial cases by their own magistrates according to their own laws.

Encouraged by the ensuing expansion of trade, by the early 14th century businessmen in Italy openly discarded the pretence of cooperating for the common good and sought profit and power. Competition replaced the ideal of community as individual competed with individual, family with family, and finally city with city. Competition, euphemistically clothed as individualism, would become one of the hallmarks of the Renaissance. In Florence the important wool processing industry fell into the hands of middle class capitalists who were then able to subject nobles and clergy and gain control of the government. Despite the Church's prohibition against usury, the Tuscans became the most famous money lenders of the peninsula as well as the continent, making Florence an important financial capital as well as an industrial center. Even today the Medici coat of arms is a symbol of the money lender and pawnbroker.

The newly enriched bourgeoisie which emerged in the numerous urban centers that dotted the Italian peninsula had sufficient capital to be able to afford some leisure and to indulge their taste for literature and the arts. Henceforth patronage would come not only from ecclesiastics and feudal aristocrats but from the nouveau riche who employed sculptors, painters, architects and writers to perpetuate their name. Thus by the 14th century the Church lost its monopoly of culture as well as its hold upon the mind of man. The results were significant.

Fortunately when the newly enriched classes transcended the ecclesiastical goals of the Middle Ages, they found secular models in the classical world of antiquity. Italians had the remains of Roman Civilization all about them and as the direct descendants of the Romans their language was the closest in Europe to the original Latin. Consequently it was not difficult for Italians to learn Latin and read the classics— including their treasure of science and the humanities. Indeed the ideal of *humanitas* was first formed in Rome. It was Cicero (106-43 B.C.) who coined the term *humanitas* to distinguish those qualities that separate man from the rest of the animal world and made him the dominant creature. This term was not only missing from Greek literature but the Greek language as well.

This Roman virtue which was based on a love of man for himself, as the best possible being above which there is no other, captivated intellectuals in 14th century Italy. Italian humanists proclaimed man the highest being in the universe and sought to cultivate his far-reaching talents. Perhaps Giovanni Pico, Count of Mirandola (1463-94), best expressed the humanist credo in his *Oration on the Dignity of Man* (1486) by pointing out that there is nothing in the world more wonderful than man.

Most men who were steeped in the culture of the Italian Renaissance, like the Romans before them, stressed life in this world and centered their interests on the here and now. The man who possessed *virtù* — which was something more than the traditional virtues of magnanimity, temperance, justice, courage, and liberality and emphasized the quality of manliness— were too preoccupied with the thoughts of the present to contemplate a possible future existence. Thus the central core of the Renaissance was an outburst of humanism, which put man at the center of the universe and stressed his creative powers.

Undeniably many aspects of Italian humanism contradicted Christian thought and practice. Humanists were inclined to reject the dogmas of original sin and man's natural depravity, raising the status of man and suggesting that his accomplishments were wholly human and owed nothing to divine intervention. Rather than medieval sanctity the ideal was the *uomo universale*— the universal man who absorbed all he could of human knowledge and participated in various ways in the exciting events of the world. The supreme being, they insisted, had created the world for man to enjoy, and this part of the divine plan they intended to fulfill.

Francesco Petrarca (1304-1374), better known as Petrarch, initiated the search for classical manuscripts and was the leading figure in the humanist movement. He more than anyone else set the style for Renaissance man, who employed his free time not in meditation or prayer but in collecting, classifying and commenting upon precious pagan documents. His leadership in the movement was recognized by his being crowned

with a laurel wreath in 1341, becoming in the eyes of some the first
poet-laureate of modern times.

Rather early Petrarch had fallen under the spell of the secular civilization of the classical world. In his *Letters to Classical Authors* he revealed the
debt he owed the ancient world. "Thou art the fountain head from which
we draw the vivifying waters for our meadows," he wrote in honor of
Cicero, whom he termed the great father of Roman eloquence. "We
frankly confess that we have been guided by thee, assisted by thy judg-
ments, enlightened by thy radiance; and, finally, that it was under thy
auspicies, so to speak, that I have gained this ability as a writer (such as it
is), and that I have attained my purpose."

Paradoxically, though Petrarch valued the use of Latin, he wrote some
of his most important works, including his love lyrics, in Italian. In point of
fact he was not only a Renaissance man in his appreciation of the classics
but also in his love of beauty, whether this be in language, art form, or
person. He loved Laura as a real woman not as an ideal, and preferred to
write his love sonnets to her in the vibrant Italian rather than the more
formal Latin. By so doing, Petrarch not only perfected the Italian sonnet of
fourteen lines— divided into sets of eight and six lines— but also proved to
be one of the founders of modern Italian literature.

Giovanni Boccaccio (1313-1375) was one of Petrarch's devoted followers and one of the first westerners to systematically study Greek. Like
his master, he sought classical documents far and wide and reveled in their
secular outlook. Though nominally a Christian, Boccaccio's literary works
and conduct were essentially pagan in spirit. Indeed his novel *Fiametta*,
written about his mistress, is sometimes hailed as the first psychological
novel. Worldly in tone and content, it makes scant reference to the Christian world of faith and morals.

Likewise the *Decameron* (1353), Boccaccio's witty and high-
spirited collection of tales told to while away ten days during the
plague, portrays a new style of life. Many of the characters in this first
prose masterpiece of the Italian renaissance are most un-Christian in
their action and attitudes, valuing above all sex, deceit, and vendetta.
Within the pages of the *Decameron*, which caused a sensation and was
widely read and copied, simplicity and stupidity are exposed as the unpardonable sins. For this reason the author of the book was nick-named
Giovanni della tranquilità— the Tranquil One, for his world seemed
complete and he appeared to express no concern for the next life. True
enough, Boccaccio, like so many other figures of the Renaissance, did not
deny an after-life. He simply discarded the thought, preferring to dwell
upon more immediate matters.

Thus in the realm of literature and even philosophy there emerged a
new outlook. In Italy, the worldly gentleman replaced the Christian Knight
as the ideal. Books were even produced to educate the novice how to

acquire the virtues of a gentleman. Such a man or *vir* always knew what he was doing and utilized his resources and opportunities to the best advantage. Perhaps the best known book of instruction was Baldesar Castiglione's *Book of the Courtier* (1528). "Now, you have asked me to write my opinion as to what form of courtship most befits a gentleman living at the courts of princes, by which he can have both the knowledge and the abilities to serve them in every reasonable thing, thereby winning favor from them and praise from others: in short, what manner of man he must be who deserves the name of perfect Courtier, without defect of any kind." In response Castiglione observed that "usage is more powerful than reason in introducing new things among us and in blotting out old things . . . ." His approach was later copied in works such as Henry Peachham's *The Complete Gentleman* (1622).

What captivated Italians of the Renaissance was the sense of man's power and potential. Unlike the earlier period when it was believed that each person somehow fitted into a hierarchy, each having his place in some estate, Renaissance man glorified in emancipation and approved of individualism. Man, it was believed, was free in mind and spirit and shaped his own destiny. To him it is granted to have whatever he chooses, to be whatever he wills. Beasts as soon as they are born (so says Lucilius) bring with them from their mother's womb all they will ever possess," wrote Pico della Mirandola. "Spiritual beings either from the beginning or soon thereafter, become what they are to be for ever and ever. On man when he came into life the Father conferred the seeds of all kinds and the germs of every way of life. Whatever seeds each man cultivates will grow to maturity and bear in him their own fruit."

This growing preoccupation with human rather than celestial matters can be discovered in Renaissance politics, philosophy, sculpture, architecture, music, and painting — perhaps the chief of all Renaissance claims to glory. The greatest figure in early Renaissance painting, to whom all his successors owe a debt, is Giotto di Bondone (1266-1337) — a Florentine artist who was the contemporary of Dante and a student of the great Cimabue. In his day all art was still religious and under the influence of the Byzantine school. In such paintings figures were impressive, eternal, and there was little specifically human about them. Giotto changed all this. Only in his work do we see depicted a Madonna who is humanly tender and shown with a real child rather than an adult in miniature. He also simulated reality in the world of art by the introduction of the third dimension. In painting as in so many other areas the rigid, more religious world of the Middle Ages was replaced by the humanism and realism of the Renaissance.

Giotto's new techniques and innovations were almost immediately appreciated and earned him fame and fortune in his day. Following in his footsteps, another Florentine Guidi Masaccio (1401-1428) made the next significant contribution in the world of art. Although many of his subjects remained religious, such as the wall painting in Santa Maria Novella in Florence, "The Holy Trinity, the Virgin, St. John and Donors" produced in 1427, his experimentation with *chiaroscuro*, the use of shading, made his figures the most lifelike ever produced. This genius in his short life span of twenty eight years effected a total revolution in painting. His figures are so real, so massive, that they appear to be in the round — virtual statues rather than two dimensional beings.

Sculpture was no less transformed. Donatello (1386-1466) who produced a statue of St. George for the guild of armourers in Florence, broke with medieval traditions. Unlike the figures which adorned gothic cathedrals and often appeared more like pillars than people, St. George produced for Or San Michele in Florence, stands with his feet firmly on the ground. His visage lacks the vague and serene beauty of medieval saints and expresses human qualities: determination and concentration Donatello's St. George like Masaccio's paintings attempts not to convey ethereal qualities but by paying great attention to details produce a new study of the real aspects of the human frame. By these means, Donatello, like Giotto a century earlier, acquired great fame in his lifetime.

As art techniques improved, governments, guilds, wealthy merchants and churchmen competed one with the other for the best talent. The guilds, very similar in may respects to our own trade unions, did more than watch over the rights and interest of their members— they had a say in the government of the city and a sense of civic responsibility. In Florence and the other Italian cities these and other corporations sought to beautify their city by commissioning various works of art.

More than ever the choice of an artistic subject was the decision of some patron, either individual or corporate, who had outbid others for the artist's service. Cities and their governments, in particular, were anxious to hire the best so that their fame would spread the length and breadth of the peninsula. In Florence, political power and patronage was in the hands of a very small oligarchy of wealthy merchants under the influence of the Medici family. Inheritors of a fortune based upon the far-flung trade of Forence, the Medici though corrupt, had a tradition of civic patronage that endeared them to their townsmen and posterity.

Cosimo de Medici (1389-1494) poured out a large part of his wealth for the construction, remodeling and refurbishing of various buildings: palaces, villas, monasteries and churches. At the same time he amassed one of the great libraries of the period, employing a group of copyists to reproduce books which he could not have brought to Florence. His son Piero followed in his footsteps. Lorenzo, Cosimo's grandson, who was a prince in fact if not in name, maintained this tradition of spending and sponsored artists and philosophers. Becoming the head of the family and the state at the age of twenty, Lorenzo's patronage of the arts was in part financed by the family's private fortune. The library which he lavishly expanded became Europe's first truly public library making accessible to everyone volumes found nowhere else.

The artists his largesse supported played a crucial role in the artistic explosion of the age, amply justifying Lorenzo's title of *Il Magnifico*. Others followed the same practice so that the talented artists of Renaissance Italy all found patrons.

The impact of the Church, though altered was not eliminated. Her calendar still governed the lives of the masses and her frequent holy days were spent in active rejoicing. Disregarding expense, displaying an almost lusty love of color and pageantry, the Italians developed the religious festival into an art form which attracted attention throughout Europe and brought northerners to the magnificently arrayed, warm cities of Italy.

The Church also played a very important role during this period by its patronage of the arts as a series of humanist Popes built up Rome and attracted artists and scholars there. The succession of Nicholas V (1447-1455) meant the truimph of humanism in Rome, and this Pope's collection of the studies of the classics served as the core for the Vatican library. Pius II who was Pontiff from 1458 to 1464 was another noted humanist as was Sixtus IV (1471-1484). Sixtus patronized writers and artists, revived and reorganized the Vatican libary, and built the Sistine Chapel. At the same time he entered boldly into Italian political affairs often acting more the part of an Italian prince rather than a great spiritual leader. His successor Innocent VIII (1484-1492) was more worldly than his name would indicate, while the Borgia Pope Alexander VI (1494-1503) showed himself all too human.

A humanistic approach was also assumed by Julius II and Leo X. Julius (1503-1513) in many ways typified the new, secularized papacy. Known as the "warrior Pope," he had a personal interest in the expansion of the boundaries of his state, leading his armed forces into battle. More than anyone else he was the founder of the states of the Church. His love of military pomp and difficult campaigns would have been questionable in an ordinary cleric, let along the Holy Father. Well versed in diplomacy, he reduced Venice to impotence by calling upon French arms which enabled him to obtain Bologna. Having achieved this objective, he later invoked Spanish assistance to dislodge the French from the peninsula. The Spanish, unfortunately, were not so easily removed.

Not all of Julius' time and interest was spent in war and diplomacy. He was a lover of the arts, among other things, and commissioned Raphael Santi (1483-1520), a young painter from Urbino in Umbria, to paint the walls of various rooms or *stanze* in the Vatican. He was also a particular patron of Michelangelo Buonarroti (1475-1563) whom he commissioned to build for him a tomb befitting the head of the Church as well as the masterpiece on the upper walls and ceiling of the Sistine Chapel. The realistic, some said sensuous art of Michelangelo, provoked an unfavorable reaction in some circles. "Your art would be at home in some voluptuous bagnio," one of his critics wrote him, "but certainly not in the highest chapel in the world."

A series of Popes thought otherwise. Julius' successor, Leo X (1513-1521), the first Medici Pope, was so preoccupied with the affairs of this world he found it difficult to fathom the fervor of Luther and his supporters. Supposedly when he was first enthroned on the papal chair, the procession carrying the blessed sacrament was accompanied by pagan images with the following inscriptions: first Venus reigned (Alexander VI), then Mars (Julius II) and now Athena (Leo X). Even if the story were not true, few would deny that for almost a century after 1450 most of the Popes and high ecclesiastics in Italy remained steeped in the ideals of the Renaissance. These Popes seemed to appreciate the humanistic approach and its emphasis on individual worth. Like so many other figures of the age they sought to enjoy the blessings of the present life and in an effort to beautify their surroundings served as sponsors of arts and letters.

Unfortunately many of these churchmen also shared the inordinate emphasis on form rather than content. As a result not a few ecclesiastics found the medieval latin of the Church corrupt. Indeed one prelate confessed that he had to wash his mouth after saying mass in order to remove the taste of the polluted latin. Another, in turn, warned his associates not to read the epistles of St. Paul, claiming this would assuredly ruin one's latin style. Thus the obsession with purity of form led to a callous disregard for more profound standards.

Not only were morality and religion profoundly affected by the Renaissance, political theory as well was radically transformed. The Italians evolved the principle of "ragione di stato" or "reason of state", the new notion that the first function of every government was to preserve itself. Implicit in this approach was the belief that a government and its representatives were justified in employing any means to maintain their regime. The end, preservation of the regime, seemed to justify any means, including deceit, violence, and even murder.

This system was reached only by abandoning the traditional thought which was built upon the subordination of practical science to theoretical science and within the sphere of political activity, on the subordination of art to prudence. Aristotle had taught medieval man that the human species can rule itself only because it knows, from the theoretical sciences, the end to which we are moved by God. Man, of course, was free to politically effect his fixed end. However even in the practical sphere of politics there was a priority of prudence over art— prudence being the virtue of finding the *right* means to accomplish a *given* end. In art, on the other hand, one determines one's own end as well as the means to achieve it.

More than anyone else it was the Tuscan Niccolò Machiavelli (1469-1527) who made politics artistic. Considered the initiator of modern political thought, he repudiated the older belief that the state derived its authority from God and therefore its power had to be exercised for Christian purposes. The state, he observed, did not rest upon any supernatural structure, but had its own practical, earthly reasons for existence. In *The Prince*, finished in 1514 and published some fourteen years later, he removed politics from Christian theology, placing it upon a purely secular plane. Rather than viewing the state as a mechanism for reaching the good, he insisted that its most important concern was simply self-preservation. Indeed the good he defined in terms of a judgment proper to art: Conformity of what the prince actually produces in terms of what he intended to produce.

Machiavelli understood the state to be an amoral force. In espousing this view he was aware that he was breaking with past political tradition. It was his express intention "to open a new route which had not hitherto been pursued by anyone." To the extent that he convinced rulers that they should hold themselves above the traditional morality, he succeeded. "Whatever strengthens the state is right," he claimed, "and whatever weakens it is wrong," a position which is frightenly modern.

For Machiavelli what was unpardonable in a prince was not his crimes but his mistakes. To many it seemed that Machiavelli was the champion of "splendid wickedness" and sanctioned any means to satisfy one's ambitions. So notorious was Machiavelli's message, so synonomous with evil his name, that the very devil was called "old Nick" because it was Machiavelli's first name. The word machiavellian entered the English language and has come to signify duplicity and craftiness.

Still the Florentine theorist was no overt opponent of religion. It must not be forgotten that the coat of arms of his family contained the Holy Cross and the nails of the passion. Furthermore he did not directly attack the medieval belief that all power is of God— he did something far worse, he ignored it. His political experience taught him that power was anything but divine. Recognizing that religion was one of the necessary elements of social life, he did not conceive of it as an end in itself. Rather he viewed it as an important instrument in the hands of political rulers.

Christianity Machiavelli considered one of the lower religions because he saw it to be in opposition with real political *virtù*. In fact, he held that Christianity had weakened Italians and was in part responsible for their present political plight. In his *Discourses on Titus Livy* he observed:

Reflecting now as to whence it came that in ancient times the people were more devoted to liberty than in the present, I believe that it resulted from this, that men were stronger in those days, which I believe to be attributable to the difference of education, founded upon the difference of their religion and ours. For, as our religion teaches us the truth and the true way of life, it causes us to attach less value to the honors and possessions of this world; whilst the Pagans, esteeming those things as the highest good, were more energetic and ferocious in their actions.

Machiavelli praised boldness, bravery, decisiveness and even deceit, if this was needed to preserve the state. Realizing that it was well for a prince to honor his word, he cited contemporary experience in his *Prince* to show that more often than not those rulers who have achieved great things have been those who have given their word lightly, who have tricked others, and have overcome those foolish enough to always abide by honest principles. "You should understand, therefore, that there are two ways of fighting: by law or by force. The first way is natural to man, and the second to beasts," Machiavelli explained. "But as the first way often proves inadequate one must needs have recourse to the second. So a prince must undertand how to make a nice use of the beast and the man."

While Machiavelli dismissed and discarded the old morality and did a good deal to destroy its hold upon the minds of man, he could not escape the fact that he was a product of that very morality he deemed irrelevant. Thus when Machiavelli wrote that a prince must learn how not to be good, he still knew that not to be good was to be bad. Ironically Machiavelli was himself not a machiavellian. When he fell ill in the summer of 1527 he confessed his sins to Fra Matteo who stayed with him to the time of his death.

Even earlier some Renaissance figures had serious doubts about the new morality. Petrarch, for example, found it impossible to reconcile the pleasures of this world with the peace of the next, which he was not yet prepared to dismiss. He was in a most difficult position, having rejected the Christian intellectual tradition while still clinging to its moral code. On the one hand he desired total knowledge, but on the other hand he well knew that this was not the best path to salvation.

This dichotomy is clearly revealed in his *Secretum*, published in 1342, which is a dialogue between himself and Saint Augustine whose thought he admired. In its pages he sought to justify his life style to St. Augustine and perhaps to God. "I do not think to become a God or to inhabit eternity, or embrace heaven and earth. Such glory as belongs to man is enough for me," he explained. "Myself mortal, it is but mortal blessing I desire."

Yet in his heart Petrarch had deep doubts and in his *Secretum* had St. Augustine express these for him. The Saint admonished, "If you have no desire for things immortal, if no regard for what is eternal, then you are indeed wholly of the earth . . . then all is over for you . . . "St. Augustine suggested that Petrarch suffered from the same delusion that had already betrayed thousands of men thousands of times and had sunk into hell countless souls. One could not hope to have one foot on earth and another in heaven, he continued. A choice had to be made, and the individual had to abandon one life-style or the other. When all these passions are extinguished, and not till then, will desire be full and free" the author had the Saint reveal to him. "For when the soul is uplifted to heaven by its own nobility while on the other dragged down to earth by the weight of the flesh and the seductions of the world, so that it both desires to rise and also to sink at one and the same time, then drawn contrary ways, you find you arrive nowhere."

His student and admirer Boccaccio shared Petrarch's concern. Although he had in his youth been known as the "Tranquil One" for his apparent disregard for the afterlife, he was not as calm and certain about his activities as some supposed. He was especially stung by the dark prediction of a dying monk who in 1361 prophesied his eternal damnation if he did not alter his mode of life. After this, the author of the *Decameron* abandoned light literature as well as his carefree ways. No matter how much he sought to concentrate upon the pleasures of this life, the thought of death and the fate of his soul continued to haunt Boccaccio.

Hence even though Italian society was becoming increasingly secular the framework of the older, Christian world prevailed. The intellectual elite that denounced the older medieval forms, found themselves, often against their will, a part of that tradition despite their preoccupation with the world about them. A feeling of guilt always prevented a relaxed enjoyment of the new freedom, a Christian conscience often lay beneath the most cynical exponent of the new morality. Not surprisingly in Renaissance Italy agnostics were rare while acknowledged atheists were even more so. The great bulk of paintings produced in this period, even those commissioned by lay patrons, were sacred in character with madonnas and miracles, saints and last-suppers, still very much in vogue. Raphael's vision and rendition of the Holy Virgin was adopted by subsequent generations just as Michelangelo's conception of God the Father won wide approval. Serious literature, as well, continued to have a religious base.

Not a few Italian humanists, moved by a heightened appreciation of man's abilities, especially his power of reason, came to the conclusion that all of these wonderful attributes were God's gifts. Marsilio Ficino (1433-1499), one of the major exponents of a revived Platonism, in conjunction with Pico della Mirandola, sought to reconcile pagan philosophy and Christianity, absorbing Plato as earlier the Church had adopted Aristotle. This task was one of the major projects of the Platonic Academy founded by Cosimo de Medici about 1450.

The neo-Platonists achieved a synthesis of sorts of philosophy, religion, and art. They maintained that man, by some accident, had become
separated from his divine realm of pure spirit so that the soul, imprisoned in
the body, sought its freedom and a return to God. This corresponded to the
Christian doctrine of man's fall and his longing for salvation. Within this
framework man's appreciation of natural beauty derived from the soul's
recollection of the celestial splendor. For some, therefore, the creation and
enjoyment of art assumed a religious tone.

This philosophical synthesis had an impact upon part of the intellectual community. For the rest Italy remained the preserve of the traditional
system. The peninsula remained what it had been for centuries, a land of
saints and ecclesiastics. There were in Italy over 250 episcopal sees—
almost as many as in all the other countries of Western Europe combined.
The wealthy and governing classes still spent large sums in building and
remodeling Roman Catholic Churches. Futhermore, from the mid 14th to
the mid 16th centuries more than eighty individuals were added to the roll
of saints.

Almost everywhere in Italy friars could still attract huge crowds at
revival meetings. There was much for such preachers to condemn including concubinage, idolatry, gambling, usury, and above all the increasing
preference for pagan literature instead of the traditional and sacred works
of the Church. Their condemnations were not without effect. In Florence,
the heartland of Renaissance Italy, the Medici remained in close and
constant contact with the priors of the local convents. Indeed Cosimo de
Medici had a cell in the monastery of San Marco where he often withdrew
for solitude and meditation.

The traditional religion remained a source of solace for many. Even
the Florentine sculptor and goldsmith Benvenuto Cellini (1500-1571) who
was boastful, vain, and ruthless, remained a Christian. Thus when Pope
Paul III had him thrown into the Castel Sant' Angelo where he remained
imprisoned for two years, Cellini endured because of his belief in God. He
even imagined he conversed with the Blessed Virgin and Saint Peter who
supported him in his time of need. When in danger, the vanities of the
Renaissance showed themselves to be shallow in comparison to the consolation offered by the traditional religion.

Cast into prison the worldly, sensuous Cellini found support in the
Catholicism of his youth. In his gloomy dungeon below the level of the
ground, full of spiders and venomous worms, he was overjoyed to have
been given his Italian bible. "I began the Bible from the commencement,
reading and reflecting on it so devoutly, and finding in it such deep
treasures of delight, that, if I had been able, I should have done nought else
but study it," Cellini wrote in his Autobiography. Unhappily the light was
poor in his cell and his troubles kept gnawing at Cellini in the damp

darkness till he attempted to dash his brains out. However he claims he was miraculously "seized by an invisible power and flung four cubits from the spot" where he had contemplated suicide.

During the following night there appeared to Cellini a youth who criticized the artist observing, "Knowest thou who lent thee that body, which thou wouldst have spoiled before its time?" Cellini admitted that all his qualities, all his gifts, all that he was or would become was the handiwork of God and realized that it was not proper for him to destroy God's work. This had a profound effect, and Cellini returned to reading the Bible, so that his eyes became accustomed to reading in that darkness. It was as if a supernatural light shone upon him. Spending his time in prayer and in communion with God, the former virtuoso now thought only of God. "There flowed into my soul so powerful a delight from these reflections upon God," Cellini explained, "that I took no further thought for all the anguish I had suffered, but rather spent the day in singing psalms and divers other compositions on the theme of his Divinity."

Thus belief in the divinity was not swept away by the Italian Renaissance. Rather the traditional system had its own champions, many of whom, though appreciative of the new arts and discoveries, urged man to cling to the lofty spiritual aims of the past. Within this group was Giovanni da Fiesole, better known as Fra Angelico (1387-1455), the friar painter. Far from being earthy, his work had an ethereal quality and has been termed a virtual pictorial sermon. He applied the new principles of Masaccio to express the traditional ideas of religious art. In his monastery of San Marco this Dominican brother painted a sacred scene in each monk's cell. Though the art of perspective posed no problem for him, he never let concern with reality spoil the simple and sacred stories of scripture.

Fra Giovanni Angelico, having a profound understanding of the techniques which Brunelleschi and Masaccio had introduced into art, could have lived very well as a layman, satisfying all his material ambitions through the practice of the arts in which he was most proficient. "But for his own peace and satisfaction and, above all, for the sake of his soul, being by nature serious and devout, he chose to join the Order of Friars Preachers," Giorgio Vasari wrote in his *Lives of the Artists*. "For although it is possible to serve God in all walks of life, there are those who believe that they must seek their salvation inside a monastery rather than in the world."

Some of the most worldly individuals in Florence were charmed by the delicate, celestial art of Fra Angelico. Cosimo de Medici was among those who admired his work so that after the Brother had completed the Church and Convent of San Marco, Cosimo commisioned him to paint the Passion of Jesus Christ on a wall in the chapter house. His fame spread beyond Florence so that Pope Nicholas V summoned him to Rome and had him paint the private chapels of the Vatican. So pleased was the Pope with his work, so struck by his modesty and great holiness of life, he decided that he would be a suitable candidate for the archbishopric of Florence which had fallen vacant. However when the friar heard this, he begged the Pope to excuse him for he did not feel capable of ruling over other men.

Fra Angelico served as a living link with the earlier age of faith. His life shows that there were in the Renaissance men who were devoted to the service of God and the benefit of his neighbors. Vassari observed in his book that religious of the 16th century could learn a great deal from that holy man upon whom it was impossible to bestow too much praise. In his words:

> Fra Angelico led a simple and devout life. It was characteristic of his good way of life, for example, that one morning, when Pope Nicholas wished him to dine with him, he excused himself from eating meat without the permission of his prior, the Pope's authority in this matter not occurring to him. He shunned all worldly intrigues, lived in purity and holiness, and befriended the poor as much as his soul is now, I believe, befriended by heaven. He worked continuously at his painting, and he would choose only holy subjects. He could have become rich, but he was not interested in wealth: indeed he used to say that true wealth consists in being content with just a little. He could have had authority over many people, but he refused it on the grounds that there was less trouble and error in obeying others.

Perhaps the spectacular if stormy career of Girolomo Savonarola (1452-1498) best illustrates the vitality of medieval ideals in the *Rinascimento*. In 1475, while in his early twenties, Savonarola left his home for Bologna, where he obtained admission as a novice in the historic convent of San Domenico. From the first, this figure, termed the "last of the great medievalists" was shocked by the state of affairs in Italy, expressing his thought in a treatise called *Contempt of the World* which he produced in 1475. On behalf of his order he preached this message in his native Ferrara, Genoa, and other towns of northern Italy. A portrait of the monk by Far Angelico reveals a dynamic if unpleasant face, dominated by deep, burning eyes.

In 1490 Savonarola was transferred to Florence and within a year was elected prior of San Marco. Appalled by the pagan secularism of life there, he warned the population of the day of retribution and charged that the clergy was neglecting to perform its duties. He prophesied that the corrupt Church would be scourged, that she would then be regenerated, and insisted that these events would occur in the near future.

Scandalized by the superfluous wealth, by the indifference to Christian morality, and the general neglect of the care of one's soul, Savonarola sought to restore the city of Florence to sanity, subtly suggesting that great scourges and tribulations were to descend. Fired by indignation, he vowed to return the influence of Christianity to what he considered a pagan capital. Before ever larger audiences he proclaimed his admonition, urging the citizenry to renounce their shallow pursuits and petty amusements and to cast their eyes upon the eternal values of the Church. Although Lorenzo was less than pleased by what he heard, he did not forbid him to preach though he did indicate his wish that the friar would not predict what would occur in the future and would be less critical. Both his requests were ignored.

Savonarola could not accept "art for arts sake." The function of art, he insisted, was to portray the glory of the soul, not the crass pleasures of the body, so he was particularly incensed by the semi-clad portraits he saw emerging from the best studios in Florence. These abominations would best be destroyed or painted over, because they were instruments that corrupted rather than corrected man's tendency toward the vile and despicable.

Initially the friar won few converts and his crusade seemed abortive. However the energetic, some said fanatical Monk, continued his campaign, convinced that he was doing the work of God. The fulfillment of his predictions made the Florentines fear if not love the outspoken Dominican. He clashed with Lorenzo de Medici, warning the worldly ruler that he would die within the year, and before the year's end, *Il Magnifico* was dead. There is a Florentine tradition that on his death bed in 1492, Lorenzo called upon Savonarola to hear his confession, but the prior of San Marco would only consent to do so if: Lorenzo would have a lively faith in God's mercy, repay all the money he had pilfered from the Florentine treasury, and finally restore full liberty to the Republic of Florence. This Lorenzo would not do, so Savonarola refused his consolation.

The story may not be true, but undeniably Savonarola's influence grew following the death of Lorenzo. Having already acquired the reputation of a holy and learned man, he now widened the range of his sermons prophesying a scourge would soon fall upon Florence and there would be a renewal in the Church. All sorts of people came to hear this prophet, including Pico della Mirandola, who it was rumored, would have become a friar had he not died shortly after hearing Savonarola.

The entry of Charles of France and his forces into the peninsula in 1494 caught the rulers and a good part of the population of Florence uprepared, but Savonarola was not surprised. Lorenzo's son, Piero, went panic stricken to Charles VIII and virtually promised the French King free passage through his territories. This led the frightened people of Florence to proclaim him a traitor and under Savonarola's guidance re-established their republic. "He preached that it was God's doing, not man's, that had freed the city from tyranny; and God wanted her to remain free and institute a popular government like the Venetian, which was more natural than any other to our peoples," wrote Guicciardini in his *History of Florence*. "His efforts in this direction were so successful either through his own talents or by divine inspiration . . . ."

Savonarola, who alone had warned that the day of reckoning was near, had invoked the Lord to hasten his scourge, and to send his sword to earth to deal with the villainy. This, many felt, took the form of the terrible Swiss pikemen and artillery of Charles. Small wonder that Savonarola who had foreseen the catastrophe and called for expiation found his influence enhanced. His determination to remake the Republic according to the laws of God enabled him to exercise a profound influence in Florence from 1494 to 1497. Although he attacked the Florentines for their intemperence and worldliness, they continued to flock to his sermons and follow his call. "The people of Florence were persuaded by Frate Girolamo Savonarola that he was speaking with God. I am not going to decide whether it was true or not, because of so great a man we ought to speak with reverence," wrote Machiavelli in his *Discourses*. "But I do say that multitudes believed him, without seeing anything unusual to make them believe, because his life, his learning, the subjects he took, were enough to get him their beliefs." Machiavelli might have added that his extremism and total commitment to reform were novel in Renaissance Italy and attracted the learned as well as the illiterate.

Determined to keep the city's moral and political life pure, he disproved of the traditional carnival festivities. Instead in 1497 his fiery, fervent preaching provoked a burning of "vanities" in the main square in Florence, the Piazza della Signoria. Under his influence more than a thousand youths, the holy children, went from door to door collecting the symbols of the sinful life for the fires of expurgation. Perfumes, mirrors, musical instruments, books, clothes as well as "immoderate works of art" were piled high to be put to the purifying flames. Alfred Austin in his work Savonarola had these youths chanting:

> Vanities! Vanities! Bring out your Vanities!
> Rouge-pots and scented girdles, spices, gums,
> Snares of the Evil One! Ferret them out,
> Unguents and patches, tresses false and tricks
> Of meretricious beauty, specious dyes
> Henna, vermillion, all of them Vanities,
> Give them all up! Vanities! Vanities!

Among those who responded to the cry was Sandro Botticelli (1446-1510) who offered a number of paintings of scantily clad females to the fire. He decided to follow Savonarola and Vasari claims that it was on his account that he gave up painting and fell into considerable economic distress for he had no other source of income. Nonetheless he remained an obstinate member of the sect and used his talent in producing engravings such as his "Triumph of the Faith of Fra Girolamo Savonarola of Ferrara."

This work brought little money. So desperate was Botticelli's situation, that if a number of friends had not come to his assistance he would have died of hunger.

Others were similarly inspired and put to the torch works by other well known painters and writers, including works by Petrarch and Boccaccio. By this and other demonstrations Savonarola taught the Florentines to loath their sinful luxuries and to consign enticing articles of all sorts, such as immodest clothing, to the fires. "Boys were almost all reformed from many wicked ways and led to a decent and God-fearing life,"according to Guicciardini. "they were gathered together in companies under the care of Fra Domenico, attended Church, wore their hair short, and pursued with stones and insults wicked men and gamblers and immoderately dressed women."

However the beginning of the end had commenced for the powerful preacher. While the French armies abandoned Italy they deprived his Republic of its most powerful friend and exposed it to attack from its many enemies. There was dissatisfaction with the slow pace of the campaign to win back Pisa which had escaped from Florentine rule when the French entered the peninsula. The city's bankers were displeased with the Monk as was Rome which had excommunicated him in May, 1497. The excommunication launched against him followed his refusal to report to Rome and accept the Pope's scheme for consolidating the priory of St. Marks to a new congregation of the Dominican order. It was not Savonarola's intention to challenge the institutions of Church or to question her authority.

Thus, after publicly protesting his innocence of the accusation of disobedience, he bowed to the papal command, ceased preaching and entered the cloister. Once silenced, all of his enemies in Florence, and there were many of these so called *Arrabbiati*, combined and openly attacked the Monk, something they had not dared to do so long as he had access to the pulpit. Once under attack, precious few of the repentent Florentines flew to his defense. In May of 1498, a month after he had promised and then refused to undergo ordeal by fire, he was hanged and burned by the secular authorities and his ashes were cast into the Arno. Even some of his early supporters were relieved that the puritanical period he had introduced to Florence was at an end, and there could be a restoration of the frivolities and vanities he had sought to banish. They seemed to relish the thought of returning to their worldly ways.

Not surprisingly, soon after his death, the Renaissance ideals once again became respectable in Florence and continued their conquest of men and the old morality. "After his death manners decayed to such an extent," according to Guicciardini, "that it proved that what good was done had been brought in by and depended upon him." One contemporary, commenting upon the attempt to stem the march of the new morality wrote, "It did not last long; the wicked were stronger than the good."

Whether viewed as a good or evil, the impact and influence of the Italian
Renaissance upon religion and morality has been far reaching.

BIBLIOGRAPHY

Autobiography of Benvenuto Cellini. Translated by John Addington Symonds. Garden City,
    N.Y.,1961.

Baron, Hans. *The Crisis of the Early Italian Renaissance*. Princeton, 1966.

Bolgar, R.R. *The Classical Heritage and its Beneficiaries*. New York, 1964.

Burckhardt, Jacob. *The Civilization of the Renaissance in Italy*. Translated by S.G.C. Middle-
    more, revised and edited by Irene Gordon. New York, 1960.

Castiglione, Baldesar. *The Book of the Courtier*. Translated by Charles S. Singleton. Garden
    City, New York, 1959.

Chabod, Federico. *Machiavelli and the Renaissance*. Translated by David Moore. New York,
    1958.

Clark, Kenneth. *Leonardo da Vinci*. Baltimore, 1959.

Ergang, Robert. *The Renaissance*. Princeton, N.J., 1967.

Gage, John. *Life in Italy at the Time of the Medici*. New York, 1970.

Guicciardini – History of Italy and History of Florence. Translated Cecil Grayon, edited and
    abridged by John R. Hale. New York, 1964.

Gundersheimer, Werner L. (ed.). *The Italian Renaissance*. Englewood Cliffs, N.J., 1965.

Hay, Denys. *The Italian Renaissance in its Historical Background*. Cambridge, 1966.

Holmes, George. *The Florentine Enlightenment 1400-50*. New York, 1969.

Italy: Machiavelli "500". *Review of National Literatures*, I (Spring, 1970), pp. 7-135.

Laven Peter. *A Comprehensive History of Renaissance Italy 1464-1534*. New York, 1966.

Machiavelli, Niccolo. *The Prince*. Translated by Luigi Ricci and revised by E.R.P. Vincent.
    New York, 1952.

Mirandola, Pico della. *On the Dignity of Man*. New York, 1965.

Molho, Anthony. *Social and Economic Foundations of the Italian Renaissance*. New York,
    1969.

Renaissance Thought: Dante and Machiavelli. Edited by Norman F. Cantor and Peter L. Klein.
    Waltham, Mass., 1969.

The Historical, Political and Diplomatic Writings of Niccolo Machiavelli. Translated C.E.
    Detmold. Boston and New York, 1891.

The Renaissance Philosophy of Man. Edited by Ernst Cassirer and others. Chicago, 1948.

Vasari, Giorgio. *The Lives of the Artists*. Translated George Bull. Baltimore, 1965.

Vespasiano – Renaissance Princes, Popes and Prelates. Translated by William George and
    Emily Waters. New York, 1963.

THE POLITICAL AND SOCIAL ASPECTS OF THE REFORMATION

Harry K. Rosenthal

Harry Kenneth Rosenthal, Assistant Professor of History at the California State University, Los Angeles, received his doctorate from Columbia University. His book on *German and Poles: National Conflict and Modern Myth* will be published by the Florida State University Press. His articles have appeared in such journals as *Slavic Review, European Studies Review, Slavonic and East European Review* and *Central European History* among others.

Europe in 1500 could only be defined as a religious community. That is, the unity of Europe was provided by the Church, its language, and its law. With its language, for instance, a Polish or German student could travel to Italy and study at one of the famous Italian centers of education. With its law, Western and Central Europe experienced a bond of unity which the later Russian writer Peter Chaadaev could only envy. Christendom existed and the European found comfort in its existence.

However, if Christendom did exist, it was troubled. The old medieval question, "How can I be saved?" seemed to many to have found an unseemly answer in the sale of indulgences. To many, the sale of salvation made a mockery of Christian faith and made religion a commercial endeavor. Furthermore, economic changes produced their own measure of discontent. On the one hand, the causes of economic depression — plague, famine, war — and the depression itself caused the rural masses to suffer while a few merchant princes prospered . On the other, the so-called "Commercial Revolution" brought on by the vigorous explorations of Western seamen and the booty they won resulted in the rise of capitalism: money came into increased use; new forms of business organization as well as new forms of accumulating and transferring capital were developed; and men and women began to be more interested in profit than a "just price." Moreover, these economic changes produced a social crisis:

feudal society was an ordered, agrarian society with the peasants at the bottom and the nobles above; the towns were of minor importance and somewhat outside the system — after all, residence in a town meant freedom from the system for the individual. Now, however, the town increased in size — perhaps ten towns (in the Netherlands and Italy) had 100,000 or more persons. But the peasant was still living in his small hut with his livestock and the noble was still defending his historical rights: conflict was inevitable with the towns by and large sharing an almost "natural alliance" with the king (against the noble as well as against the tax demands of the clergy) and the peasant experiencing an increasing sense of frustration. To complete the picture, the observer must note that the territorial state had begun to emerge in some areas of Europe — Spain, Portugal, France, England — while in other parts — Germany in particular — the modern state was far from supreme.

This political and social turmoil obviously involved the Church. For example, when the ships of Europe reached non-European shores, the missionary was there. And, when the ships returned with riches or intra-European commerce produced wealth, the Church was there. The Pope in Rome was a product of his times, the Italian Renaissance. It produced the subsidy of scholarship, shameless nepotism, and such secularization that Alexander VI (1492-1503) spent a considerable portion of his time striving for wealth and political power. Outside Rome, the Popes seemed to be turning local clergy into salesmen for indulgences and the Church into a collection agency. Thus, the Church appeared to have been deeply corrupted by the economic and cultural changes around it.

As might have been expected, there was a continuing reaction. Various movements and individuals had attempted to fill the gap which they felt had resulted from the lack of religious devotion on the part of the official Church. Some religious orders and popular preachers had sought to re-establish a purer religion by frightening the masses into proper behavior. Various cults had sought support in the glory of one or another saint. Mysticism had gained followers in the Northwest while Erasmus of Rotterdam used his giant intellect to try and preserve the unity of Christendom. But none of these attempts had resolved the many dilemmas of early 16th century Europe nor had they given the Church either a new leadership or a new image. Then came Luther.

Martin Luther, born in 1483, had received a good education in a pious Christian setting. In fact, his environment was so permeated with religious influences that he disobeyed his father's wishes and turned to religion instead of law. Ordained a priest in 1507, he stood in awe of his responsibilities and his overwhelming need to gain salvation. Moveover, he was troubled both by his father's rejection of his career and his doubts as to his own salvation. He indeed wondered if he could accumulate sufficient good deeds to assure God's acceptance of his salvation. In this dissatisfied and troubled state of mind, he went in 1508 to Wittenberg to continue his theological studies and then in 1509 he went to Erfurt to study and lecture.

After an unhappy visit to secularized Rome in 1510, he returned to Wittenberg to teach and learn: and his conclusions resulted in the concept of justification by faith. They also led to a condemnation of the business of selling salvation or indulgences. His public condemnation of this practice (in Latin) in 1517 in the famous *Ninety-Five Theses* warranted in turn a Papal condemnation which provoked a complicated political situation which involved German princes, Papal interests, the European balance of power, and the question of the allocation of financial resources. As far as religion was concerned, his Leipzig debates of 1519 as well as Luther's other activities intensified and clarified the religious issues which included, beyond the problem of indulgences, the questions of the authority of the Bible and the authority of the Papacy. It should also be noted that these issues were discussed in articles which were now printed and distributed throughout Christendom in which an increasing, portion of the population could read.

As the conflict assumed a life of its own — as often results in human as well as institutional divorce — both sides increased their level of attack. The Papacy issued a Bull condemning Luther. Enjoying popular support in Germany for political, social, economic, and religious reasons, Luther not only burnt the Papal Bull but also wrote and had circulated three important pamphlets: the *Address to the Christian Nobility of the German Nation, The Babylonian Captivity of the Church,* and *The Freedom of the Christian Man.* In the first, he demanded radical reform of the Church: he wanted an end to papal absolutism, an end to the papal use of German monies, an end to papal political interference in Germany, the formation of a German Church, the placing of the study of the Bible at the center of an education at German universities, and the supremacy of civil as opposed to canon law. It should be noted that, with these pleas, Luther had touched upon the political, economic, cultural, and social issues of his day which were all interwoven with the religious controversy.

Luther's second and third pamphlets were more strictly theological. That is, he summarized his teachings on man's justification by faith alone, on the Christian community as a priesthood of believers, and on the supremacy of the Bible in religious matters. Thus, the theological issues were clearly ennunciated and they would have to be resolved along with the questions of papal authority; moreover, the various other stresses and rivalries of the time would also have to be included in this process of resolution. And, in this setting, Luther proceeded to that climatic, and fabled, Diet at Worms.

That Diet was the Emperor's Diet which the newly-elected Holy Roman Emperor of the German Nation, Charles V, had called for the first part of 1521. Charles, unaware of the popular passions aroused by Luther's denunciations of what to many was a vile and unbearable *status quo* and perhaps underestimating the support which the various German princes were prepared to give, finally heard Luther in April. Luther, encouraged by the support he had received, answered his accusers, "Unless I am convinced of error by the testimony of Scripture or by clear reason I cannot and will not recant anything, for it is neither safe nor honest to act against one's conscience." Then he left Worms for almost a year of residence at Wartburg castle. His condemnation by the Emperor and his excommunication by the Church made him (in what might be termed a period of exile in his own country) an even greater symbol of rebellion against the *status quo*. After the Diet of Worms, Luther would be at the center of all religious, social, and political strife.

As far as the religious controversy was concerned, Luther worked both to reform the Church service and to resist what to his mind were unwise experiments. In the wide area of dissatisfied Europe, preachers and pamphlets spread his call for change. The printing press facilitated the call and, in turn, was fully employed and further developed by those issuing the call. Portraits and hymns, woodcuts and dramas, all served the cause and later experienced distinct Protestant patterns of development. In the end, not only did a new Church service and a new set of Church dogma emerge from the creative chaos of the age but also new uses for and new conception of art and music were vouchsafed to future generations.

Concerning social strife, the great problem was the peasant and his dissatisfactions. In a world of increasing urban wealth and increased demands upon them, the peasants as well as the unsuccessful townspeople despised the pretensions and wealth of the higher clergy, the merchant, and the noble. Encouraged by the seeming equalitarian implications of Luther's community of Christian believers, the "Peasants' Revolt" of 1524-1525 burst spontaneously upon the German scene. Suppressed by force of arms, it left the peasants disillusioned and not at all eager to support Luther in his difficult task of reorganizing Christianity in Germany. Moreover, the revolt enabled Catholics to claim that religious dissent inevitably led to social and political revolt. Luther, for his part, by stressing the need for order and obedience to the princes' authority, cemented his alliance with the princes.

Politically, the struggle for power aided Luther's cause. In the West, the Holy Roman Emperor battled the forces of France. Since even a military victory in 1525 failed to resolve Charles' "Western Problem," he could not confront Luther with all his forces: it is indeed ironic that a struggle between Catholic France and the Catholic Habsburg Empire enabled the religious reformers in Germany to consolidate their position. In the East, the Muslim Turks battered the fortresses of Christendom: Belgrade fell in 1521; Rhodes in 1522; and, in 1526, the Turks gained supremacy in the Balkans with a resounding victory at Mohacs. Moreover, after occupying

Hungary, the Turks advanced to Vienna and, in 1529, besieged the central European capital of the Habsburgs for the first time — 1683 would be the last time. Thus, Charles also faced a considerable "Eastern Problem." Furthermore, within Germany, the imperial knights attempted — in vain — to use Luther's creed as a banner under which they could regain political power. What, then, could Charles do but wish to suppress Luther's creed without being able to take decisive military action to accomplish that end?

Yet, wishes can become threats and threats may become realities: words can and do precipitate actions. In this case, Catholic threats — even without the presence of an adequate Catholic army and treasury — caused the "'Protesting Estates" or Protestants in1530 to form the Schmalkaldic League. Saxony, Hesse, Brunswick-Luneberg, Anhalt, Mansfeld, Madgeburg, and Bremen were original members of this anti-Habsburg, Protestant league which, in Germany, disputed the extent of the Holy Roman Emperor's powers as well as the validity of his religion. But, again, what could Charles, confronted by a Turkish threat and a French threat, do? And so the Protestants consolidated their hold on churches in their territories and expanded their areas of control.

The political balance of power continued to aid the Protestants for, in the period lasting until the death of Luther (1546), the Habsburgs were under great pressure. France allied herself in 1535 with the muslim Turks — perhaps the first indication that religion was losing its position as the dominant influence in Western Civilzation — and battled the Habsburg Monarchy once more. Less than half a decade after this war with its inconclusive peace, another war confronted the Catholic Habsburgs: this time, they faced the forces of France and the Turks as well as the hostility of the Protestant North. Thus, it was not until 1545-1546, after various peaces and armistices had been arranged, that Charles of the House of Habsburg and Holy Roman Emperor could turn his attention to the Protestants.

How powerful were the Protestants? Obviously in Germany they had been given sufficient time to resolve their internal dilemmas and to organize an effective Protestant society: indeed, they seemed to have a chance of uniting most, if not all, of Germany under their banner. In the North of Europe, the Lutheran preacher produced in Denmark what was to be the usual result of the spread of Protestant influence: the first Danish version of the New Testament. These translations served to create an accepted form of the written language in many countries. Another usual result was civil strife which ended in 1536 with a new king, Christian III, and a new state religion — Lutheranism. In Norway, the Danish king imposed Luther's beliefs on a resentful people while the Icelanders reacted in the same manner as the people of Norway: finally however, the Bible was translated into Icelandic and the people were won over. In Sweden, a Danish claim to the country was rejected and the Vasa dynasty gained control: and the new monarch, Gustavus, championed the Protestant cause both out of personal conviction and a need for Church monies. Since Finland belonged to Sweden, it too became Protestant: and the first Finnish translation of the New Testament appeared. Finally, in East Prussia, another ruler, Albert of Hohenzollern, converted his land into a Protestant state: the Kurland, Livonia, and Estonia likewise followed in so far as the upper classes embraced the teachings of Luther.

In East Central Europe, the situation remained less clearcut. Most people associate Poland with a fanatical devotion to Catholicism: in fact, a German author once called Poland "the Spain of the East." Yet, the teachings of Luther did attract a considerable following in Poland. The urban centers, somewhat German, were receptive to Lutheran belief: in Königsberg, East Prussia, a resident of Poznan (Posen) even published a Polish translation of the New Testament. Moreover, many Polish nobles accepted the new belief either for reasons of personal conviction or for reasons of political opportunism: in Poland, the king represented the Catholic side and, therefore, adopting the Protestant persuasion was a political act designed to weaken royal authority. In point of fact, so many Polish nobles accepted Protestant teachings that these nobles dominated the Diets of the 1550's and 1560's. They even secured a pledge of religious toleration from the newly-elected king. Thus, it seemed as if Poland might be won over to the Protestant side.

The Bohemian-Moravian situation was also complex and, as usual, the local political and social situation influenced the form of the religious issue. At the turn of the fifteenth century, a religious movement which was at the same time a Czech-national movement had burst upon the European scene and had found its leader in the person of John Hus. A century before Luther, Hus, a clergyman in Prague, had attacked the theory of indulgences and had preached the supreme authority of the Bible. But, unlike Luther, his condemnation by the Church had resulted in his burning at the stake: it also had resulted in the Hussite or civil war in Bohemia. Thus, when Luther's teachings came to the Czech lands, they came to an area which was not only well-prepared to receive them but also had already accepted many of these ideas and had organized the Bohemian Brethren of the Unity to perpetuate them. This series of events resulted initially in several Protestant sects, later in a Czech version of the New Testament, and finally in a Protestant solidarity against the Catholic Habsburg ruler of Bohemia.

In Hungary, the situation was complex but different. Local German settlers embraced Lutheranism while many Hungarian nobles adopted a Lutheranism which came with an education at a German Protestant university. But, back home in Hungary, it would have proven to be nearly impossible for the Germans and Hungarians to unite in one church even if they could have agreed on one set of religious doctrines. Still, as in so many other lands, the religious controversy aided the development of the native language: the New Testament as well as other religious works appeared in

Hungarian translation; the New Testament also appeared in Slovene and Croatian translations.

Thus, when Charles finally freed himself from the French and Turkish threats, he discovered a transformed Europe which had changed not only in the sphere of religion but also politically, socially, and culturally. Not only had the Protestant belief spread to many parts of Europe but its adherents had seized political control of large areas. Thus, the Protestants in less than three decades had become an organized and integral part of the European *status quo*.

In 1546, Charles reacted with military force which, combined with Protestant ineptitude, resulted in a victory in 1547: it resulted in the recovery of southern Germany for the Catholic cause. But, as usual, the balance of power upset the conqueror; the Pope feared Charles' power as did France; the Turks appeared to be on the move again; and the German princes intrigued against the power of their Holy Roman Emperor — they even concluded an alliance with France. As would happen again and again in European history, the victor, Charles, was compelled to retreat and, in 1555, the Peace of Augsburg followed.

This peace was extremely interesting and fateful. As regards its terms, the permanence of the Protestant political leadership in Germany was recognized, peace was pledged, and each political sub-division was given the right to choose either Catholicism or Lutheranism for its people. Thus, the power of the local princes as well as the Protestants had been formally acknowledged. Moreover, the provision which allowed the local prince to choose the religion of his people revealed the absurdity of later religious hatred. After all, three or four *hundred* years later, some average Catholic or Protestant would hate his non-Catholic or non-Protestant neighbor and not realize that, had the prince of his ancestors' territory chosen the other religion, he would believe in the religion he now despised!

Political decisions also influenced religious belief in England. Of course, there were sincere English religious reformers such as William Tyndale who had translated the Bible into English. But the needs of Henry VIII resulted in the break with Rome. Henry had to divorce his wife, Catherine, because of her politics, her inability to produce a male heir, her previous marriage to his brother, and his love for one of Catherine's ladies in waiting, Anne Boleyn. Due to the international balance of power, a papal annulment could not be expected, Henry was therefore forced to challenge papal authority. Using his powers of persuasion and intimidation on parliament, he succeeded in creating an independent Church under his supervision. A division of the Church's wealth among Henry's allies in the nobility and the townspeople then followed.

In Geneva, also, political and social rivalries helped the emergence of a new Church. Geneva, coveted by France and Savoy as well as by Bern and Fribourg, found itself at the center of an obvious international conflict:

to compound its difficulties, its various neighbors represented the interests of differing religions. In 1536, this political-religious conflict ended with an affirmation of the validity of the Protestant belief. Moreover, a young man by the name of John Calvin was invited to help make Geneva a proper Protestant city: from this beginning, Calvinism developed.

Perhaps, politically, it would have been best if this mid-sixteenth century state of affairs had continued: the South of Europe as well as France would then have remained Catholic while the North of Europe would have developed, undisturbed, along its own lines. Without the experience of a fearful war with all of its terrible consequences, Europe could have possibly developed along the lines it would have to accept a century later. However, there was an obstacle: the beliefs of man. After all, many Catholics sincerely believed that their cause was the cause of God and their opponents' cause was hateful to Him; this feeling was known to Protestants as well.

In any event, forces did emerge within the Church of Rome which both put new vigor into the Catholic cause and perpetuated the political struggle. The most noted of these was the Jesuit order which Ignatius Loyola founded. Loyola, a military officer and a firm believer in military discipline, turned to religion as his life's work after injury ended his military career. Possessed of a strong will and iron discipline, he stressed both: in his *Spiritual Exercises*, he ordered that the Jesuit would have to learn to detest sin and to understand the meaning of Christ's existence by a prescribed meditation. Only in this fashion could the individual develop that spiritual discipline which would be needed for a renewed battle with the forces let loose by Martin Luther.

In 1540, the Pope gave his sanction to the formation by Loyola and his followers of a Society of Jesus which won an ever-increasing influence. The Jesuits educated the young and sought to heighten religious consciousness among the masses. Their means consisted of discipline and still more discipline: they developed a progression of classes, regular examinations, and a series of textbooks which the student had to master. And they did such an excellent job of educating the young and old alike that large numbers of influential people sent their boys to Jesuit schools and invited Jesuit priests to their courts. Political influence thus flowed to the Jesuits who made the most of it in their campaign to win the Protestants back to the "true faith." In the romance language countries of Western Europe, their overseas colonies, and in Poland, they succeeded. They also became an important force in Germany.

Yet, the Jesuits alone could not regain Europe for Catholicism: a disciplined force may represent a disorganized center and attain local successes but a true Catholic revival required Catholic unity of purpose and doctrine; this, in turn, necessitated a general church council which could produce such a unity. In 1542, Pope Paul III summoned such a council to Trent in the Austrian Tyrol. The first sessions were held in late 1545 and were primarily attended by Italian churchmen. Later — in 1551-1552 and 1562-1563 — the council reconvened. When the council had come to an end, the delegates had secured a Catholic unity of doctrine and an agreement on papal supremacy although the doctrine of papal infallibility had to wait until 1870 for its final acceptance. Now that the Catholic church had placed its house in good order it was ready to counter-attack.

Philip II of Spain, recognized by the dying Pope Paul IV as the strongest pillar of Catholicism, led the attack. Personally devout, austere, a champion of Spanish culture, and responsible for the Escorial — a massive, palace near Madrid — Philip worked long and hard at the tasks of government. An absolutist ruler before Louis XIV of France, the Sun King, made the issue of absolutism a standard chapter in any treatment of Western Civilization, Philip established his bureaucracy which was a dependable instrument for converting his wishes into reality. And he labored long and hard in defense of Catholicism — an activity that gained him popularity with the Spanish rural masses.

Within Spain, Philip demanded a strict obedience to the Catholic church (not only because of his faith but also because of the danger that certain Spanish nobles might use Protestantism — as had so many nobilities in Europe — as an instrument of opposition to their king). Therefore, the Inquisition was given encouragement in its work of converting or liquidating all Jews, Muslims, and Protestants in Spain and proved successful in its appointed task.

In the Mediterranean, Philip's Catholicism also achieved success. This time, the enemy was the Turk who, in the Southeastern half of Europe, had besieged Vienna and who, in the Southwestern half of Europe, threatened Malta. Spain, in union with Venice and the Pope, sent its fleet in 1571 to the Bay of Lepanto. This resulted in the virtual annihilation of the Turkish fleet as well as the end of the dream of Turkish naval domination of the Mediterranean area.

In the Netherlands, however, God did not seem to bless Philip's cause. Ruling in the Netherlands but separated from this bit of hereditary territory by the great bulk of France, Philip faced a dual challenge: the quest of the native population for local autonomy and the spread of Protestant teachings. He reacted by attempting to organize these lands along Spanish lines. When this attempt provoked resistance, Philip sent the Duke of Alva to the Netherlands in 1567. The Duke suppressed disobedience "to the word of God": terror ensued and the number of executions mounted. But these executions in turn provoked bitter anti-Spanish feelings especially in the Protestant North. Eventually, the North gained Europe's recognition as an independent state while the South remained under Habsburg control.

Philip's efforts in France likewise produced a less than satisfactory result. Appalled by the prospect that the Protestant Henry of Navarre would become King of France and might also gain sovereignty over the Netherlands, Philip joined forces with the French Catholics. While, in the end, Henry of Navarre did become France's ruler, he also became a Catholic: thus, Philip could rejoice at France's adherence to the "true faith" but the establishment of Bourbon rule reduced his prospects of gaining territory and made France the next Great Power in Europe. As a Catholic, he could rejoice but, as a Spaniard, he could only weep.

Philip's efforts vis-à-vis England resulted in a total disaster. The English problem had several dimensions: English adventurers plundered Spanish shipping; there was a potential Catholic ruler of England— Mary Stuart; and England might be won by a marriage to Elizabeth, the unmarried Queen of England. Thus, Philip's activities began with the wooing of Elizabeth and ended with the despatch of a great Armada to England: the later activity resulted in the destruction of the Spanish fleet. Although Philip hoped to rebuild his fleet, his and Spain's time of power had come to an end: the English looted Spain's principal port, Cadiz, in 1596 and Philip died in 1598. Spain was bankrupt and Protestant Europe had no longer to fear the schemes of the Spanish Monarch.

Unfortunately, however, for the people of Europe, Europeans still had to fear themselves: they could bring forth religious wars without Spanish assistance. In France, for instance, the Protestants or Huguenots had found support in the growing bourgeoisie while the Catholic side consisted of the higher nobility, the peasants, and the masses of the large urban centers. This religious struggle— *as others*— merged with a political conflict. In the St. Bartholomew's Day massacre of 1572 organized Catholic bands provoked an attack upon the Protestants and left about 20,000 dead when the rioting finally ended. But these massacres failed to eliminate the Huguenots and, more than two decades later, a religious peace within France was reached just as a political peace had been reached with the succession of Henry of Navarre to the throne.

Some results of this process should be noted. First of all, the Edict of Nantes in 1598 represented an acceptable compromise of the religious issue for a great many Frenchmen. Under its provisions, the Catholic Church was recognized as France's official Church while the Huguenots received religious rights such as freedom to worship in religious centers established prior to 1597, civil rights such as the protection of law and the ability both to hold public assemblies and to hold public office, and communal rights such as permission to maintain fortified places. Secondly, the *Politiques* organized: they treasured political unity above religious confession and, therefore, championed the concept of a political sovereignty within France which refused to allow private beliefs to disturb the public peace. Finally, Henry reduced the power of the traditional, feudal institutions such as the Estates-General and the Parlement of Paris by ignoring them and relying instead on non-noble officials. Thus, with the largest population in Western Europe, France was ready to begin its climb to a pre-eminent position in Europe.

The Thirty Years' war provided the opportunity: its beginnings were as inconspicuous as its results were epochal. It began with a typical feudal dispute: the Bohemian estates claimed the right to elect their ruler while the Habsburg Monarch claimed the right of hereditary succession. Of course, the religious co-existed with the political: the estates were largely Protestant while the Habsburg ruler in Vienna was Catholic. Thus, enough tinder existed so that only a match was needed to set the Czech lands ablaze with strife and it came with the defenestration, the tossing of two Imperial officials out of the window of the royal palace.

Immediately thereafter, there was no conflict of arms for the Habsburgs had other problems to resolve and the Bohemian forces lacked the strength to besiege Vienna. However, the level of conflict did rise: the Bohemian estates elected Frederick V of the Palatinate as their ruler. Crowned in 1619 in Prague, Frederick inherited the conflict with the Habsburgs over the rights of the Bohemian nobles and inherited the religious conflict. His presence in Prague added a German conflict since the Palatinate and Austria were both members of the Holy Roman Empire and it added an international conflict since some Protestant states did recognize his rule in Bohemia. Thus, a feudal conflict had quickly developed into a complex struggle.

The original conflicts were speedily resolved. In 1620, the Habsburg army advanced to Prague and within an hour defeated the Protestant forces at the Battle of the White Mountain. It is astonishing that in such a short time several thousand men could settle the fate of a nation for 298 years but it happened: until the destruction of the Habsburg Empire in 1918, the hereditary rule of the Habsburgs in Bohemia was acknowledged by all and Bohemia, after much of its land had been divided among Habsburg officials and after the Jesuits had effected a "re-education," was once again a Catholic area despite the fact that its national hero, John Hus, had been an early reformer of the church!

The struggle, however, continued since the German and international considerations remained. Issues of power within Germany and standing in Europe— as well as the religious issue— propelled Denmark into the war. Moreover, these issues enabled Christian IV, the Danish king, to gain promises of English and French support. However, the realities of the respective English and French domestic scenes as well as the organizational abilities of Wallenstein, the Habsburg commander, resulted in an abandoned Christian being soundly defeated by the Habsburg armies and forced to flee to his islands in the Baltic. Thus, in 1629, the Catholic cause had truimphed throughout Germany.

But the consequences of military victory can be just as troublesome as military defeat. On the Catholic side triumph brought spoils and disputes. Moreover, triumph had so increased the Habsburg power that such Catholic forces as France, Bavaria, and the Pope feared the possibility of the Habsburgs' achieving hegemony over Europe. As a result, they pressured the Habsburg Monarch, Ferdinand, to fire Wallenstein: and they succeeded. On the Protestant side, anger and apathy co-existed. On the one hand, the Protestants were outraged when, in 1629, Ferdinand issued an Edict of Restitution which, in effect, removed from Protestant control all Church lands gained since 1552. On the other, they were helpless. There was even the possibility that a united Germany under Habsburg, Catholic leadership would emerge.

This was prevented by the Swedes who entered the war with the usual mixture of religious fervor and territorial ambitions: Gustavus Adolphus, the Swedish king, wished at the same time to crush the Catholic power and make the Baltic a Swedish sea. And although few Protestant leaders could believe that he had a chance to achieve these goals, he had some advantages. For one thing, he and his army had years of military experience behind them as well as a well-organized government and economy supporting them. For another, without Wallenstein, the Habsburg forces were much reduced in effectiveness. Moreover, the French at this time did financially support the Scandinavian troops.

And so the war resumed but with a new ferocity. The Catholics burned Magdeburg and plundered Saxony. Then the Swedes defeated the Habsburg army in 1631 and proceeded to plunder Bavaria while the Saxons captured Prague. At this point, Wallenstein resumed his service in the Habsburg cause and checked the Protestant advance: his forces even claimed the death of Gustavus Adolphus in 1632. But Wallenstein's assassination in 1634 likewise deprived the Catholic side of its best commander: a stalemate had been reached which ended in the Peace of Prague of 1635.

This treaty represented an end to an epoch even though the war continued for another thirteen years. It was epochal because religious motivation had ceased to determine political behavior: now Catholic France and Protestant Sweden openly co-operated out of Great Power motivations and they continued the war purely for political reasons. Furthermore, a religious settlement for Germany had been accepted by all: whoever possessed Church lands before the Edict of Restitution retained them; all religious leagues were disbanded; and the Imperial Court was to have an equal number of Catholics and Protestants. As the Treaty of Westphalia confirmed in 1648, open religious strife in Central Europe had come to an end.

A period had also come to an end. This was the period in which religion ceased to dominate the politics of Europe. This was a period in which a major impetus was given to the development of literatures in the native tongue. This was a period in which the unity of the Christian world was tested and shattered. This was a period in which men with new concepts sought to clarify and codify them while men with old traditions sought to recast their convictions in the light of a new day. It was a challenging and terrifying time.

And, in some ways, it remained and remains. For example, the Edict of Nantes was revoked and the Huguenots were forced to leave France. Even in the 1950's, the Catholic-Protestant rivalry in Germany demanded the presence of a Protestant President with a Catholic Chancellor (in West Germany). And, in the 1970's, armed Protestants and armed Catholics face one another in Northern Ireland. The traces of the era remain.

BIBLIOGRAPHY

Bainton, Roland H. *The Age of the Reformation*. Princeton,1956.
Bindoff, S.T. *Tudor England*. London,1950.
Boehmer, Heinrich. *The Jesuits*. Philadelphia, 1928.
Corbett, James A. *The Papacy*. Princeton,1956.
Geyl, Peter. *The Revolt of the Netherlands, 1555-1609*. New York,1958.
Grimm, Harold. *The Reformation Era*. New York,1966.
Hughes, Philip. *A Popular History of the Reformation*. New York,1957.
Janelle, Pierre. *The Catholic Reformation*. Milwaukee,1963.
Kidd, Beresford. *The Counter-Reformation 1550-1600*. London,1937.
Mattingly, Garrett. *The Armada*. New York,1959.
Murray, Robert H. *Political Consequences of the Reformation*. London,1961.
Ogg, David. *Europe in the Seventeenth Century*. New York, 1960.
Smith, Preserved. *The Age of the Reformation*. New York,1962.
Walsh, William. *Philip II*. New York,1953.